The Celts

Their Spirituality and Their Place in History

PREVIOUS PAGE: Cwbelin Cross, highlighted in the video of the 850th Anniversary Celebration of The Margham Abbey (1147–1997) in South Wales is presented here. The cross, attributed to be one of the oldest, if not the oldest Celtic Cross in existence, stands 7 x 14 feet tall and dated circa 600 A.D. It can be seen today in the Stowe Museum in Port Talbot, South Wales. The museum is located adjacent to Margham Abbey and is open daily from 9:00 to 5:00.

To Patricia —

Your time and talent are reflected in this book!

The Celts

Their Spirituality and Their Place in History

[signature: Paul Evans]

Paul F. Evans

Diolch yn fawr!
Thank you very much!

© 1999 by Paul F. Evans. All rights reserved

Printed in the United States of America

Packaged by WinePress Publishing, PO Box 428, Enumclaw, WA 98022. The views expressed or implied in this work do not necessarily reflect those of WinePress Publishing. Ultimate design, content, and editorial accuracy of this work are the responsibilities of the author.

No part of this publication may be reproduced, stored in a retrieval system, or transmitted in any way by any means—electronic, mechanical, photocopy, recording, or otherwise—without the prior permission of the copyright holder, except as provided by USA copyright law.

Copyright © Albert Hyma and J. F. Stach
From: *World History—A Christian Interpretation*
By: Albert Hyma and J. F. Stach
Reprinted with permission of Wm. B. Eerdmans Publishing Co. Inc.

Copyright © Alan Luff
From: *Welsh Hymns and Their Tunes*
By: Alan Luff
Reprinted with permission of Hope Publishing Co.

Copyright © John Davies
From: *A History of Wales*
By: Jonn Davies
Permission of Penguin Books Ltd. Pending.

Copyright © Barry Cunliffe
From: *The Celtic World*
Reprinted with permission of St. Martin's Press, Inc.

Unless otherwise noted all scriptures are taken from the Revised Standard Version of the Bible. Copyright 1946, 1952, 1971 by the Division of Christian Education of the National Council of the Churches of Christ in the U.S.A. Used by permission.

ISBN 1-57921-200-X
Library of Congress Catalog Card Number: 98-89782

---

* Front Cover: The Celtic Knot was found in excavations both at LaTene and Hallstatt and is considered to be dated as early as 1200 B.C. Samples of these are also found on Celtic Crosses. The Celtic Knot was drawn by the Druids in a continuous formation to prove, in some cases, there is neither a beginning nor an ending. Later in Celtic spirituality and history, it became known to signify "Eternity" and "The Celtic Symbol of Life."

Gweddi'r Orsedd

Dyro, Dduw, dy nawdd;
Ac yn nawdd, nerth;
Ac yn nerth, ddeall;
Ac yn neall, gwybod;
Ac yng ngwybod, gwybod y cyfiawn;
Ac yng ngwybod y cyfiawn, ei garu;
Ac a garu, caru pob hanfod;
Ac ym mhob hanfod, caru Duw;
Duw a phob Daioni!

Gorsedd Prayer

Grant, O God, your protection;
And in protection, strength;
And in strength, understanding;
And in understanding, knowledge;
And in knowledge, the perception of rectitude;
And in the perception of rectitude, the love of it;
And in that love, the love of every existence;
And in the love of every existence, the love of God;
The God of all goodness!

NOTE: Gorsedd is the throne of the Bards, who were the early historians and storytellers of the ancient Celts, going back to the time of the Druids. This Bardic blessing in Welsh and translated into English dates back to about A.D. 1200.

WITH DEEP APPRECIATION

I am sorry that a simple word like "Thanks" has become such a trite and forgotten word in our international and national vocabulary.

Oh, how I wish someone would plant the seed of graciousness and courtesy in the hearts and minds of people like my Grandpa Isaac Evans, a great Celt, and others like him, who emigrated to America. When he and other immigrants said "Thanks!" for what they received in this new land of tremendous opportunity, it came from the heart.

Or, when my parents said "Thanks" to us for doing the little chores we children did, that sweet perfume of appreciation meant something!

Or, when "Daddy" Hays (Dr. Arthur Hays, my professor of church history at McCormick Seminary in Chicago) prayed before each lesson, his prayer was a "classic prayer of thanksgiving." He passionately prayed that "the eyes of church history characters would be opened" and, when they were, the words of "thanks" and "thanksgiving" bubbled with glorious meaning!

These folks gave rich meaning to the word "thanks" that I have not heard in quite a time. Oh, that such richness of heartfelt speech would return. It is this depth in the word "thanks" that I wish to convey to those who spiritually nudged me along the road of life, who made Celtic spirituality more than just two words with a current appeal; leading me, not only to be grateful for my heritage, but also for my deeper Christian faith and experience.

I would also like to express this kind of thanks to those who made this book possible.

Thanks for those who have been any part of my Celtic heritage, especially my wife Norma, who also has a rich Celtic family heritage, and our children who inherited both this Celtic heritage as well as this Celtic spirituality. The great congregation at Capel Cymraeg, Bryn Seion in Beavercreek, Oregon, has been a tremendous encouragement.

To those who proofread this text, gave encouragement, and offered changes, I would like to thank them personally.

Carol J. Evans
M.A. University of Oregon
Professor of English
Clackamas Community College
Oregon City, Oregon

Harold Fisher
Ph.D. Indiana University
M.Th. SanFransisco Seminary
Prof. Em. Bowling Green University
Writer, Researcher, Pastor, Missionary

Douglas Jones
Creigiau, Wales
Trinity College, Carmarthen, Wales
Teacher's Certificate
Secondary Education

Don Kohl
M.Ed. Wayne State University
Adm. Asst. Superintendent Schools
Teacher, Educational Research
Doctoral Class Work Completed

Beverly Kohl
Office, Secretary of State
Proofreader Skills
Salem, Oregon

David McCreery
Ph.D. University of Pittsburgh
Professor, Willamette University
Old Testament—Hebrew Bible
Near Eastern History and Religion
Archaeologist, Dyro-Palestinian Digs

Patricia McKinney
M.A. Portland State University
English Professor
Oregon State University

James F. Moore
Pastor, Theologian, Author
B.Th. Princeton Seminary
MST. SanFransisco Theological Seminary
DST, SanFransisco Theological Seminary

Gretchen Williver
University of Oregon
Peace Making and Social Justice Advocate
Presbyterian Church USA

Virginia Rainey
Historian
Ph.D. European History
University of North Carolina

Patrick Thomas
M.A. English and Medieval Welsh
St. Catherine's College, Cambridge
Examining Chaplain—Bishop of St. David's
Rector Brechfa, Wales—Celtic Author
Honorary Member, Gorsedd y Beirdd

Thanks to the typists whose ardent and meticulous word led to this production.

A deep appreciation to WinePress Publishing for their advice and placing this book in final form.

And readers, thank you for passing along such a rich heritage without forgetting your own and holding it dear.

One note of thanksgiving I cannot omit. I must say, "Thanks be to God with whom all things are possible." For without God, these words wouldn't even be a thought!

PAUL F. EVANS
SALEM, OREGON
1999

Contents

An Introduction to Celtic Spirituality:
My Early Background xiii

CHAPTER 1
From Their Beginnings
2250 B.C. to the United Kingdom 17

CHAPTER 2
The Road to Celtic Spirituality:
2250 B.C. to the United Kingdom 55

CHAPTER 3
Historical Development in the United Kingdom:
From the Migration to the Reformation (1558) 99

CHAPTER 4
Celtic Spirituality in the United Kingdom: From the
Migration to the Reformation (1558) 143

CHAPTER 5
Historical Development in the United
Kingdom (1558—1950) 179

Chapter 6
    Celtic Spirituality in the United
        Kingdom (1558 to 1950) 205

Chapter 7
    Present Day Celts:
        Our Spiritual Mentors? (1950–present) 239

Afterword 263
Notes 265
Addendum
    Celtic History/Church History Chronology 277
    Kings in the United Kingdom 299
    Celtic Poems 301
    Translation of St. Patrick's Works 309
Bibliography 317
Index 323

An Introduction to Celtic Spirituality: My Early Celtic Background

> The future is never quite a thing apart from all that has gone before. We bring into the present ingredients and cargoes from the past, and all these are with us as we take the unknown road. All that we have learned, felt, and thought; all our experience from birth to now; all the love that nourished us at other times; all the yearnings rooted in our spirits—all these are still with us as we move into the unknown way.
> —*Howard Thurman*

When I was a child, my grandfather kept telling me, "Remember your heritage! You are both a Welshman and a Celt!"

At seven years of age, I knew what a Welshman was because Grandpa was a Welshman, but what was a "Celt"? My curiosity aroused, I asked Dad what Grandpa meant. Dad replied, "I have an idea, but I think Grandpa could give you a more complete answer." When Grandpa came home from his work in the "pit" at the Continental Coal Mine in Scranton, Pennsylvania, I asked him, "Gramps, what is a Celt? Am I a Celt?"

Dirty as he was, still black as could be from coal dust, he did not make me wait for the answer but asked me to accompany him upstairs while he took his bath. While he bathed, he shared with me many stories about his life and the lives of his parents.

"Celts were people who lived long before the time of Jesus," he explained to me later as we sat at the dining room table with a map spread before us. "In fact, some claim before people in Old Testament times. My father before me told me they came from somewhere in Germany around the Danube River."

He showed me the area on the map from which the Celts possibly had come, explaining how the Celts had migrated across Europe through France and into what he called the "United Kingdom of the Celts." He continued, "This place includes Wales, from which Grandma and I came with your Aunt Esther and Uncle Abie; and Ireland, from where Mr. and Mrs. Murphy came; and Scotland, the homeland of Mr. and Mrs. McNulty; and England, from where the Wordsworths emigrated." Again he said, "Remember your heritage! You are both a Welshman and a Celt!"

Every Christmas, always a family reunion, before we opened our presents or sat down to Christmas dinner, Grandpa would gather the grandchildren around his favorite chair and place the smallest ones on each knee. When everyone was seated, he would send the eldest grandchild to the sideboard for his Welsh Bible. Then he would read the Christmas story from Luke's Gospel in Welsh, *"Yn y dyddiau hynny aeth gorchymyn allan oddi wrth Cesar Agwstus i gofrestu'r holl Ymerodraeth."*[1] He would translate those funny looking words into a language we could understand, telling us the story in his own words. Then he would pray a short prayer in Welsh, translate it into English, and admonish us, "Remember you are a Celt and a Welsh person! Remember your heritage because you have a good one!"

He also taught us that nightly prayer, "Now I lay me down to sleep . . ." in Welsh: *"Rhof fy mae'n i lawer/ i gysgu/ Rhof fy Heniad i Grist Iesu/ Os byddai farw cyn y bore/ Iesu cadw fy heniad heno. . . . Duw bendith mam a tad, mam-gu a tad-cu . . ."*[2]

When I was attending McCormick Seminary in Chicago, I noticed that the only reference to the Celts in our textbook on church history was this paragraph:

> Beyond a certainty that a Christian Church existed in Britain in this period (the Nicene Age—A.D. 325–590), very little is known about it. The population was Keltic. From later data it is to be inferred that this church had an independence and character of its own.[3]

"What about Celtic spirituality and the Celtic saints?" I asked Dr. Arthur "Daddy" Hays, Professor of church history, pointing that there was nothing else about the Celts in the book. Dr. Hays was sympathetic, but he could offer no solutions to my question and asked if perchance my grandpa could come to the seminary and talk to the class. Unfortunately Grandpa had died by then.

In fact, aside from a few words in Zenos' *Compendium,* there was nothing about the Celts or Celtic spirituality in any church history text that I could find. It wasn't until many years later while rummaging through books at a church book sale that I found my first reference book about the Celts. Now out of print, it was titled *The Celtic Realms* and written by Miles Dillon and Nora Chadwick. (I bought it for 25 cents.)

In 1995, I was invited to attend a one-week seminar called "Celtic Spirituality" at Pacific School of Religion, Berkeley, California. The course was taught by Dr. Arthur G. Holder, professor of religion at the Church Divinity School of the Pacific (Episcopal). Because of the interest generated by the course, Dr. Holder later taught classes in Celtic spirituality to seminary students in 1996 at both Pacific School of Religion and the Church Divinity School of the Pacific.

Subsequent to attending the course by Dr. Holder, I was invited by Dr. Cynthia Campbell, president of McCormick Theological Seminary, to write an outline for a new course on "Celtic

Spirituality" in church history, which I completed in 1996 and has led to the writing of this book.

Before we proceed with the body of material on *The Celts: Their Spirituality and Their Place in History*, most people are knowledgeable about history, but "spirituality" is an ambiguous word to many. In order to define the parameters of this presentation and the direction of this adventure, I will use Oliver Davies' definition of spirituality, which is:

> A complex grouping of theological ideas, sacramental experiences, religious forms of life, and a spiritual inner piety, that makes Christian experience what it is both in time and space.

Join me as I try to express the ways in which spirituality has evolved through Celtic history; how their devotion and reverence for gods and God are unique; how those qualities have changed; and the ways in which the Celtic people have contributed to this special kind of spirituality in the history of Christianity and the Church.

PAUL F. EVANS
Salem, Oregon
Bugail Capel Cymraeg, Bryn Seion[4]
Beavercreek, Oregon

CHAPTER 1

FROM THEIR BEGINNINGS: 2250 B.C. TO THE UNITED KINGDOM

> The subject of History is the life of peoples and of humanity. To catch and pin-down in words—that is, to describe directly the life, not only of humanity, but even a single people, appears impossible.
>
> —Count Leof Nikolayevich Tolstoy

Writing history is no easy task, as some might think. There are many problems such as when does history begin? How does one find history, which has been handed down by word of mouth from one generation to another, and be able to vouch for its authenticity? Where similar and duplicate stories are found, which one is the most authentic? Who decides? What have historians done about pieces of history, like that of the Celts, which have been dangling since about 2250 B.C.?

A problem exists regarding Celtic oral traditions and written history. Oral history, as differentiated from written history, has always been suspect. There is suspicion that such memories in the oral tradition still exist. People forget that written histories too can be distorted or misrepresented according to the prejudices or vantage point of the author.

To begin with, the word spelled C-E-L-T-I-C is pronounced with a hard *c* (Kel-tic, not Sel-tic.) The pronunciation *Keltic* was the only one given in the first edition of the *Oxford Dictionary*. In the second edition of the *Oxford Dictionary*, the alternate pronunciation *Seltic* was included. "Why is the second or alternate pronunciation given?" seems to be a fair question.

Several reasons were given, but none can be verified. However, since the alternate pronunciation was first printed in the second edition of the *Oxford Dictionary* (printed in England), the English must have had reason to give credence for such an insertion.

One story, seemingly handed down from one generation to the next, and giving reason for the change, comes from conversations of the author with Irish Gaelic Celts, Scottish Gaelic Celts, and Welsh Celts. In general, the story is this. The Welsh referred to the English as *Saesneg* (the Welsh word for English). The English took offense to this word, believing it to be demeaning and profaning the English people. Hence, the alternate pronunciation made out of spite. It was at this juncture that the English began referring to the crosses in the United Kingdom as "Seltic" crosses.

Another story appears: The inhabitants of the United Kingdom changed their linguistics from the early Celtic pronunciation to the Anglo-Saxon pronunciation, which uses the letter *c* to be pronounced both hard and soft (i.e., *c*old and *c*elery.) They evidently then believed that it was proper for them to use the alternate form "Seltic."

Does this give them the authority to change the name or pronunciation of a language or people? Let me share a quote here concerning dictionaries. "A dictionary editor cannot change the facts of a language any more than a map-maker can change the position of a mountain, a river or a city, in making a map."[1]

As early as the fifth century B.C., these nomadic people were referred to by the early Greeks as *Keltoi* and by the early Romans as *Galatae*. At a later time, some of these Celts became known as *Cymry* (pronounced COME-ree by the Welsh), and *Gaelic* (earlier pronounced "Gah-elic" before it was anglicized into "Gay-lick"), thus making up the Gaelic Scots and the Gaelic Irish. There also were Manx (earlier spelled Mancs, since there was no *k* or *x* in the Celtic languages), and Bretons and Cornish.

All the Celtic alphabets included the letters *c* and *s* and never contained the letters *k* and *x*. The *c* was pronounced hard, like a *k*, and the *s* pronounced soft. Earlier historical writers, to make sure the word Celt was pronounced properly, wrote the word *Kelt*.

Let's look at another bit of linguistics among the early Celts. In their grammar among the Celts (Cymraeg) and the Celts (Gaelic), all nouns were either masculine or feminine; there were no neuter nouns. However, in these two cultures, there were two nouns separate and distinct from all others. These two nouns were God and angels. Evidently these early Celts grew up to believe that God was God and angels were angels. There was no "Father" God or "Mother" God. Although they were akin to the Hebrews, for them God had both male and female attributes, but for the Celts no pronouns were used in reference to God or angels. God was simply God and angels were simply angels.

THE EARLY EUROPEAN PEOPLE

When talking about the Celtic people, it is natural to question *who* are they, *where* do they come from, and *how* were they divided? The closest we can come to portraying such a division is to present the following outlines.

For clarity, I am going to divide the following schematic into two sections. First are listed the Indo-European people among the Celts; the Primitive Celts will be listed separately.

The Indo-European People[2]

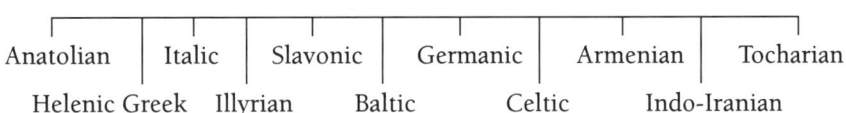

| Anatolian | Italic | Slavonic | Germanic | Armenian | Tocharian |
| Helenic Greek | Illyrian | Baltic | Celtic | Indo-Iranian | |

Anatolian was the name given in the 1900s B.C. to the part of the Middle East that is now Turkey. Its boundaries were roughly those of Asia Minor. The main plateau of Asiatic Turkey is called the Anatolian Plateau. The languages here have been long extinct.

Helenic Greek was a language and civilization beginning circa 300 B.C., when Alexander the Great controlled Greece. It lasted until the Romans conquered Greece circa 100 B.C.

Italic (Latin and Romance languages) was the early Roman name for the area we now know as Italy. From the fall of the Roman Empire (early in the A.D. 400s until the early 1500s) all writing was in Latin. In the early 1200s, writing began in Italian and was called a "Romance language."

Illyrian—People from Illyria (a section of Albania) were captured by the Romans about 200 B.C. When the Roman Empire was divided in A.D. 395, Albania became a part of the Byzantine Empire.

Slavonic (Russian and Polish) was a division of the old Aryan speaking Indo-European people. They lived in the Ukraine and Southeastern Poland. Between A.D. 200 and 500, the Slavs began to emigrate to other parts of Europe and went into the regions of Germany, Albania, and Russia.

Baltic (Latvian)—Scientists believe that these people lived in Latvia around 3000 B.C. They traded with the Romans, Arabs, Slavs, and Anglo-Saxons. About 700 B.C. they built a chain of frontier forts to protect their land.

Germanic—Julius Caesar campaigned against the Germans (58–55 B.C.). In A.D. 9, the Germans under Arminius destroyed a Roman army, ending Rome's plan to conquer Germany. From A.D. 376–600 German invaders conquered Rome's western provinces. Charlemagne began the First Reich Empire in A.D. 800, which lasted until 1806.

Celtic—(Recorded in second schematic.)

Armenian—A region of Southwest Asia south of the Caucuses Mountains, from the Black Sea to the Caspean Sea. The Hittites lived in this region. According to tradition, Noah landed his ark on Mt. Ararat. Armenians cling to their own language. They have been Christians since about A.D. 300 through St. Gregory the Illuminator.

Indo-Iranian (Persian Sanskrit)—This kingdom ruled in Southeast Iran from before 1200 B.C. to 642 B.C. Some folks called this area Persia. In 700 B.C., the Medes and the Persians came under partial Syrian control. In 600 B.C., the Medes overthrew the Assyrians and became dominant in Iran.

Tocharian—Tocharians lived in Asia until the tenth century A.D. Tocharian, a language with eastern and western dialects, was known for the preservation of many documents by the historian Strabo.[3]

The second section is of the Indo-European people called the Celts.

The Primitive Celts[4]

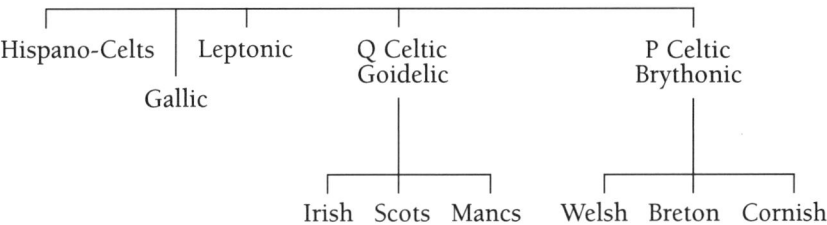

Hispano-Celtic and Gallic—These extinct members of the early Celtic tongues are only partially known from tiny fragments so small as to only notice their existence.

Leptonic—Little is known of these people, except that they existed about 1400 B.C. and lived around Lake Moggiore (pronounced mhad-JOH-ray) in northern Italy and projecting into Switzerland (Helvetia).[5]

Most historians agree that the latter six languages spoken by the Celtic people belong into two groups: *Goidelic* (or Q Celtic) includes Irish, Scottish, and Manx (earlier spelled Mancs) and *Brythonic* (or P Celtic) includes Welsh, Breton, and Cornish.

This distribution is the result of immigrations in the fifth and sixth century A.D. Before that, Brythonic was spoken in Wales, and Goidelic was spoken in Ireland. The migration of the Irish westward introduced Goidelic into western parts of Scotland, where it became known as Gaelic (pronounced GAH-elic). In Celtic languages every letter is pronounced. There are no diphthongs. The Brythonic remained in use in Wales and Cornwall.

There are no contemporary written records or documents of any kind from which we can obtain even an incomplete or sketchy account of how our ancestors lived; but geologists, anthropologists, and archaeologists have contributed to our knowledge.

Discoveries by geologists and archaeologists have been greatly assisted in recent years by nuclear physicists, who have been able to date rocks and artifacts. Aerial photography has also played a very important role in archaeological discoveries.

Because of these findings, we can report such things as the ages of humankind in Europe and in what we know as the United Kingdom, setting them apart roughly as follows:

1. Paleolithic or Old Stone Age: Began circa 500,000 B.C.
2. Neolithic or New Stone Age: Began circa 6000 B.C.
3. Bronze Age: Began circa 1800 B.C.
4. Iron Age: Began circa 1100 B.C.[6]

As a prelude of life through these ages, we can view the panorama of people's existence, see where and when the Celts arrived on the scene, and notice how they functioned as well as their contributions to the world.

THE PALEOLITHIC OR OLD STONE AGE—BEGINNING CIRCA 500,000 B.C.

The Paleolithic person was equipped with instruments of unpolished stone. He was a cave-dweller, with a knowledge of fire, as well as an ardent hunter. There is evidence of early occupation in Europe, and what we know now as the United Kingdom may have been swept away by glaciers and sheets of ice during the Ice Age.

The only satisfactory remains relating to the Paleolithic times (50,000 to 8000 B.C.) show our aborigine ancestors as cave-dwellers who may have been tall, dark, and long-headed with prominent cheek bones.[7]

Nearly all caves found are in limestone regions of Europe, fringing on the Bristol Channel, in the south of Ireland and Scotland, and on the edges of the Irish Sea, and in Wales at Vale and Clwyd.[8]

NEOLITHIC OR NEW STONE AGE—BEGINNING CIRCA 6000 B.C.

In the United Kingdom, Neolithic people still lived in caves, partly in open settlements not far from the sea. Traces of this age have been found in Wales, along the coast of Aberystwyth, the Cliffs of Gower, and the sand dunes near Porthcawl. In Ireland, Neolithic people lived in the south from Bantry Bay to Wrexford; in Scotland, on the west coast no farther north than the Firth of Forth; and in England, from Bristol Channel on the west and around to Dover on the east.

An important difference between Paleolithic and Neolithic times was that stones were now ground and polished. This influenced greatly the settlement of human beings. Flintstones were lacking, but there was a plentiful supply of igneous rock in such places as Caernarvonshire, Pembrokeshire, Kilarney, and Norfolk. The outer skin of igneous rock, when polished, made it tougher and more durable than flint. These sharpened stones were made into axes and sickles for cutting grain.

Until the 1960s, it was believed there were no agriculturalists in the United Kingdom until about 2000 B.C., and the Neolithic Age, the age of farmers lacking metal, was considered to have lasted for about 400 years.[9] Nuclear physicists have also documented that there were fairly numerous communities of agriculturalists in the United Kingdom by 4000 B.C., and the Neolithic Age came to an end around about the time when previously it was thought to have begun.

THE BRONZE AGE—BEGINNING CIRCA 1800 B.C.

Bronze Age is a term describing that period in the development of a people when bronze, rather than stone or soft copper, was used as the material for weapons, implements, and ornaments. The Bronze Age varied from place to place. In some areas it lasted for a long time, and in others it was short. The people of some regions skipped the Bronze Age altogether.[10]

Bronze settlers arrived in what we know now as the United Kingdom, about the time of Abraham, nearly 2,000 years before the birth of Christ. The indigenous pre-Celtic people were still around, as well as others who had migrated into the area. They were collectively known as Iberians. The Iberians, who originated in the area of Spain and Portugal, were mixed with the Celts and were called *Celtiberians*. They introduced into the islands metal working in bronze, gold, and copper. In addition, they hunted and tended herds of sheep, pigs, and goats. They were the first archers and were skilled in weaving and other crafts. People soon noticed that they initiated a revolution in agriculture by introducing well-balanced farming through rotation of crops and plow tillage.[11]

Both the Romans and the Greeks declared the Celts clearly of good intelligence, having changed from primitive culture of the Stone Age into a recognizable civilization. From these folks came the great poets of Ireland and Wales.

THE IRON AGE—CIRCA 1100 B.C.

Many historians report the Iron Age as having begun circa 1100 B.C. and continuing through to the present day. During the Iron Age, carpenters and masons abandoned their crude tools of the Bronze Age and began to use stronger and better tools of iron. Because iron was abundant, tools were more available. In addition, such tools and armaments improved trade and helped civilization expand and progress.

Some historians claim that middle and southern Europe came into the Iron Age long before northern countries did.[12] This substantiates the findings of the La Tene and Hallstatt cultures and that iron was used about 1,000 to 1,500 years earlier among the Celts, who produced metal plows, iron tires for wheels, etc.

People began to use iron long before they learned how to write. Some historians believe that men first obtained their knowledge of iron from meteors that fell from the sky. Others believe that men discovered iron accidentally by building a fire on top of a vein of rich iron ore. In whatever manner this hard metal was discovered, it began a technical revolution by the Celts.

The blacksmiths of this age did not possess the technology to melt down iron for casting. Instead they were able to use a type of forge to soften the metal so it could be hammered into a desired shape or form. Such techniques of forging and smelting must have taken them much time and much patience to accomplish such a feat!

The encyclopedia has this to say:

> For thousands of years, men made iron in a simple way. The ore was put in a hot deep fire of charcoal. The carbon in the charcoal slowly combined with the oxygen in the iron ore and escaped as gas. The fire was not hot enough to melt the resulting iron, but was hot enough to soften it so it could be pounded and forged into some form or shape in manufacturing simple tools.[13]

Some information has been found through archaeologists who discovered a palace near Dorset, England. Here they unearthed tools, crucibles, and an implement resembling a forge. After scientific analyses, these findings tell us of the composition of the materials and something of the techniques that the blacksmiths employed. Above all, they used charcoal as a method of heating the iron. It wasn't until years later that a method was found to melt the iron, and still later a method to make steel. A claim can be made that the Celts were the pioneers of the industrial age.

The invention of the plow was most vital to those who tilled the soil. Previous to this invention, those planting used a stout digging stick or hoe to loosen the soil just enough to sow seeds. Later these Celts used an *ard* (a curved stick with a pointed end for digging) made entirely of wood. The inherent weakness of this implement was the actual point of the ard. Under normal conditions, the wooden point would quickly wear out.

It would not have taken a great feat of inventive genius to realize that a larger ard or a hoe dragged through the soil would create an acceptable furrow, and it was only a matter of time before a man who pulled the plow would be replaced by yoked oxen as a means of locomotion.

Later an iron tip was fastened to the ard which would be more effective and rip deeper into the soil. It was not much later when the first large plow would be formed and pulled by a yoke of oxen. This plow was provided with an iron *coulter* (or contoured knife blade), which would turn over a furrow of soil.

> The regular plowing of defined areas gave rise to regular fields, which soon became distinctive landscape features, as soil accumulated on downhill slopes, and rocks were thrown off the field and piled along the boundaries where hedges grew. In this way checkerboards of little fields blanketed the landscape.[14]

Rock engravings depicting agricultural scenes occur in Scandinavia, the Ligurian Alps (engraving), and in particular at Val Camonica, north of Milan where this example was found.[15]

Celtic Migratory Routes

Migration is the mass movement of people or animals from one place to another. Throughout history, entire groups of people and animals have left their homes and moved to new ones.

Migration includes both *emigration* (the movement of people out of an area), and *immigration* (the movement of people into an area).

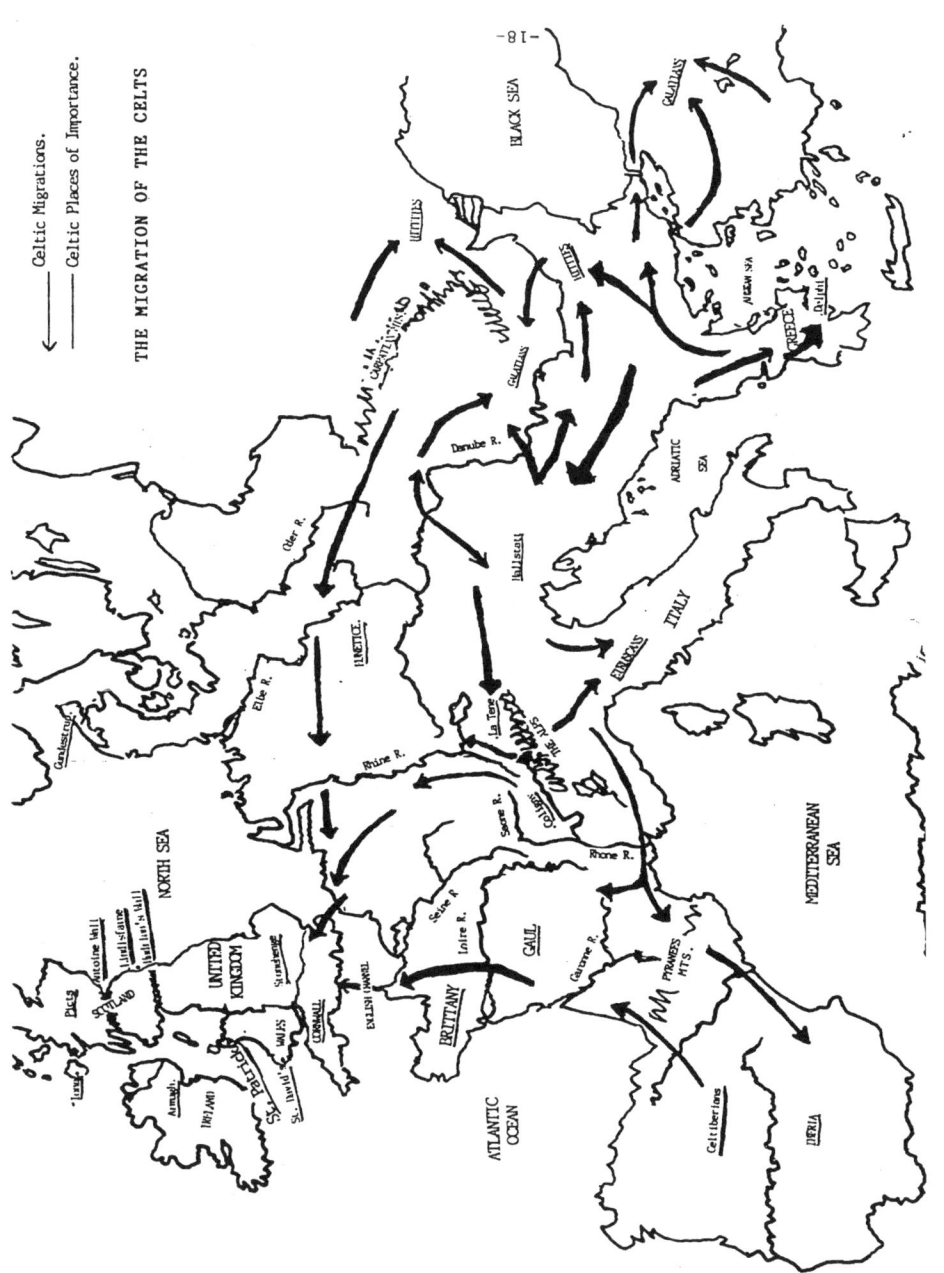

Since early times people have migrated chiefly for three reasons: (1) They have used up or destroyed their natural resources; (2) They seek to improve their way of life; or (3) They have been displaced by invasions, wars, or famine. For the Celts, we can add a fourth reason: They were for the most part inquisitive people who wanted to explore areas beyond their sight. It has been suggested that they were inquisitive because they wondered about what the gods were doing in other places.

The first migration of the Celts into the United Kingdom was about 6000 B.C. followed by the Iberian Celts (Celtiberians) circa 2000 B.C., followed by more Celts between 600 B.C. and 400 B.C.

On the mainland of Europe, the Celts fought the Hittites twice: first on the northwestern corner of the Black Sea around 1400 B.C., and drove them south to the southwestern corner of the Black Sea, where their second encounter all but annihilated them about 1200 B.C. These were the same Hittites of Old Testament Bible times. The Hittites were thought to be descendants of Heth.[17]

When the Celts first appeared to be recognized by historians about 500 B.C., they seem to have spread over much of the Alpine region and the areas immediately north in central France and parts of Spain.

Beginning in the fifth century B.C., they were found in a zone stretching from northern France to Bohemia. A new culture arose, named after the archaeological site of La Tene in Helvetia (Switzerland).

Soon after 400 B.C. the La Tene Celts erupted over the Alps, seizing and settling in the Po Valley. They sacked Rome in about 390 B.C. Here they were known to the Romans as "Galli" or "Galatae."

Others migrated through the Balkans, attacking Greece and sacking Delphi in 279 B.C., and were known to the Greeks at Keltoi. Some crossed the Hellispont and carved out a kingdom in central Turkey (Galatia). While in this area the Celts fought the Galatians circa 300 B.C., the same Galatians referred to in the New Testament. It was here that the apostle Paul, speaking to the Galatians (because of their use of warlike powers to amass land and take people captive), says to them, "O foolish Galatians! Who has bewitched you . . ."[18]

In the third century B.C., the Celtic world constituted a shifting mosaic of autonomous tribes and states stretching from Ireland to Hungary with isolated pockets and partly Celtic populations from Portugal to Turkey.

During the latter part of the second century B.C., the Celtic lands were beginning to come under pressure from the Germans and to fall under the sway of Rome.

This brings us to the Roman invasion of Britain by Julius Caesar in 46 B.C., in which some suggest Celtic mercenaries were a part of their armies. The only documented information we have is that Caesar's armies invaded the United Kingdom in 46 B.C., following two armed reconnaissance missions in 55 and 54 B.C. His army occupied only a part of the United Kingdom, and departed about A.D. 407 without conquering the land.[19] (See p. 106)

Most of the migratory routes of the Celts have been noted as being west, south and north. No historian has presented any data concerning migrations going "east," with the exception of the Celts fighting the Hittites just west of the Black Sea.

Yet from our vantage point, some questions need to be asked.

1. The Celts fought naked, wore blue and red pigment on their skin in battle, and also wore a woven belt around their waist on which to hang a dagger. What other tribes fought naked, wore blue and red pigment on their skin during battle, or wore a dagger on a woven belt? Answer: The Alaskan and American Indians (Native Americans)!
2. The Celts were also known to have totems; among them—the Raven. What other tribes had totems, including "the Raven"? The answer: the Alaskan Indians! The Thlingits call their Raven, "Creator Raven."
3. The early Celts were basically pantheistic and had many gods. So did Alaskan and American Indians!

Could it possibly be that there was a Celtic easterly migration over the ice cap into Alaska and down into the Americas? Could these people have a Celtic background? Are they really Native Americans?

How Do We Know So Much About This Literal Culture?

They could write, but they didn't. It wasn't that they didn't have anything important to write about. Very important facts of which they were knowledgeable, could have been written down. They were ahead of their time in methods of farming, such as rotating their crops, fertilizing, and plowing their fields. They were the first wheel-wrights and builders of wagons and chariots. They were the first to mine ores and make them into metals for spears, shields, and implements of protection and war. They also tamed horses. They were certainly not without important things to write about!

It is difficult to pinpoint the origins of people, either in space or time, for throughout the story of humankind there are only small threads of continuity. These threads reach backwards through millennia of the preliterate past in such a manner that significant transitions are rarely perceptible. The origins of the Celts belong to this historic past.

How do we know as much about the Celts as we do, especially as far back as about 2250 B.C.? Nora Chadwick, a noted historian on the Celtic people, mentions three ways we have secured this knowledge:

1. By classical authors
2. By archaeology
3. By languages and linguistics[20]

By Classical Authors

The Celts seemed to have little use for writing. However, Peter Berresford Ellis in his book, *The Druids*, makes a case that the Celts did some writing in Latin and other languages.

Certainly the Druids saw little evidence of the need for it, especially when it came to presenting their faith. The Druids believed that writing was improper and spoiled the spirituality of the thought process. They believed people would misinterpret their words and thoughts. So they considered it was safer to pass information down from generation to generation, so the word might be received by their own people in all of its purity.

Caesar infers that because some Druid students spent more than twenty years in study, their spirituality could be complicated and was apt to be misinterpreted. But Caesar seems to be more concerned about the powerful influence these Druids had on the Celtic people. Note the number of times that he raided Druid strongholds and desecrated their places of worship.

Gaul during the latter Iron Age, however, also presents evidence that even though the Celts wrote little, they did write.

> Early Celtic writing was basically for census records and for prominent events. (Caesar captured such documents, in Greek characters, from the Helvetii). The Gauls were recorded to have placed letters to the dead on funeral pyres. . . . Writing in early times was confined to southern and central Gaul and was only used in a limited way by certain groups.[21]

What makes the Celts live is that our knowledge of them does not depend solely upon dead scattered relics. Archaeological and linguistic reports (which will be shared later) will enhance our knowledge of the Celts. It will be greatly enlivened by descriptions of the Celts as they come to us from many classical authors but even more remarkably by the survival of a considerable body of Celtic literature. These writings were derived from an oral tradition. They came from heroic folk tales that were written down in Ireland and Wales in the latter part of the first millennium A.D.

To read them today, says Cunliffe, puts us in direct communication with the world of the Celts, while to hear some spoken in Gaelic, Welsh, or Irish is to experience an eerie echo from the past.

From the interpretations of the early classical writers concerning the Celts, we get a varied glimpse into who they were and what they were about. As portrayed by the early Greeks and Romans, the Celts were fearsome and dangerous, nonliterate barbarians who even fought naked! The Greeks and the Romans said many crude things about the Celts. Later on the Greeks and the Romans, in a complete turnaround, wrote of the Celts as an intelligent, complex, wealthy, and accomplished family of societies who came to play a pivotal role in the making of Europe.

Let's take a look at the views of a few of the early classical writers. *Strabo* (Stray-bow) 63 B.C.?–A.D. 24? was a Greek geographer and historian. He became famous for his seventeen-volume *Geography,* which described all parts of the then-known world and its people. These volumes are the best source of geographical information about the Mediterranean countries just before the beginning of the Christian era. He studied in Rome and Alexandria. In addition to his travels in Arabia, he traveled in southern Europe where he gleaned extensive information about the Celts through direct experience, which is evident in the following quotes.[22]

Strabo designates the Celts by name as a specific people and talks of them as a multi-sided people. Here Strabo talks of their name.

> This then is what I have to say about the people who inhabit the dominion of Gallia Narbonensis (Southern France), when the men of former times called "Celtae"; and it was from the Celtae, I think, that the Galatae as a whole were by the Greeks called "Keltoi" . . .[23]

Strabo talks here of their actions and their character and realizes what the Celts mean when they talk about power:

> The whole race of the Celts, which I will further refer to as Gallic or Galatic, is madly fond of war, high-spirited and quick to battle, but later otherwise straight forward and not evil of character . . . being ever-ready to sympathize with the anger of a neighbor who thinks he has been wronged by another, or has

been warred upon and has his land and belongings taken from him. . . . There seems to me to be two kinds of Celts. One who will fight and challenge as a sport, and who has no place, and is a roamer; the other, who for the most part, remains in one place for a while before moving on. He will only fight on principle.

    This Celt believes that power is not found in the amount of land he possesses, but power is found in the family, his cattle, and the land he resides on and farms. He will also reserve this principle for all people; and would fight for his neighbor's land against that enemy, take booty, and return most of that booty and his land to his neighbor.[24]

This quote is basic to power as presented in other chapters in this book. It is here that Strabo presents the motivating power in the Celtic family ambitions and the nonbarbaric side of their life:

The country of the Celtic people produces grain in large quantities, and millet, and nuts, and kinds of livestock. And none of their country is untilled, except these parts where tilling is precluded by swamps and woods. Yet, these parts are too thickly peopled—more because of the largeness of their population, than because of the industry of the people; for their women are not only prolific, but good nurses as well, while the men are fighters for their principle as well as good farmers.[25]

    The Celti who lived about the Adriatic joined Alexander the Great for the sake of establishing friendship and hospitality. . . . The king received them kindly, and asked them as they were drinking, what it was they feared most, thinking they would say himself, but they replied that they feared nothing, unless it were Heaven might fall on them, although indeed they added that they put above everything else, the friendship of such a man as he.[26]

Alexander the Great was equal, if not superior, to the Celts. The Celts felt that they were Alexander's next intended conquest. This was tact and diplomacy used by the Celts, even though some historians tagged this as arrogant. The result? No combat!

One can imagine here that the Greek and Roman historians first write of the Celts as "barbarians" and paint a most horrible picture of their bloody incursions, and then they reverse their whole perspective and portray them as normal people like themselves. Could it have been that the spirituality of the Celts was beginning to show an evolutionary change in their character?

HERODOTUS (HAIR-ROD-OH-TUS) 484?–424? B.C.

This Greek historian undertook the task of writing the history of the world up to his own time. The Roman orator Cicero called him the "father of history." Herodotus named the early residence of the Celts.

> The Danube traverses the whole of Europe, rising among the Celts . . . (who) dwell beyond the Pillars of Hercules, being the neighbors of Cynesii, who are the westernmost of all nations inhabiting Europe.[27]

THE PILLARS OF HERCULES

This was the name that the Greeks gave to the rocks on either side of the Strait of Gibraltar. Greek legend states that Hercules placed these rocks there. Later these two rocks were pictured as pillars bound together by a scroll bearing the Latin words *Ne plus ultra,* meaning "no more beyond." The Cynesii are unknown.[28]

DIODORUS SICULUS OF TARSUS (DIO-DOOR-US SICK-YOU-LUS)?—A.D. 394

A praised theologian of this time period, and founder and leader of the Antioch School, says Siculus was the early name for Sicily. Chrysostom practiced extreme asceticism and pursued theological studies here under Diodorus. Diodorus was also a historian who has been quoted (oftentimes secondhanded) concerning the Celts. About the early residence of the Celts, he is quoted as saying:

> At the time that Dionysius was blessing the Rhegium 391 B.C., the Celts, who had their home in the regions beyond the Alps, streamed through the passes in great strength and seized the

territory that lay between the Appenine Mountains and the Alps, expelling the Tyrhenians who lived there.[29]

Diodorus the Roman does not say until much later that the Tyrhenians were holed up in a small Alpine ravine so that the Romans could not get at them. Or that the Celts wanted to get out without loss of life and protect the Tyrhenians from the Romans. The Celts made it possible that they had a place to live, and it was wrong for the Romans to take their land. Diodorus Siculus also talks of the Iberians and the Celts concerning their amiable solution as well as their common definition of power. This is what he had to say:

> In ancient times these peoples—the Iberians (Spain) and the Celts, kept warring among themselves over the land, but later, when they arranged their differences and settled on their land together, and they went together and agreed on inter-marriage with each other, because of such inter-mixture, the two peoples received the appellation "Celtiberians" . . . and since it was two powerful nations, and united, and their land was fertile, it came to pass that the "Celtiberians" advanced far in fame.[30]

The last were quotes of classical writers (and there may be other possible quotes to prove who the Celts were and how they were thought of). Here we present still another view of the Celts, this time through the eyes of the archaeologist.

By Archaeologists

The author has not found in print, but has heard lecturers on the Celts declare, "The premise that the Celts belong to a prehistoric past must be proven!" What kind of proof are they looking for? The proof, as Nora Chadwick claims in her volume *The Celts,* has already been presented through three avenues of approach: classical writers, linguists and linguistics, plus archaeologists and anthropologists. Through use of scientific methods, other authors have attempted to unveil many minute details of Celtic ancestry, such as physical types, nutrition, and death rates. Even fears, hopes, and aspirations have been presented, and the Celts emerge as one of the most important peoples of Europe, at least through the first millennium B.C.

Chadwick states "Archaeological evidence suggests that in the prehistoric period, the contribution of this region to what was to become distinctively European culture, was no less seminal."[31]

The findings of the Hallstatt culture, the La Tene culture, as well as the Urnfield period, the Battle-axe era, the Beaker Folk, and others confirm Chadwick's statement.

THE HALLSTATT CULTURE (700–500 B.C.)

Hallstatt is a site in Austria where many objects have been found dating to the Early Iron Age (circa 1000–918 B.C.).[32]

The most prolific source of archaeological materials relevant to the Celts comes from the excavation of many of their cemeteries in this area. Despite the unceremonious grubout of many of their graves to satisfy the contemporary lust for collectible objects, we have been afforded much information about our ancestors.

In 1846, on the shores of Lake Hallstatt in Austria, Georg Ramsauer, director of the Hallstatt mine, began to excavate the graves in prehistoric cemeteries where a flourishing community had buried their dead. Between 1846–1862, he uncovered no less than 980 gravesites, excavating bodies and artifacts.[33]

It is surmised that, since this volume is about the Celts, these findings were labeled Celtic in origin.

LA TENE CULTURE (600–200 B.C.)

La Tene is a shallow area at the northern end of Neuenburg Lake in Switzerland. It was here that an amateur archaeologist, a Colonel Schwab, unearthed thousands of artifacts: swords, tools, pottery with designs and animal figures that scholars never had seen before. These finds were clearly recognized from the beginning as being Celtic.

The art-form that is properly Celtic, as it seems to have been evolved by the Celts, is that of the late Iron Age, known as La Tene. Overshadowed by the prestige of Greek and Roman art and architecture, it has only gradually been recognized as a precious contribution to the culture. In contrast to the realism and natural beauty of classical art, this Celtic art is imaginative, even wild, delighting in symbol and pattern rather than in direct representation.[34]

About the same time as the Hallstatt culture, excavations and important discoveries were being made at Lake Neuchatel in 1858. Archaeologists sent from Zurich, Switzerland, discovered the remains of several prehistoric settlements along the shores. Vast quantities of Iron Age metal work were found, such as swords in their decorated sheaths, spears and shields, horse harnesses, bits and bridles, tools of all kinds, coins, ornaments, wheels, ornate carvings, and pottery.[35] These were all designated by the excavators as Celtic in origin.

THE BEAKER PEOPLE

About 2000 B.C. came the Beaker People, whose burials were in single graves. The remarkable Wessex culture of the Bronze Age, which appears about 1500 B.C., is thought to be based on this condition. Their gravesites seemed to portray a warrior-type existence.

However, these people were named not for their warrior mentality but by a certain artifact found in their graves—a bell-shaped beaker or drinking vessel. Also found among their artifacts were archery equipment, such as bows and arrows (flint tipped), and metal arm braces that took away the stings of the bow-string when it was spent.

> These people were distinguished archaeologically by a characteristic artifact commonly found in their respective graves.... For these people it was a Bell-Shaped Beaker or drinking vessel, and this was sometimes accompanied by archer's equipment, including flint-tipped arrows, and an occasional metal-tanged dagger.[36]

THE BATTLE-AXE PEOPLE (CLOSE TO THE THIRD MILLENNIUM B.C.)

The Battle-Axe People were so named by an artifact found in their graves. In addition to the formation of various types of battle-axes with intricate detailed markings, these people were also refuted to be the forerunners of a historically attested language with archaeological culture, including the modern Celtic languages.[37]

In addition, other cultures, such as the Unetice and the Timulus, provide evidence of flourishing barbarian societies in Central Europe, which were allowed to develop without any disruption by local people. Within a century of their discovery, however, they disappeared. There is no historical indication as to how or why.

OTHER ARCHAEOLOGICAL FINDINGS ABOUT THE CELTS

Archaeology has unearthed many things about the Celts that have aided humanity:

1. *Wheelwrights*: 5,000 years ago the Celts learned to shrink an iron tire on a wooden wheel. The wheel was first constructed with wooden parts, then an iron tire was made fractionally smaller than the wheel.

    The iron tire was then heated so it would expand. It was then put on the wheel and immediately cooled, so the tire shrank to the felly (the rim of the wheel supported by spokes), binding all parts of the wheel tightly together. These wheels were first used to aid them in farming, and then they used them in making chariots, which they sold or traded to the Romans and others.[38]

2. *Tamed horses*: The horse was essential to the Celts in both war and peace. The Greeks and the Romans, in their history, naturally emphasized the military aspects, but this gives a very one-sided impression. We look at the other kinds of evidence, and we find the horse everywhere present: in the graves and the farmland, on coins, and in one unique and resplendent example, on the British Chalkhill at Uffington, carved into the landscape.[39]

3. *Farming*: The Celts were once great hunters, and then they turned to farming. The same shops that made wheels first made them for farm carts and wagons, but they also made and manufactured iron plows for tilling the soil, which

opened up areas of agriculture (corn, wheat, millet and hay, as well as nuts and fruits of many kinds). They also tamed cows and goats; the cows and goats for milk and meat, as well as pulling carts. They were also the first to let their agricultural land lay fallow for a year every seven years.[40]

4. *Salt Mining:* Extensive Celtic salt mining operations were known in the Eastern Alps, with tunnels running up to 350 meters (about 1,200 feet) into a mountainside. A nearby stream was diverted to flood into the mine shaft. The rock salt was washed out of the mine and led through a conduit system into large vats where the water was evaporated off, using heat from the sun or by wood fires under the vats. The salt water was also poured over straw, and when dry was shaken into dry vats or leather pouches and stored. This salt was used to preserve and season their food. Prior to this the blood of animals they killed for meat or used for sacrifices was stored and used for seasoning.[41]

In addition, these Celts minted coins; built houses to live in and sheds for their tools and animals; made metal tools, including plows; and fashioned jewelry and adornments. These ingenious creative inventors were called "barbarians," "uncouth," and even "animals."

Celtic Languages and Linguistics

The Celts were known by the language they spoke, rather than the place from which they came, i.e., Germans from Germany, Italians from Italy, French from France, Spaniards from Spain.

As early as 500 B.C., Strabo believed that the languages of the Celts belonged to the great Indo-European family of languages and generally acknowledged the fact that the Celts had a special language. He believed that the Celtic languages were composed of a cacophony of Celtic guttural labial and nasal sounds, which were later combined into dialects as they migrated across Europe. They became able to communicate and understand each other, but were seemingly unable to speak each other's language, even by the time these Celts arrived from Europe into the "United Kingdom of the Celts."

These dialects either melted down into several distinct languages, or some of the dialects survived as what we know now as Irish Gaelic, Scottish Gaelic, Mancs, Breton, and Cymru (Welsh). These dialects or languages seemed to be particular to large communities, which we know today as England (Breton), Ireland (Irish Gaelic), Scotland (Scottish Gaelic), Isle of Man (Mancs), Cornwall (Cornish), and Wales (Cymru).

Over the years, several of these languages are spoken no more. Others have merged, such as Irish Gaelic and Scottish Gaelic, into one language simply called "Gaelic." There is now a present effort to revive some of these languages, especially Gaelic. Gaelic, for instance, is spoken more today in Nova Scotia than in Ireland or Scotland.

The only language that has been continually spoken over the years is Cymraeg (Welsh). It has been noted by many historians and linguists as *the oldest continually spoken language in the world.* Even if one considers Roman (Latin) surviving to the present time through the Mass of the Roman Catholic Church, Greek surviving through the worship of the Greek Orthodox Church, or Hebrew surviving to the present through the Hebrew Bible, and even including the various dialects of these languages, the historians still believe Cymraeg (Welsh) to be the oldest continually spoken language in the world!

Celtic people paid great attention to the development of an advanced use of oral technique in their language as a better vehicle for the transmission of their thoughts through their language. This included not only a choice of words but what some linguists call "an oratory inflection in their chosen words." Hence, their artistic speech became highly cultivated, and a high standard of eloquence became a great plus for orators. It is heard especially in the Irish and Welsh in church sermons and in political oratory. Already in the middle of the second century B.C., Cato attributed to the Celts a high degree of skill in the art of eloquence. It is still considered an art. Competition in eloquence is still on the program of present day *Eisteddfodau*. Eisteddfodau is the plural of Eisteddfod, a term denoting a meeting or assembly of poets in Wales. It is the time designated when orators compete before Yr Gorsedd, the throne of the Bards. One may be named "Bard of the Year" for their presentation of prose or verse.

This is also a music festival where choral offerings are presented and awarded honors much like the Olympics. Competition is open for choruses of various size (male, female, or mixed); solo, duet, trio, quartet etc. (male, female, and mixed). The Eisteddfod is an annual affair and open to citizens of all nations. (Also see p. 256)

How the ancient speech of the people in the United Kingdom of the Celts, after battling for eighteen centuries against profound languages such as Latin, French, Greek, and English, has survived at all is a mystery. The fact that it is today more studied, more written, and more read that ever before is a miracle!

The Celtic Law

There has to be, in any community, both written and inferred common laws, plus people to enforce those laws for the security and safety of the people in that community. This was as true and necessary for the early Celts as it is for us today. The laws of the early days of the Celts may not have been as structured as are ours in the twentieth century.

Early historians have determined that the early Celtic laws were both formulated and enforced by the Druids, an esteemed group of people within the Celtic society. No person has been able to pinpoint the beginning of the Druids, nor does anyone have any knowledge as to who gave them authority to enact laws. No one knows how such laws were formed or enforced except that the decrees were by the Druids and determined by the instruction of the gods through the Druids. The Druids had both spiritual and legal responsibilities, and it is thought, therefore, that the judgments in each case were spiritually based. Caesar put it this way:

> [The Druids] are concerned with divine worship, the due performances of sacrifices, public and private, and the interpretation of ritual questions: a great number of young men gather about them for the sake of instructions (this could be interpreted as moral instruction and a deterrent to criminal activity). In fact, it is the Druids who *decide in almost all disputes,* public and private; and if any *crime* has been committed, or *murder* done, or if there is any *dispute* about succession or boundaries. They also decide determining *rewards* and *penalties* . . .[42]

The following is one of the Druidic laws among the Irish regarding concubines and is an example of a kind of justice in relation to women.

> The first wife is completely free from liability for anything she may do during the first three nights (after the concubine has been introduced into the house), short of killing. . . . The concubine has only the right to inflict damage with her fingernails, and to utter insults including scratchings, hair tearings, and small injuries in general.[43]

This startling regulation has much to say about gender relations and levels of interpersonal violence and polygamy tolerated by medieval Irish society. Concubinage was permitted, but wives did not have to acquiesce without a fight! Medieval Celtic women often had more rights than their English and French sisters, just as their foremothers had more right than GrecoRoman women. The laws of all Celtic society can be grasped by reading between the lines of Irish epics.

Often the Druids' judgments involved entire families. Under Celtic law, as spelled out in the old Irish tracts, all of the culprits' immediate relatives—not just the wrongdoer himself—could be held responsible for their misdeed. If they faulted in the Druid's judgment, the whole family was disgraced. The Celtic family comprised everyone descended through four generations back to the great-grandfathers. One can imagine that any Celtic family must have presented many knotty and inherited problems for the Druids or the one designated to arbitrate such a court matter.

Also, sometimes families were not included in the crime of the wrongdoer (probably at the discretion of the Druids). Often when the criminal was single, or without a family, they were fined according to their economic status. And, when a surety was granted over a period of time, when that period of time had elapsed and the fine had not been paid, there was no extension time allowed. The Druids had a right to seize any of the criminal's property to pay the debt or fine.

Finally, in any criminal litigation, when all else failed, the Celts could seek to enforce a ruling from the Druids to exert pressure to exclude the offender's right to partake in the tribe's sacred ceremonies. This meant censure as well as ostracism. This meant unknown punishment from the gods.

It also has been noted that a fine or debt might be paid by the clan or tribe should that person's work or position in the clan merit such an act.

Laws for the Church

In *The Penitential of Cummian* (Abbot of Durrow, written to Segene, bishop of Iona [623–652]), the abbot's writings show how even the clergy are not outside the law. He presents two sets of laws for the clergy—one, outside the confines of the Church, and the other related to duties inside the Church.

THE LAWS OUTSIDE THE CHURCH
1. A bishop who commits fornication shall be degraded and shall do penance for twelve years.
2. A presbyter or a deacon who commits natural fornication, having previously taken the vow of a monk, shall do penance for seven years. He shall ask pardon every hour; he shall perform a fast every week, except between the days between Easter and Pentecost . . .

3. If (the culprit) is a monk of inferior status, he shall do penance for three years, but his allowance of bread shall be increased. If he is a worker, let him take a pint of milk and another whey and as much water as the intensity of his thirst.
4. If a presbyter or a deacon without monastic vow has sinned, he shall do the same penance as a monk not in holy orders.
5. But after the offense if he wants to become a monk, he shall do penance in a designated place of exile for a year and a half, until his obedience is satisfactory to God and his own abbot.
6. He who sins with a beast shall do penance for a year, with a perpetual pilgrimage.
7. He who defiles his mother shall do penance for life.
8. Those who befoul their lips shall do penance for four years; if it happens the second time, they shall do penance for seven years.
9. So shall those who commit sodomy do penance for seven years.
10. For masturbation, two years.

THE LAWS INSIDE THE CHURCH
1. He who fails to guard the host carefully, so that a mouse eats it, shall do penance for four days.
2. But he who loses it in the church, that is, so that a part falls and is not found, twenty days.
3. But he who loses his chrismal (holy oil vial) or only the host in whatever place, if it cannot be found, three forty-day periods of a year.
4. One who pours anything from the chalice upon the altar when the linen is being removed shall do penance for seven days; or if he has spilled it rather freely, he shall do penance with several fasts for seven days.
5. If by accident the host falls from the officiant's hand into the straw, he shall do penance for seven days from the time of the accident.

6. He who pours out the chalice at the end of the solemn Mass shall do penance for forty days.
7. One who vomits the host because his stomach is overloaded with food, if he casts it into the fire, twenty days, but if not, forty.
8. If moreover dogs consume this vomit, one hundred days.[44]

The above laws by Cummian are laws from the Roman Catholic Church and have nothing to do with the Druids.

Marriage Laws

The Druids' concern seemed to be instructive in regard to marriage laws. They also were very specific regarding whatever situation might occur, regarding parents as well as the bride and the groom. Here are the laws laid down by the Druids.

1. Three types of marriages related to different proportions of the wealth brought to the marriage by each party:

    - Equal proportions
    - Wealth brought only by the man
    - Wealth brought only by the woman

2. Forcible seduction were only temporary marriages. This was called a base and sinful act.
3. Union accepted by the man's invitation

Marriage seems to have been far more a partnership than found in the Roman world. In Roman life, daughters seemed to be no more than chattel passed off to gain land or riches. In most Celtic marriages, the husband and wife pooled equal amounts of money and shared their gains. At death the surviving spouse inherited everything.

This is probably true because the early Druids were integrated so closely into all society on a daily basis, including family life. Whether each tribe had its own special group of Druids, or if the

Druids were over several tribes, or if the Druids functioned individually, we cannot be positive. It has been intimated that, however they acted, the Druids counseled parents about their personal life and about the lives of their children in the growing-up years.

The Druidic laws, including marriage laws, were oral laws and were not defined in any written form until many years later. We can only infer from the writings of historians that Celtic marriages were more of a partnership than those of the Greeks and the Romans, wherein the husband made all decisions and was the prime benefactor in all marriage relationships.

Concerning marriage laws in the earlier years, we can only infer that the Druids knew of couples who were wed in some manner, with or without ceremony, because of their careful control of polygamy. The Druids allowed polygamy, similar to the later Hebrew concept, only when the first wife was without child.

> Neither were the Celts as rampantly licentious as their contemporaries pictured them to be. What the Greeks and the Romans took for promiscuity was often no more than a difference in codes of social conduct.[45]

The Celts had an acute sense of the rights and duties of every member of society, from the humblest laborer to the king. Although these laws and contracts were not written down publicly, they were known by the Druids, including the contract of marriage, because they functioned as both law-giver and priest. So when someone's moral conduct was thought to be out-of-bounds in the marriage, or with children, the Druids' prescription for the malady was to be carried out!

Whatever the outcome in any family situation, it was always assumed to have been cared for through divine intervention. In Irish epics of earlier years, and translated later, it is noted in Celtic affairs that religion cemented not only the king's position after he came into office. Likewise, if he were deposed in any way for any matter, it was noted that "he betrayed a sacred trust." The same was true of husband and wives, no matter how they came to be wed. It was reasoned by the Druids that they probably betrayed a sacred trust.

By the time the Celts migrated into the United Kingdom of the Celts, marriage laws came to be written down. Such writings, it was believed, were the result of Druidic information handed down through the ages.

According to the Laws of Hywel Dda, between 800 and 1282, it was assumed that the union of a man and woman was a contract rather than a sacrament; as Dafydd Jenkins put it, "The law kept the Church in its place."[46] It recognized, as canon law did not, that a marriage union could come to an end, and the law books provide detailed guidance as how the family property and the responsibility for children were to be shared if this should happen.

Several forms of a marriage union were discussed (see p. 45), and it was suggested not imposing that the church had a special status, and other forms were not invalid.

The chasm between legitimate and illegitimate children at this time was foreign to Celtic law, however, a later ruling under Hywel Dda came about that all children inherited equally. His matter stated, "It was not the nature of the union between father and mother, but rather the father's readiness to accept and acknowledge his son, which gave the son the rights that stemmed from his ancestry; thus, a bastard could inherit the property and status of his father."[47]

The Justinian Code

Justinian I, ruler of the eastern Roman Empire from 527–565, commanded ten of the wisest men in his realm to draw up a collection of the Roman laws. This collection is known as the *Corpus Juris Civilis,* which means "body of civil law." Also called the Justinian Code, this body of law is recognized as one of the greatest Roman contributions to civilization. It was a compilation of early Roman laws and legal principles, illustrated by cases, and combined with an explanation of new laws and future legislation to be put into effect. The Code clarified the laws of those times and has since served as a basis for the law codes of many countries.

The scholars who compiled the Justinian Code divided it into four parts. *The Institutes* served as a textbook in law for students and lawyers. *The Digest* was a case book covering many trials and decisions. *The Codex* was a collection of statutes and principles. *The Novels* contained proposed new laws.[48]

As to "Laws Pertaining to Marriage," very little is said except that Roman marriages, and the number of wives, were at the man's discretion.

WOMEN IN THE CELTIC WORLD

In the Celtic world, Greek women surrendered to her husband all of her possessions upon marriage. The Roman wife was to be a moral supporter of her husband, above reproach, and to bear as many children as he desired, thus making sure his name would be perpetuated.

It is only natural to assume that marriage in Celtic life would be a prelude into how women were thought of and treated in the Celtic world and to show the contrast.

Celtic women possessed a high ranking in the community, but Nora Chadwick also notes that among the Celts there were women warriors,[49] as well as "instructors in arms" until the ninth century, when bans against them were passed. There were other women warriors among the Celtic women, but none were among warrior heroines like Boudicca (the name means "victory"), the queen and commander of the British Iceni. Huge in frame, with a spear grasped in ample fist, a heavy torc around her neck, and knee-length red hair billowing like a flag, she ploughed the ranks of the Roman Legion IX in her sickle-hubbed chariot.[50]

In addition, Celtic women were also proud of their deportment and dress. They cared for their complexions better than their contemporaries, and their descendants were proud of them. The fabric of their skirts were wool, linen, and occasionally some imported silk. Golden torcs of varied style accented her clothing. They used special soaps and perfumes that added to her charms, and her beauty was enhanced by jewelry and other adornments given to her by her husband. Such women were not only beautiful but they proved to be powerful in government as well![51]

Celtic Tribes

In the early years, when the Celtic people were recognized by the Greeks as Keltoi, and by the Romans as Celtae or Galatae, nothing was mentioned about tribes of Celts. They were just a group of people.

It wasn't until much later (no B.C. date can be given), that they were referred to as "tribes" during an invasion or battle with or by these same Greeks and Romans. Such tribes usually numbered about 300, and they exhibited more drive and stamina than organization. Celtic tribes were formed around a prominent leader, often a warrior type. The tribal leader was either imposed or chosen and later formed as designated in the tribal structure below.

These Celtic tribes were classified into two distinct branches. The larger group held a deep inner conviction about power residing in the family, the land on which they resided, their cattle, and their possessions. They upheld this deep belief even to the extent of valiantly fighting the non-Celts. These non-Celtic people believed power was found in invasions of others' land and taking along with their land, their possessions as booty. The smaller Celtic tribes, like the Greeks and the Romans, gained power by invasions and amassed great wealth of lands and possessions of others. About the first millennium A.D. a tribal structure became apparent. The best manner in which to portray their tribal structure is to present it in outline form.

    King (Ri)—head of the tribe
        Either appointed himself or named by the people.
    Tribe (Tuaith)—the people
        Usually about 300.
    Society—three classes.
        1. Nobles:
            Warriors
            Specialists
            Master craftsmen
            Jurists

Carpenters
　　　Metal workers
　　　Men of learning
　　　Druids
　　　Bards
　　　Priests
2. Free-Commoners:
　　　Peasant farmers
　　　Craftsmen—lesser ability
3. Unfree: The majority of laborers
　　　Prisoners
　　　Subjugated communities
　　　Slaves
　　　Providers

Note: Knights could be among the warriors or chosen from the societies.[52]

NAMING OF PEOPLE

Peoples' names are important to Celtic families. Being genealogically arranged, they are a boon to those who are tracing their family tree.

There are two types in the Celtic naming of people.

1. The child is named after his father but not like John Smith Jr., John Smith III, John Smith IV. The child is given only his first name, then "son of . . . ," then the father's name.
    - In Welsh, 'ap is used (map means son of), so the child's name could be "Twm 'ap Gruffudd"—Tom son of Griffith. "Catrin merch Prys"—Catherine daughter of Price. In *Gaelic* (Irish or Scottish) Mac used to mean "son of" for the Scottish, like Mac Pherson, or "Ian MacPherson." The Irish for "son of" used to be Mc, like "Padraeg McGuffy," or Patrick McGuffy. Later Mac and Mc are used by both the Scottish and the Irish.

2. Later, when the children grew up and became employed, they were named after the manner of their employment. If a man ran a saloon, he might be called "Billy Saloonie." If he worked in a brewery, he might be named "Sam Brewer." Of if a single woman did special work with thread, she could be called "Ann Weaver."

THE FIGHTING CELTS—BUILDERS?

As Fighters. Although the Celts had a reputation as being fighters, what was it that made them fight? They were known as fighting for sport. This kind of fighting, one might say, was a vital part of Celtic aristocratic life. They were also known as fighting as mercenaries in both the Greek and Roman armies.

There was greater reason why a greater majority of the Celts fought. It was for justice! All other warriors fought to take people prisoner, amass territory, and to gather booty for a kind of personal pride. This is how they defined power. The reason the majority of Celts fought was because of a deep-seated ethic and an inner belief they possessed from early times.

The greater number of Celts believed that it was wrong, and against the desires of the gods, to take land from others when land not in use was available for the taking. This is why some Celts fought against those who caused such injustices against themselves and their neighbors.

As Builders. The majority of the Celts built hill forts to protect themselves against invasions. Hill forts were usually built circular, complete with moats, high banks of dirt, wooden cross timbers fashioned together, and rocks for basic support.[53]

Other construction techniques give us a glimpse of how the Celts lived: their homes, barns for their cattle, and storage places for tools and farming gear; their erection of food silos dug in the earth for food storage; the building of their temples of worship.[54] These Celts believed as spiritual beings that they were responsible to the gods and desired to show their stewardship. Much has been gained from what archaeologists have found at various sites, but much is unknown about the tools they used to do such work. We can only imagine the kinds of cumbersome tools they possessed, but we can marvel at the results of their workmanship.

The Celts Left Varied Impressions

One can more easily mark the different impressions that writers have about people and events in our age, and such impressions are fueled by the media as well as present-day historians. In addition, in our time, we possess what might be called higher ethics or a greater moral restraint, written into our laws and prescribed by our religious community.

However, we cannot use the criteria of our present day to make such impressions of the Celts. Here we must report the impressions left by the Celts during their time and place rather than ours. Usually what we call negatives are more prominent than the positives; such was true in their day as in ours. The following are impressions made during their time:

Head Hunting

> When their enemies (speaking of the Celts) fall they cut off their heads, and fasten them about the necks of their horses; and turning over to their attendants the arms of their opponents all covered with blood, they carry them off as booty, singing a paean over them and striking up a song of victory, and these first-fruits of battle are fastened with nails upon their houses, just as men do, in certain kinds of hunting, with the heads of wild beasts they have mastered.
>
> The heads of most-distinguished enemies they embalm in cedar oil and carefully preserve in a chest, and these they exhibit to strangers, gravely maintaining that in exchange for this head some one of their ancestors, refused to offer them a great sum of gold for the head they show.[55]

It seems that the Greeks and Romans reasoned that the Celts carried on in this manner for the same reason they did. They never made an inquiry into the Celts' reasoning that the heads contained the person's soul. The heads, by being cut off, allowed the soul to go on to an afterlife. Also the soul could not further be contaminated by the body, thus that person could do them no harm.

Human Sacrifice

Human sacrifice existed among many ancient people other than the Celts. It appeared especially among the Hittites (until 180 B.C.), and the Galatians (until 165 B.C.) in early biblical times. Peter Berresford Ellis, author of *The Druids,* makes an excellent comment on "The Ritual of the Druids," that the Romans also sacrificed humans to their gods but also fed Christians to the lions for "sport." (See Ellis, p. 144 f.)

> Human sacrifices seemed also to be a practice in Old Testament times. Lest we get into an argument here, that Abraham was led to sacrifice Isaac, a human that would have destroyed the lineage, according to the Scriptures; it was God that called Abraham to sacrifice Isaac, to test his faith, and made a way to provide a lamb for the sacrifice.[56]

It was the Hittites and the Galatians, the Celts and other cults, who instituted this type of sacrifice to the gods, believing the gods would make them better persons.

> The whole nation of the Celts are greatly devoted to ritual observances, and for that reason those who are smitten with the more grievous maladies, and who are engaged in the perils of battle, either sacrifice human victims, or vow to do so, employing the Druids as ministers for such sacrifices. They believed, in effect, that unless for a man's life a life be paid, the majesty of the immortal gods may not be appeased.[57]

Aside from what we would term the negative side, there is also the domestic side. The *Druids* provided the law and leadership of the Celts. The *Bards* made available their entertainment and historical presentations.

The Celts portrayed their enterprising agricultural expertise. Rotating of crops; fertilizing their fields; taming animals, especially horses, cows, and goats; planting and harvesting of crops; harvesting of fruits; mining ores; forging, smelting, and making metal tools; crafting jewelry and other ornaments from gold and silver; inventing the plow, sickle, and farm tools; building homes, wagons, and storage for their crops; manufacturing salt; weaving and making clothes.

These are just some of the things for which the Celts will be remembered. They will well impress their peers and will have handed down much to generations yet unborn.

In the eyes of this author, the greatest impression the Celts, or any other culture, left was their spiritual and moral ethics. However, the Celts left a greater impression by their definition of power as residing in the family, the land on which they resided and farmed, their belief that all their gifts were from their gods, and to these gods they were responsible.

Of course, they had their ups and downs, and that's natural. But this early spirituality, which they kept with them across Europe, was carried with them into the United Kingdom of the Celts and beyond.

We have just followed the historical background of the early Celts from circa 2250 B.C. until their migration into what we know now as the United Kingdom. Here we have been able to note their frustrations as well as their accomplishments. In the next chapter, we will traverse the same journey but note another stage of their life—their spirituality—and how it evolved over the years.

CHAPTER 2

THE ROAD TO CELTIC SPIRITUALITY: 2250 B.C. TO THE UNITED KINGDOM

> There is something in the thought of being surrounded, even upon earth, by the Majesty on high, that gives a peculiar elevation and serenity to the soul. It gave such a feeling even to our ancient families.
>
> —Anonymous

When we look at Celtic spirituality, which some historians trace back to about 2250 B.C., we have to gear our brains to a completely different attitude, vision, and viewpoint. We have to shift into a mind-set that parallels the minds of the Celts living in those early ages.

If somehow we could be transported back in time and live among the ancient Celts, and see life in the way they saw it, how do you think we would behave while living the events of that time?

We are able to look back over this road of history by means of classical writers, archaeologists, languages and linguistics, as well as historians. We will see that these Celts have rewarded us, not only with a historical and cultural perspective, but also with a panoramic view of what we call Celtic spirituality.

> A complex grouping of theological ideas, sacramental experiences, religious forms of life, and a spiritual inner-piety, that makes Christian experience what it is both in time and space.[1]

Our view of the Celts is seen from a present-day perspective, including all the written histories and lore that are at our disposal, as well as the stories shared with us from past generations. We need to view Celtic spirituality, as the Celts did, from their day by day existence; then we can see more clearly how that spirituality evolved.

For example, we understand and view the existence of the life of Christ after years have passed, and much has been written concerning his life and ministry, and from many angles and various approaches to his life and works. The disciples of Christ, like the early Celts, were unable to view such a panorama as we do now. They were held to view only the present day-by-day activities and act and react to the events and challenges of their time and according to their perspectives as did the Celts.

In order to understand the early Celts, we need this type of mind-set into which we must seek to place ourselves. These early Celts, we need to remember, did not have the same spiritual history that we have or the background that we possess. We have to set our minds, to think and reason, as the Celts did.

Church history has left us with a void about the Celts. We have only a few words like these in church history texts, which read:

> Beyond the certainty that a Christian Church existed in Britain at this period, very little is known about it. The population was *Keltic*. From later data it was to be inferred that this Church had an independence and character of its own.[2]

We have nothing before, during, or after these few words about the Celts in most church history texts. Referring to the quote above, we have to ask: What later data? What was to be inferred? If we are to know anything about Celtic spirituality, we also must understand what went before these words, what happened during these words, and what happened after these words. For these are the folks whose lineage took part in what we know now as the pre-Reformation period, the Reformation period, and the post-Reformation of church history. It was their children's children who are the very core of the "Reformed" and "Reforming" Church then and continuing through the present time.

We are grateful that we have a starting point for this adventure. The few words we have about the Celts have been pinpointed for us at least in Zenos' church history text, as being the latter part of the Nicene Age (A.D. 325–590).

From this statement, as a focus, we need to amass some documentary evidence on what was previous to, during, and after this statement, to show both the evolution and the growth of what we are calling Celtic spirituality. Such evidences will fill this void in our texts on church history. Such evidences will also show the roots of our Christian heritage and culture as well as the evolution of faith people have received that is called Celtic spirituality.

Little is known about the beliefs of the pre-Christian Celts. What is known about their early spirituality must be picked up in bits and pieces, here and there. We will find them from classical writers, from the later divulging of such facts from the stories of the early Druids (who earlier committed such beliefs and rituals to memory, and who much later transcribed them for our use), plus what spirituality could be revealed from early graves and archaeological finds. So, what is written here is of such a nature.

There is more confusion also. Some earlier historians refer to places by names not yet in existence, i.e., England, Great Britain, and the British Isles. (See examples below.) They know these names from their vantage point in history. Some historians also have referred to Great Britain long before Henry III named it officially in 1267. Up until 1267, the only official name of this area was either the United Kingdom of the Celts[3] or the United Kingdom.

If it is true, no historian is quoted as saying, "I am writing this history from my vantage point in time." Such can only be inferred as history is read.

The only official name given to this kingdom is the United Kingdom. It was given by Parliament in 1267, when Henry III was king. This official name replaced the common name prior to that time, used by the Celts themselves: the United Kingdom of the Celts.

Writing from their vantage point, some historians used England and Great Britain, or these words were perhaps penned in by the copyist. For example:

- Caesar in A.D. 4 writes, "The Romans conquered 'Great Britain.'"[4]
- Around A.D. 449 Angles, Saxons, and Jutes invaded "Great Britain."[5]
- About 500 B.C., the Celts settled in what is now France; their country was Gaul. . . . In England they became known as "Britains."[6]
- The title of this section reads: *How Great Britain Became Anglo-Saxon.*[7]

Early Celtic Spirituality

This author believes that the major tenet of the earliest Celtic spirituality must have begun with an innate response to a primal belief that there was a "Holy Other" in existence who sought the best for each individual and who seemingly demanded a human response to which they later made idols, or called gods, or later named a personal God.

From our hindsight other people have emerged in nearly the same manner but evolved to the present day in different faiths—Muslims, Hindus, Buddhists, etc. At first there was an oral tradition, and later holy writings appeared such as the Koran, the Bhagavad-Gita, the Bible, or pithy sayings by Confucius.

But in this text we are concerned about the spirituality of the Celts—how it began and evolved over the early years and down through the centuries.

Let's travel this Celtic road to spirituality together. It will be a long walk that leads us from circa 2250 B.C. to today—over a road paved with romanticism and intrigue—while we notice the growing and maturing faith of these Celts. This section of the trip, however, will take us only from their beginnings across Europe up to the time they entered the United Kingdom of the Celts.

The intention here is not only to give an introduction to Celtic spirituality, which is particularly unique, but also to whet your investigative appetite to further study the Celts and your own heritage whatever it may be.

Where Do We Begin?

For the road to Celtic spirituality, there seems to be a natural division to follow: (1) the spirituality of the Celts in Europe, or their earlier beginnings, and (2) the spirituality of the Celts in the land that began to be known as the United Kingdom of the Celts, now known by the United Kingdom, including England, Ireland, Scotland, the Isle of Man, and Wales, plus the land where the Cornish folks resided. The latter will be discovered in chapter four.

Such information concerning the beginning and the maturing of their early faith can only be secured from early classical writers, archaeology, language and linguistics as well as some historians. From these we know that the faith of the early Celts could angle off in several directions, but in the Celtic tradition that we will follow, we must state that not only will other cultures have influence over the Celts, but the Celts will, by their feelings and understanding and actions, communicate both their culture and spirituality to the world. Thus, shortly after one's primal faith (whatever that may have been), there is no pure faith but a kind of an amalgamation of beliefs woven into an evolutionary faith, which becomes personal.

It appears in the ancient histories and writings that have come down to us from time immemorial when these ancient forefathers and foremothers came into this world, they came with many inborn attributes; among them at least these three innate senses:

1. They realized that their life was physical, but that there was much in the world that was spiritual and made their life possible. This higher spiritual feeling was attributed to gods and goddesses. They believed that this higher power was responsible for the land on which they lived and used, their family of children, and their cattle and tools; and to this power they felt responsible. They also depended on that power to give them strength to lead better lives.
2. It seems that later they came to believe there was not only an entrance into this life by birth, as they experienced it with growing up years, but there was also an exit from this life by death, plus a better life beyond death! This thinking was later verified by the Druids.

> Duncan Norton-Taylor captures the Celts' belief in the hereafter. "The Celtic heaven was like the earthly world, only far better. It was a land without sickness, calamity, or old age, Where all people are beautiful, especially women. The sun always shone, birds always sang, and no one wanted for food or drink, which appeared in abundance, as if by magic."
>
> In the ancient Irish legends, goddesses often invite heroes to join them there. One enticing deity called it *Tir Inna'm Bio,* the Land of the Living. The Celts' hereafter was perhaps the most rhapsodically evoked in these stanzas by an anonymous Irish poet who referred to the heavenly abode as *Magh Mar* (literally, Great Plain), and *Tir Mar* (Great Land).
>
> > There, there is neither "mine" nor "thine,"
> > White are teeth there, dark the brow,

> The delight of the eye the array of our hosts,
> Every cheek there is of the hue of the foxglove.
>
> Purple the surface of every plain,
> A marvel of beauty the blackbird's eggs;
> Though the Plain of Fal be fair to see,
> 'Tis desolate once you have known Magh Mar.
>
> Fine though you think the ale of Ireland,
> More exhilarating still is the ale of Tir Mar.
> A wondrous land is the land I tell you of,
> Youth does not give way to age there.
>
> Sweet warm streams flow through the land,
> The choice of meat and wine.
> Splendid people without blemish,
> Conception without sin, without lust.

In preaching such a heaven, the Druids made the Celts formidable adversaries in war, for death became an alluring prospect. Little wonder Caesar especially singled out their sanctuaries for destruction. So long as the Druids existed, he argued, they were a threat to Rome. Caesar claimed to be wiping out "barbarous and inhuman religion," but in fact he was probably more bent upon "undermining the Druids hold on their followers."[8]

3. They realized that while they existed, they came to understand that life had some meaning, which resulted in the direction their life would take in their growing-up years, and that direction would have either a positive or negative result.

There were three earlier actions of a spiritual nature which motivated the Celts and for which others needed explanation. One dealt with their belief in their definition of power; another in their belief in fighting naked; and still another, their singing while going to and coming from battle.

THE CELTS' DEFINITION OF POWER

Their idea of power was not only a belief but a practice as well. It was stated previously that power for them resided in their family, the land on which they farmed and lived, and their cattle. (See pages 32–33) It was what the gods gave them, and to the gods they were responsible.

> The Celts also believed that they were responsible to their gods, who gave them strength to fight against enemies who would destroy their property and the property of their neighbors.[9]

Other nations around them believed that power was gained by warring and taking over other people's land and properties. The more land they were able to amass, the more power they possessed. This use of power to a majority of the Celts was absolutely wrong! This was not what the gods desired of their creatures. So they believed they were right to fight because the gods would want them to fight against such a wrong belief and practice of power. This is why the Celts fought hard against those who believed in such a practice—like the Romans, the Greeks, the Hittites, the Galatians, and others. And when the Celts won, and they often did, they also took a superfluous amount of booty. The greater amount of this booty taken away from the enemy, they returned to the people who had been wronged. Victims were also allowed to repossess their land.

There were some Celtic tribes who were known to have made treaties with the Romans. Whether some of these were Celts who believed that power was centered in the family, or whose power centered in amassing land, booty, and prisoners through conflict, we cannot be certain. Among those who made treaties with the Romans (Claudius) were the tribe Trinovantes. This occurred in A.D. 43.

This was the basic reason for the fighting of the Greeks and the Romans, whom the Celts often "beat to a pulp." This may be why, before these wars, they spoke of the Celts as barbarians, and after they were beaten, they wrote about them as "intelligent and inventive people."

Maybe to get on their good side? Or maybe they saw the Celts for who they really were!

THE CELTS AT WAR

Giraldus Cambrensis (Gerald the Welshman), a historian in the early 1200s, knew the Celts well. The following is a cryptic comment of his pertaining to the Celts.

> The Celts are light and active and hardy, rather than strong, and entirely bred up to the use of arms; for not only the nobles, but all the people are trained to war, and when the trumpet sounds the tribesmen rush as eagerly from his plough as does the courtier from his court.[10]

The Celts seen through Roman eyes were ferocious, flamboyant, and tensed with energy. These qualities were self-evident to their non-Celtic neighbors, even before 500 B.C. They fought with grace and a kind of fierce joy. They did not ever conceive of warfare as an investment in nationhood. According to Nora Chadwick:

> The warlike tendencies of the Celts, which appear to have been thought significant by classical writers, might be better classified as nonessential in that territorial aggrandizement was less frequently involved.[11]

The Celts did believe in warring for the gods, however, and felt it was their moral obligation to war against those who were using power by taking other people's land and possessions that were given to them by the gods.

> The Celts also believed that they were responsible to their gods, who gave them strength to fight against enemies who would destroy their property and the property of their neighbors.[12]

The Celts also fought the Galatians and the Hittites for plundering small tribes, making them captive and usurping their land. They also brought back prisoners as well as goods, and following their return sold slaves and had a reputation for sacrificing prisoners. People were known to commit suicide rather than fall into their hands.[13]

Celts Fought Naked

Fighting naked was another characteristic of the Celts at war. The only pieces of their attire when fighting was a braided belt (on which they hung their dagger), and a brass helmet, plus a shield and a spear.

Their nakedness in war had a spiritual meaning to it as well. They reasoned that, whatever they did to protect themselves and their neighbor, was for the gods, including war. (See endnote 9 above.) The bravery and ferocity of the Celts has never been in doubt.

When early writers (Strabo, Diodorus Siculus, and Caesar) either saw for themselves, or heard about the Celts fighting naked, one would think they would have asked why? We have been given vivid descriptions by them as to what limited apparel they wore: "only helmet, torc, braided belt on which hung a dagger," but nothing was said about why they fought in this manner. The writers didn't even hazard a guess!

Some lecturers, millennia removed from the scene and heard by this author, said, and I quote: "The Celts replied to an early historian, 'We brought nothing into this world, and we can take nothing out!'" They could give no verification for such a quote except the apostle Paul's word to Timothy.[14] Such a statement only proves "speculation is rampant, but factual data here is nil."

Many of these bronze and stone fighting figures of the fourth and fifth centuries B.C. feature the Celts stark naked. Such figures may be found in the museum at Hallstatt, Rome, at Bologna and St. Maur-en-Chausee, France.

Celts Sang Going into Battle and Returning

Why? No other group at that time is reported doing such a thing! Later Zulus and the Masai were reported as singing their war chant on their way to battle to inspire bravery and invoke their gods' presence in battle. The Celts probably were no different, with the exception that the Celts sang after the battle, whether they were victorious or were defeated.[15]

Fight songs are sung at sports events. The U.S. Army, Navy, Air Force or Marine bands were not only formed for just playing at football games or in a parade. They were formed many years before, for other reasons such as reminding the nation of its freedom, and the fact that others paid the price for that freedom.

Reminiscent of such a procedure is the Welsh Folk Song, *"Rhyfelgyrch Gwyr Harlech"* (Men of Harlech). The full translation of this music is "The War Song of the Men of Harlech." The following is an English translation.

> Men of Harlech! In the hollow,
> Do you hear, like the rushing billow,
> Wave on wave that surging follow,
> Battle's distant sound!
> 'Tis the tramp of Saxon foe-men,
> Be they knights, or hinds of yeomen,
>
> They shall bite the ground!
> Loose the folds asunder,
> Flag we conquer under!
> The placid sky now bright on high
> Shall launch its bolts in thunder!
> Onward! 'tis our country needs us,
> Freedom! God, and Right!
>
> Rocky steeps and passes narrow
> Flash with spear and flight of arrow;
> Who would think of death or sorrow?
> Death is glory now!
> Hurl the reeling horsemen over,
> Let the earth dead foemen cover!
> Fate of friend, of wife or lover,

Trembles on a blow!
Strands of life are riven!
Blow for blow is given
In deadly lock, or battle shock,
And mercy shrieks to heaven.
Men of Harlech, young and hoary.
Would you win a name in story?
Strike for home, for life, for glory!
Freedom! God, and Right.[16]

The Celtic Gods

The names of over 4,000 Celtic gods and goddesses have been recorded. However, this count includes gods and goddesses, local deities as well as some gods adopted from other non-Celtic tribes. If we suggest that individual deities could have been known by several titles, then the plethora of divines could be reduced to a manageable sum.

The Celts did not have an organized pantheon of gods like the Greeks and Romans. Several historians reported some things entirely different than what is true of other early people. Although the Celts have no organized pantheon of gods, they do possess a notion of a single divine spirit. Despite the cruelty found in some of their rituals, their moral comprehension was considered well developed.

You will notice that the Celts were both polytheistic and believed in pantheism. They believed not only in many gods but that all forces and manifestations of the universe were of the gods. Dealing with the deities, and perhaps a host of other spirits and supernatural forces, was to them a serious every-day business and practice.

About the religion of the Celts, Julius Caesar writes that the Celts worshipped Mercury, Apollo, Jupiter, Minerva, and Mars, and a pantheon of Roman gods:

> Among the gods (the Celts) worship Mercury.... There are numerous images of him; they declare him inventor of the arts, and

guide for every road and journey, and they deem him to have the greatest influence for all money-making and traffic. After him, they set Apollo, Mars, Jupiter, and Minerva; of these deities they have the same idea as other nations: Apollo drives away diseases, Minerva supplies the first principles of arts and crafts, Jupiter holds the empire of heaven, and Mars controls wars.[17]

Caesar, at this point, is probably equating Celtic deities with his own Roman gods. If these assertions are true, nothing of this has ever been repeated outside his Roman writings. In fact if any sleuth tried to substantiate his contention, he would find that Caesar, in none of his other writings names any Celtic god parallel to any Roman god. The logic seems to make his statement about Celtic and Roman gods being parallel either a fabrication or a bit of wishful thinking.

These early Celts were seemingly born with an intense sense and belief that there was much of an otherness; a kind of spirituality in the world into which they were born. They possessed an inner belief, not only that there was something of a higher nature, but it was an active force in their time. It was a force responsible for their being, and that same something gave them all that they had, and to that something they had to be responsible.

Believing in this "spiritual something" that was responsible for their life and enjoyments, they began to believe in "gods and goddesses, male and female" just prior to the Druids coming on the historical scene. Their reasoning seemed to be because of their needs being fulfilled, and their enjoyments were a deep satisfaction. They believed that all of this could not be handled by just "one spirit" or "one god" who was titled "male only." Such a belief was probably patterned after Greeks and Romans beliefs but to a much higher degree.

The Celts believed that they needed these gods to sustain them in their living and in their dealing with their neighbors. It should progressively lead them toward a greater and better life than existed for them at the moment. What we need to notice at this early time, with all this deep thinking about "spiritual matters" and "deities," there appears to be no thought of sin, and therefore no need of forgiveness. In addition, there is also no such mention of these two words being related to their belief in an afterlife.

> The Celts apparently had no conception of heaven or hell as a reward or punishment for their conduct during life: birth into the afterlife was, it seems, thought to be automatic.[18]

The oldest of the stories of the Irish gods are stories of rebirth.[19]

In addition, how some Christian theorists can read into the sacrificial practices of the Celts thoughts of any practice containing *penitential offerings* or of presenting any evidence of a *substitutionary atonement* is far beyond the comprehension of this author! For these two practices to occur, an awareness of sin is certainly a necessity. No author in the scope of my reading has presented any evidence that any Celt or other groups of people living at this time had any such thought in mind. It wasn't that they disbelieved in sin or forgiveness; it was the fact that they had not yet been confronted so that they might believe. We will see how Celtic spirituality evolves into their faith, and how they handled it.

From the facts at hand in the life of the Celts, we can't help noticing that they possessed a strong belief and faith in the gods and felt a responsibility to them. These were the gods who not only made it possible for them to exist, but who also supplied their needs, the needs of their family, their land and cattle, plus their possessions and gifts as well. Therefore, it is highly plausible to assume that some kind of worship must have taken place.

What kind of worship? Without Scriptures or hymns available, it was certainly not impossible for them to have had, if nothing else, prayers of thanksgiving to the gods for placing them here, supplying their needs and gifts that were so precious to them. In addition, since they had such a strong belief that their gods would make them better people, and help keep their confidence that their belief in power was the right thing, there could even have been prayers of petition.

Where could this worship take place? Any place at all! It could have been held within the family unit, or a gathering within the neighborhood, or among the clan, or all three. It could have been formal, with a leader gathering them together and using the first bidding prayer, or it could have been a spontaneous act. In any case, with a knowledge of the Celts' thinking and reasoning about the deities, worship in some form could have been held, before the Druids arrived, at any special time and place.

Remember, the early Celts had a multiplicity of gods, not only a god responsible for each chore, but more necessary a god to aid them with the jobs that needed to be done. There were the gods of the clans, and gods with overall responsibilities, and gods who were mentioned only once. i.e., in certain ceremonies.

Let's take a look at the more important Celtic gods; the gods that were mentioned often and the gods who played a major part in their lives.

Lugh

Lugh is one of the most important and highest of the Celtic deities. In addition to being kind of a supervisor, he is the god of light. We will hear more about him, as he is referred to in the United Kingdom and in his relation to Stonehenge.

His name was Lugh; in Wales, *Llew;* in Spain (the Etruscan territory), *Lugoues;* in Holland, *Leiden;* in Silesia (a region in Central Europe, between what is known as Poland and Czechoslovakia), *Liegnitz.* In Ireland he was the god of *Lugnastad.*

He must have been important because many places have derived their name after him, namely Liegnitz, Lyon, and Lieden.

His feast day was August 1. (Check the Celtic calendar.) His sacred symbol was a spear, and he was always accompanied by ravens and had a single eye. The German god Wotan had similar attributes. It was the Irish monks who converted Lugh into superhero, who excelled in every art and defeated his enemies with a magic spear. After all, who would want a god without that god being godlike?

Cernunnos

Cernunnos was at the lower end of the Celtic divinities but nonetheless powerful. The "god of the dead," he is usually shown wearing reindeer antlers and being close to animals. He is pictured on the Gundestrup cauldron holding a snake in one hand and a torque (a collar of gold, brass, or silver) in the other hand. Sometimes he is shown holding a bag of money. Some say it is a sign of a payoff he received from the dead for a better life in the next world. Others say it is a sign of being the god of fertility also, keeping himself busy, so that he may keep his part of the other-world occupied.

His special day, called Samhain by the Celts, was held on November 1.[20] This was the birthdate of Halloween. We will learn more about this in reference to the Celtic calendar found in Coligney, France. The early Christians identified Cernunnos as Satan.

There seems to be some confusion and disagreement among various authors whose works I have read concerning Cernunnos. Most of them agree that Cernunnos means "horned one" or "antlered one." He is variously called "the god of beasts" or "the god of wild animals" because he is usually shown in association with the animals of the forest and sea.[21]

Goddess Brigantia and Mapinas

Goddess Brigantia was said to preside over sacred healing groups at this early time but later over such as the one in Bath, England. *Mapinas* was her male companion, and they both were responsible for many miraculous cures. These two deities were spoken of all over Europe. Archaeologists have discovered many carvings that depict what were thought of as being affected human body parts. These carvings of human body parts were probably done by ailing people, who presented these as offerings to this goddess.

As Brigantia, the goddess, was adopted later by some early Christian missionaries in Ireland as St. Brigid. The goddess and the saint shared the same sacred day, February 1, and St. Brigid's shrine at Kildare, Ireland, is built over an earlier shrine of Sulevra, an earlier goddess who presided over healing springs. There is more about St. Brigid in a section on "The Early Saints." Springs sacred to Brigid are near Fouchart, Ireland and Llyn Cerrig Bach in Wales on the Isle of Anglesey.

Dagda

Dagda or *Daghda* is the most prominent of the older Celtic gods. His name literally means "the good god," but the epithet does not imply that he is good in the moral sense. When Dagda states his qualifications in the council of war before the battle of Moytura, he declares, "All that you promise, I will do, myself alone." "It is you who are the good god," they respond. And, from that day, he is called "Dag-da," i.e., "the god good for everything"—a leading magician, a redoubtable warrior, an artisan, all-powerful, omniscient, the lord of great knowledge. Dagda was the father of Brigid. Dagda was the nearest the Irish had to a universal god, though he was often subordinate to Lugh.

Nodens and Ogimos

Nodens, Nodons, Nudens, identified from the Irish god *Nudan, Nudau, Argetlam.* He was called "Nuada of the Silver Hand," and was connected with the Welsh tradition *Lludd Llaw Ereint,* or "Lludd of the Silver Hand."

Ogimos. The Greek historian Lucan of Samosata, writing about 150 B.C., relates that "as he was traveling in Gaul, apparently in the neighborhood of the Atlantic, he came upon a picture of an old man, clad in a lion's skin, leading a group of followers whose ears were attached to his own tongue by little gold and amber chains of great beauty and delicacy. The men are not being forced along but follow him eagerly and heap praises upon him, and it was clear that they would regret their liberty. A Greek-speaking Gaul, who was standing near, explained to him that the old man represented eloquence because "eloquence is a greater power than physical strength, and also that eloquence attains its climax in old age." His name is Ogimos.[22] It is said that Ogimos invented Ogham, a system of writing developed by the Celts. He is called the "god of eloquence."

Lesser-Known Gods

There were other lesser-known gods who probably could be equated with the gods of the family or clan. They were used less prominently in some ceremonies and were brought into the mythology of the later Celts. *Belenus* is sun god and a healer. *Epona,* a horse goddess who is always seated on a mare. She is pictured individually as a mother goddess. *Teutates* means "the god of the tribe." Teutates was also a common name and was probably the name of more than one god: *Lir, Matroma, Morrighan, Oegnus, Sequona, Sucellos,* etc. Some of these, and others, were considered cult gods and goddesses. Some mythology and religion of the early Celts was intertwined, and a certain unity of belief prevailed despite the earlier indigenous and localized cults.

The Pagan Trinity

One of the gods most often represented as a part of Celtic spirituality is a triad of gods (three-headed), of whom there are as many as thirty-two effigies.

These threesomes placed together seemed to represent more power, i.e., *Epona—Matres—Matronae,* mother goddesses who can be traced back to the Upper Paleolithic period. *Lugh—Dagda—Tuatha* were often associated together, usually in reference to the power to disseminate light. Light needs all powers available because light is created in so many different ways. (See Stonehenge later.) *Morrigan—Macha—Bodb* are known collectively as *Morrigana* (the great queens). Referred to as the "goddesses of fertility," they are accompanied by fruits, cornucopia, and infants. *Teutates* (god of the tribe)—*Esus* (Lord)—*Taranis* (thunderer god of the sky) clearly have their counterparts in Ireland and Wales. Taranis comes from the same word as the Welsh "taran" and the Irish "torann," meaning thunder, while Teutates comes from the same root as "tuath" or tribe in Irish. They reveled in sacrifices of those drowned in cauldrons, according to Caesar. *Esus* (Lord) had a savage shrine that makes strong men shudder. Many gods were venerated in triads. They were depicted as having three faces and were found in the excavations at Hallstatt and La Tene.

Gods in Human and Animal Form

Gods were not depicted in human form until about the middle of the Bronze Age (about 700 B.C.). In addition to the gods in human form, the Celts also had gods in animal form and gods who could transform themselves from one form to the other and back again. This was done for their own reasons and at their own discretion, not to harm but to benefit the people. Such actions of these Celtic gods were much like animal forms portrayed in the beliefs and myths presented in the totems of the Thlingits, Hydas, and Tsimsians of Southeast Alaska. Could it be that some early Celts migrated east over the arctic ice cap?

Some animals may have been regarded as totems or at least as symbolic of certain groups of Celts. This is suggested by use of the boar figurines on their helmets and representations of this animal on other pieces of their military equipment.[23]

There was also an apparent taboo against eating certain animals designated as totems in thoughts mentioned by Caesar. Early poles as high as forty feet have been topped by some Celtic cult figure or object, much like the totem poles of Southeast Alaskan Indians, which present a series of animals telling a story. (See later how the Druids used certain animals in their worship and sacrifices.)

CELTIC CULT PRACTICES

Cultic practices were many and varied, but religion permeated all aspects of Celtic life to a degree that most Westerners would find strange, yet the distinction between secular and religious is a quite recent western concept. The Celts probably worshiped in their home and in other domestic settings as well as at specific holy places. Much of their worship, however, was out-of-doors and animistic. Certain gods were associated with particular locations, remote places such as mountains, forest glades, springs and streams of water (obvious sources of life). Water cults were not solely Celtic. Germans and other parts of the classical world also shared them.

The gods of the Celts never lived in the sky or on mountain tops. They lived individually—either underground or on earth, often across the seas, or in distant lands. For them, worship was a reminder of what the gods did for them, which in turn made them feel responsible to the gods—without calling their gods "personal." You can see why their worship of the sacred remains an enigma to the western world.

In the Bronze Age, the Celts began to make figures of their gods, carved in wood and stone, as well as forming them on their cauldrons, implements of war, jewelry, and art forms. Some of these figures were about twenty feet high while others were twelve feet or less and may have been used as household gods. There are no records or even intimations that these sculptures or forms were ever worshiped as idols! They were used, however, as a reminder that these gods were the ones who were responsible for their being. The images made them (people) both appreciative of their creation and responsible to the gods for their life.

> A regular and systematic practice of the Celts after every battle victory was to dedicate such things they may have taken in battle. They dedicated the booty they would keep for themselves as well as the booty they would return to a group who had been sacked by some to amass power. They would gather all effects in one place. In many places, heaps of such objects were piled up in hallowed spots. Seldom has anyone, in defiance of religious scruple, dared to conceal such spoils in his house or remove them from their sacred places. The grievous punishment, with torture, was ordained for such an offense.[24]

The Druids as Worship Leaders of the Celts

When did the Druids come on the scene? No one seems to be able to pinpoint their beginning. Roman and Greek historians just seemed to come upon them and their doings in progress. In this manner historians picked up many of their achievements and antics as well.

Since we have already shared Celtic laws, schools, setting of boundaries, and settling of disputes, in this section we will look at the Druids in their leadership role as a kind of priest and shaman.

It is believed that the early Celts possessed a wonder and awe about everything, including a high respect for their environment, as well as a deep innate sense that some higher power made all things that they saw and felt. Chadwick claims, "The Celts reflect a ritual preoccupation with their environment."

References to the creations of the gods, honor given to animal totems, their worship in groves and by streams, and the fact that they treated the supernatural as natural declare their voice concerning their environment.

The nature of Celtic poetry has much to say about their environment. Hear what one author comments about the Celts' relation to their environment.

> The nature poetry the Gaelic muse may vie with that of any other nation. Indeed, these poems occupy a unique position in the literature of the world. To seek out and to watch and love Nature, in its tiniest phenomena as in its grandest, was given to no people so early and so fully as to the Celt. Many hundreds of Gaelic and Welsh poems testify to this fact. It is characteristic of these poems that in none of them do we get an elaborate and sustained description of any scene or scenery, but rather a succession of pictures and images which the poet, like an impressionist, calls up before us by light and skillful touches.[25] (See Celtic Poems on p. 291*f.*)

We can see what the coming Druids did was to build on this spiritual awakening, and continue support, encouragement, and direction, opening further the evolution of what we are calling Celtic spirituality. No monumental changes seemed to have been reported.

The early Druids had evidently already practiced and put together an amazing capacity for memorization. They studied the stars and their motion, the size of the earth and the world, plus the spheres and actions of the immortal gods. They also taught without books.

> The education of the young and the intellectual life of all classes was carried out by two classes of men known a Druids and Seers, who taught entirely by means of poetry orally transmitted. Their subject matter was saved by the use of metrical form from the inevitable disintegration which it would otherwise have suffered.... Despite the absence of books their teaching was on a lofty plane and included such subjects as the stars and their motions, the nature and greatness of our earth, the power and majesty of our immortal gods and other matters which comprised natural and moral philosophy.[26]

If we look at the Druids, and evaluate them based on the knowledge we have today, they probably do not make much of an impression. When we see them in their time and sphere of action, however, they become the moral and intelligent giants of their day.

The wildly familiar testimony of Julius Caesar is the most valuable testimony we have in some respects. He tells more about the Druids than do others. He felt that they possessed a rather poor trait by relying on their memories and the memories of their students. Their spiritual beliefs, mythologies, and other bits of historical knowledge, were to be passed on only by oral tradition. Caesar showed a concern that much would be lost by either embellishment or forgetfulness. Some of this could be true, but how much we will never know. Again, by this kind of thinking, we fail to look at Celtic spirituality in their time. Instead we look at it in ours.

The Druids believed that in societies without books and the written word, all knowledge is regarded as a spiritual possession and acquired by spiritual means or inspiration.[27] They seemed to believe that if these words were not handed down by oral tradition, there was a greater possibility of them being misinterpreted and debased because others' thinking was contrary to their thinking and reasoning.

But we have to ask two questions. (1) How can we rightly accept their memorized literature and spiritual acumen, in relation to their time, when receiving it centuries later? (2) Wasn't there a better chance if they revealed their spiritual knowledge back then? Wouldn't they have had a better possibility of a spiritual outreach? Could not an awakening have occurred in other areas so minds could have accepted their belief that power was in the family rather than invading other lands, breaking up families, and taking their possessions? This didn't happen, however, and we will never know, but it's worth the thought. This is another reason why we need to set our thinking on the things that really happened at that time and not let our minds stray, trying to place their actions in our time.

It is very difficult to determine which stories are true about the Druids. Either the writers place the Druids in our time; or some, like Lucan and Tacitus, slant their writing according to patriotic purpose; or Caesar, who wanted to prove himself an emancipator from the barbaric past, who really couldn't help himself from being anti-Druid. Caesar also wanted Senate approval to plunder Britain, and the Druids got in his way. Strabo and other philosophers had their own axes to grind. Some "Johnny Come Lately" types painted the Druids conditionally illiterate or gave alibis, saying there was a "lack of available information."

Spiritual Happenings Because of the Druids

Spiritual happenings are not always accompanied by ritual prayers, certain physical positions, or intoned incantations. According to our earlier definition of spirituality, the following actions by the Druids have resulted in clear spiritual happenings. They are not written down step-by-step in prose form that can be read or copied from a book or manuscript. They are buried here and there by sensitive writers who have caught a glimpse of significant spiritual performances.

For example, Druids, as sun-worshipers, engineered the monument at Stonehenge as one of their worship sites. Here a stone marker eighty yards to the east cast a shadow directly on the center of the altar during both the vernal equinox (about March 21), and the autumnal equinox about (September 22).

Peter Berrsford Ellis makes the claim:

> ... Great megaliths and stone circles, such as Stonehenge ... were constructed with highly advanced skill in astronomical observation. ... [W]e cannot claim all these constructions for the Celts for they date to a period well before we can safely identify the spread of a Celtic civilization ... [28]

In addition, Celtic heritage would have been lost if not for the Druids and the Bards. I believe we need to credit the Druids with the evolution of Celtic spirituality, beginning in those early years and continuing down through the centuries, even up to the celebrations in our day called Eisteddfodau,[29] and directed by the Druids.

Who were the first healers? The Druids! There can be little doubt that early Druidic medicine was practiced by using herbs. The oak might be called the sacred tree of the Druids, and from it they ritualistically gathered mistletoe for use as one of their medicines and for ritual purposes. Only the Druids collected the mistletoe and only in their white robes. This herb was so sacred to the Druids that it must fall into a white cloth. If any mistletoe fell on the ground, it was immediately contaminated and was burned. In addition:

> From Pliny's time down to the present it was thought to be a cure for epilepsy and hysteria and, in fact, its pharmacologically-active ingredient guipsine is actually employed by modern medicine in the treatment of hypertension and nervous disorders. This gives some backing to the belief that the Druids practiced psychiatry and even had clinics devoted to it.[30]

Consider the Druids' use of extracts from fungi and sea urchins, secretions from angry snakes, a magic egg, and even hypnosis borrowed from the Greeks for major operations.

The Greeks and Romans are in agreement when they say, "They practiced 'magic,'" although they do not describe the type of magic the Druids practiced or the results they achieved, or failed to achieve, with their magic.

They scorned the Druids' dissection of the viscera of sacrificed animals, but the writers do not say if they considered these acts as magic; nor do they claim that they followed the same procedures in their sacrifices themselves.

OUTWARD FORMS OF EARLY CELTIC RELIGION

The Cult of the Mothers

The Cult of the Mothers was a very prominent Celtic practice. There is a confusing mass of material, however, in the Celtic supernatural that came through the Romans, flowers in the Irish and Welsh literature, and centers in female deities. The female deities, in various ways, come in reflection of an earth mother goddess.

The female counterpart of Dagda (good god) in Irish literature was Morrigan (the great queen). She has many attributes but basically is a mother goddess, a goddess of fertility. Morrigan, the goddess of fertility, is also named Sheela-na-gig and is named the goddess of creation. She can be found in a *corbel* (a bracket of stone, wood, or other building material projected from the face of a main tower of a church or public building). In this case the goddess can be found on the tower of the medieval church at Kilpeck in Herefordshire in England.[31] The fertility god is carved in a squat position with each hand holding apart the lips of her vagina.

Beneath this corbel are printed these words:

> I am she that is the natural mother of all things, mistress and governess of all the elements, the initial progeny of worlds, chief of the powers divine, queen of all that are in hell, and principal of them that dwell in the heaven, manifested alone and under one form of all the gods and goddesses.[32]

Samhain, one of the early Celtic seasonal celebrations, marked its beginning on November 1. During Samhain, the limbo period between the ending of one year and the beginning of the next, sacrifices were held and feasting celebrated in concern for the fertility of both herds and crops. During this time, it was a practice to honor Morrigan and all the goddesses of fertility. Several such holy places are found in Caerwent, Wales.

To make such a cult prominent and more powerful, the gods and goddesses of fertility were often worshiped as triune gods. For example, the gods in triple form were mother goddesses—Morrigan, Macha, and Bodb or Epona, Matres, and Matronae.

Such triple goddesses can be traced back to the Upper Paleolithic Period (500,000–10,000 B.C.). We find surviving dedications on monuments in Gaul. These goddesses are engraved in both Latin and Celtic with the goddess pictured with baskets of fruit, cornucopia, or with children in their laps.

There is also a Welsh place called *Y Foel Famau* (the Hill of Mothers), which preserves this tradition. Beliefs in these goddesses of fertility, found in such places as Caerwent, Wales and Herefordshire in England, were no doubt a part of the faith of the early Celts.

Reminder Gods—Household Gods

In the Bronze Age (beginning circa 1800 B.C.) the Celts began to make small figurines of several of their gods, at first in wood and stone and later in bronze.

It is believed that the earliest mention of household gods appeared to be such a part of the Celtic culture, however, household gods also appeared in other cultures, i.e., Greek, Roman, and Hebrew cultures.

Lares (pronounced LAY reez) and Penates (pronounced Pee NAY teez) were gods and spirits of the home and hearth in Roman and Greek mythology which were used to protect home and family from physical harm. A family was known to offer some of its food to these gods at every meal. Safety and success, the family believed, depended on their faithfulness to these family gods and spirits. Lares and Penates were associated with the cities, as if each city was a big family.[33]

In the Bible we find these words concerning household gods: "Laban had gone to shear his sheep, and Rachel stole her father's household gods."[34]

"It is thought that household gods were images for religious use; penates, household gods were either worshipped or consulted."[35]

Among the most prominent household gods were:

Taranus, a naked god, a figure just over five inches tall and made of bronze, was found in France. He is pictured with a sunwheel in his left hand and a thunderbolt and a spiral of lightning, which he uses for protection in his right hand. This tiny figure has been thought to be a household god to whom a Celtic family could pray for protection against all enemies.

God of the hunt. Although the Celts were, for the most part, an agrarian society, they did hunt for hides and meat. It was believed that many households had copies of this six-inch high god of the hunt (no special name given), which they would take with them on hunting expeditions. The model is recognized as the god of the hunt by the typical hunting jacket worn by the figure. Copies can be found in the museum in Touget, France.

Brigantia, the goddess of healing, was the most prominent of all the household gods! One can hardly miss this reason. Like us, the Celts had babies and suffered sickness, accidents, and catastrophes. Modern medicine as we know it did not exist. The only ones able to come to their aid were the Druid and the shaman for healing and the goddess of healing, Brigantia.

A household god of healing, located in a prominent place, gave easily seen assurance that help was available not only for physical healing but also for dealing with death, depression, and mental and spiritual maladies.

God of the unknown. This sounds like the altar the apostle Paul found on Mars Hill in Athens, to which he responds, ". . . I perceive that in all things ye are too superstitious. For as I passed by, and beheld your devotions, I found an altar with this inscription: TO THE UNKNOWN GOD. Whom therefore ye ignorantly worship, him I declare unto you."[36]

This god of the unknown was usually carved about six inches tall and depicted sitting cross-legged in a yoga position. He wore a torque about his neck, giving him magical protection to the household. Being the god of the unknown, he has knowledge of things before they happen, and therefore it was believed to be a wonderful god to have on your side.

It has been assumed that this household god was carried into battle to alert the Celtic warrior to the intended action before he made his move, giving the Celtic warrior a distinct advantage. This belief in the unknown god could have led the later Celts to accept the belief in the One God who had a knowledge of all things. In addition, they could be reminded of their other gods who gave them strength and to whom they were responsible.

The gods carved small enough to be household gods, and those carved much larger, were always pictured as anthropomorphic (humanlike). The more prominent gods, however, such as Lugh, Cernunnos, Dagda, and Ogimos, have not been found even in gravesites. Could the reason have been because they served a different purpose? Were they too important or too spiritual to have been carved for this purpose?

Household gods have been found in burial sites unearthed in both the Hallstatt and La Tene areas, in Switzerland and along the Danube River, and were often found in the hands of the deceased.

The early ones were hand-carved and wooden. The reason they had been preserved for so long is that they had been treated with oil and had been hand-rubbed. Later household gods were made from stone and bronze. These household gods can be found in museums housing Celtic artifacts. Many of these household gods are being counterfeited and sold as originals.

Keep in mind, however, that nothing has been found written that any Celt used household gods or any replica of a god as idols to be worshipped. The prominence of these figures in their household helped them realize the power given them by the gods and were a present reminder to them of their responsibility to the gods. This, in turn, would make them proud of their creation, as well as help to make them better people.

Holy grounds of the early Celts, before the Druids arrived on the scene regarded the mountains, forest groves, streams and pools of water with a holy awe and considered them as holy ground. However, it is believed that the early Celts held in greater veneration: the gods who gave them their home, family, the ground on which they tilled, plus their gifts and pleasures. In a sense, they considered their lives as "Holy Ground."

At their coming, it seems that the Druids began using what the early Celts called sacred or holy ground and added to the Celtic belief, rituals and other sacred places that might be termed holy ground. The following are a few of those very special places:

There were the *deep forest glades* where trees (especially the oak) had become sacred to the Celtic worshipers. From them they carved anthropomorphic figures they called "gods."

Writers like Caesar made these areas appear gruesome places with sacrificial blood splashed on trees and trees defaced by branches being lopped off to carve epitomes of their gods. Even today, however, without any clue to induce worship, one can naturally find in such areas not only aesthetic beauty but also an awe bringing to mind a sense of "the Other."

> And there were many springs there, and grim-faced figures of gods, uncouthly hewn by the axe from the untrimmed tree to witness.[37]

Pools, springs, and running waters had a long tradition for the Celts—going back before the Bronze Age to a part of the Neolithic Age, which began about 2500 B.C. Holy waters provided a kind of purification and spiritual calmness for the early Celts. Archaeologists later proved that such areas were a place where the gods met the Celts and where the Celts met the gods. This was also a place of sacrifice, proven by the fact that many artifacts and what might be referred to as votive offerings were found.

For the Celts water and foliage came from the earth, so it was appropriate that such gods be female because these things came from Mother Earth.

In addressing themselves to deities and cult objects, classical chroniclers never really offer explanations. Pliny, the Roman procurator, reports witnessing a Druid ceremony at the base of an oak tree that stood in a grove of trees with a stream nearby, which proved to be a natural sanctuary.

Dillon and Chadwick write concerning early Celtic worship, "A feature of Celtic religion that emerges early is by rivers and sacred trees which were objects of devotion."

Pools of water were later Christianized in such pools of water as Bath in England and Lourdes in France. Later, water was used in Christian circles for baptism, signifying cleansing from sin.

The places of sacrifice, whether at an altar, where the sacrifice was human, animal, or food; whether in a forest glade under an oak; or by a lake, stream, or well, such locations were considered specific places of sacrifice over the years and in a sense might be called permanent places of sacrifice and holy ground.

There were other specific places of sacrifice, such as a funerary sacrifice, which were not considered permanent places of sacrifice due to the varied places of burial. The sacrificial rite of cutting off the heads of the enemy in battle to let them depart to the after-life might be considered a sacrificial rite.

There is also a possibility that a family might have made sacrifices of some sort; if not in their homes then in buildings such as temples, ritual shafts, storage places, etc., known as places of worship and sacrifice.

Ritual shafts. One of the most surprising and most impressive aspects of Celtic religious practice was their practice of digging shafts deep into the ground. Some archaeologists have suggested that they represented a Celtic expression borrowed from an earlier Mediterranean belief. It was thought that if shafts were dug deep enough, people would be able to communicate with folks in the underworld.

There is no evidence found in any Irish or other Celtic literature to substantiate such an idea. These shafts were deep but not deep enough to imagine such a communication. Celtic shafts dating back to the Bronze Age (circa 1800 B.C.) were dug well before the Romans expanded northward. These Celtic ritual shafts were called *bothros* by the Greeks and *mundus* by the Romans.

There were many examples of Celtic religious shafts found especially in what might be called religious centers, especially Holshausen in Bavaria, where three ritual shafts were found within a square enclosure (probably fenced to signify holy ground). These shafts were dug at various depths from fifty to one hundred feet deep but only about forty inches wide. The mystery is not the depths or the contents of these shafts but how they were able to dig such a pit. From the vantage point of today, a pit forty inches wide could be dug with an augur—but there was no such tool in their time.

In Vendee, France, there were about thirty of these deeper shafts within the radius of a square mile, always three and four inside what might be termed a fenced area or sacred ground. At Vendee there was found a shallow shaft, approximately eight meters in depth, but with only a forty-inch opening. In it was found a cypress pole, and upon later examination an organic substance on the pole was found to be decomposed human flesh and blood. Whether this was a sacrificial pit, or the person digging the hole died there, we do not know.

Other earlier ritual shafts have also been found in the area of Zurich, Salzburg, and Frankfurt. Some of these shafts have been dated back as far as the Neolithic Period (8000– 4300 B.C.)

Some ritual shafts have been found in the United Kingdom at Hampshire and Norfolk in Northumberland and at Wilsford near Stonehenge. In some of these shafts water was found, and since water was a ritual substance, many of these shafts took on a superstitious nature. Concerning these shafts in the United Kingdom, 1000 B.C. seems likely.

All of these ritual shafts were thought to have been considered holy ground by the Celts and, by the nature of their content of what was considered votive offerings, it has been agreed that sacred rituals were also held here.

Votive offerings were animal and human bones, small wooden figures (probably household gods), and wooden and bronze forms of fertility gods of both male and female sexual forms. Other articles were also found, such as antlers, pottery, torques, jewelry, etc.[38] (See artist's drawing of ritual pits on next page)

Storage shafts. In addition to what we have called ritual shafts, storage shafts have also been found. These pits have been found mostly on the top of small hills or hillocks where there was less chance of water seepage. Such pits were dug in hard clay or lined with hard clay.

Archaeologists suggest that Celtic storage practices were before their time. To explain, such an earthen storage needed an airtight seal. If these pits were completely dry, no problem. If the walls of the pit became damp, the seeds would germinate using the available oxygen and release carbon dioxide. This would put the bulk of the grain into suspended animation. The grain would keep for months until the seal is broken.

Both Rutherford and Norton-Taylor suggest that the area where these storage shafts were dug was "holy ground." At these places it could be inferred that a kind of dedication rite or ceremony might have been held by the Celts three-times—once when the shaft was dug or prepared, again at harvest-time when the crops were placed in storage, and yet again when the seal was broken and the contents were used.

Structured holy ground. From the forest glades under oak trees or beside pools or running water, Celtic worship evolved into sacrificial altars, which in turn evolved into permanent sanctuaries—shrines and later temples. The worship of the Celts, led by the Druids, did not take place exclusively in the out-of-doors.

In the 1940s, when workers were preparing for the building of London's Heathrow Airport, a Celtic settlement dating back to circa 300 B.C., including a temple, was excavated. As the Celts became

RITUAL SHAFTS WITH DIVINE OFFERINGS

BECAUSE THEY BELIEVED THAT SOME OF THEIR GODS LIVED INSIDE THE EARTH, THE CELTS BORED DEEP HOLES IN THE GROUND AND FILLED THEM WITH VOTIVE OFFERINGS TO PROPITIATE THE UNDERWORLD SPIRITS. NO ONE CAN BE SURE HOW THESE RITUAL SHAFTS WERE DUG—SOME ARE AS DEEP AS 100 FEET—BUT THEY PUNCTURE THE LAND IN EVERY REGION OCCUPIED BY THE CELTS.

MANY OF THE SHAFTS, SUCH AS THOSE DIAGRAMED AT RIGHT, HAVE BEEN DISCOVERED IN CLUSTERS, SUGGESTING THAT THEY WERE CENTERS OF CONSECRATED AREAS WHERE THE CELTS CAME TO WORSHIP.

THESE TWO EXAMPLES, CONSTRUCTED MORE THAN 2,000 YEARS AGO, WERE FOUND ALONG WITH 30 OTHERS IN AN AREA ABOUT A MILE SQUARE IN THE VENDÉE REGION OF FRANCE. THE ONE ON THE LEFT WAS CAREFULLY FILLED IN FOUR DISTINCT ZONES, WHICH WERE SEPARATED BY LAYERS OF STONE. IN CONTRAST, THE CONTENTS OF THE OTHER SHAFT APPARENTLY WERE DEPOSITED IN A HAPHAZARD FASHION. BOTH OF THESE PITS CONTAINED SIMILAR OBJECTS: WHOLE AND BROKEN POTTERY, HUMAN BONES AS WELL AS THOSE OF DEER, COWS, PIGS, DOGS, AND FOXES. THE LEFT SHAFT ALSO CONTAINED A 20-INCH WOODEN FIGURINE OF A FEMALE DEITY, ALONG WITH PIECES OF DEER ANTLER. THE OTHER ONE YIELDED A 12-FOOT CYPRESS TRUNK AND A HOLLOW OAK LOG FILLED WITH BONES, REFLECTING THE CELTIC BELIEF IN THE SACREDNESS OF TREES.

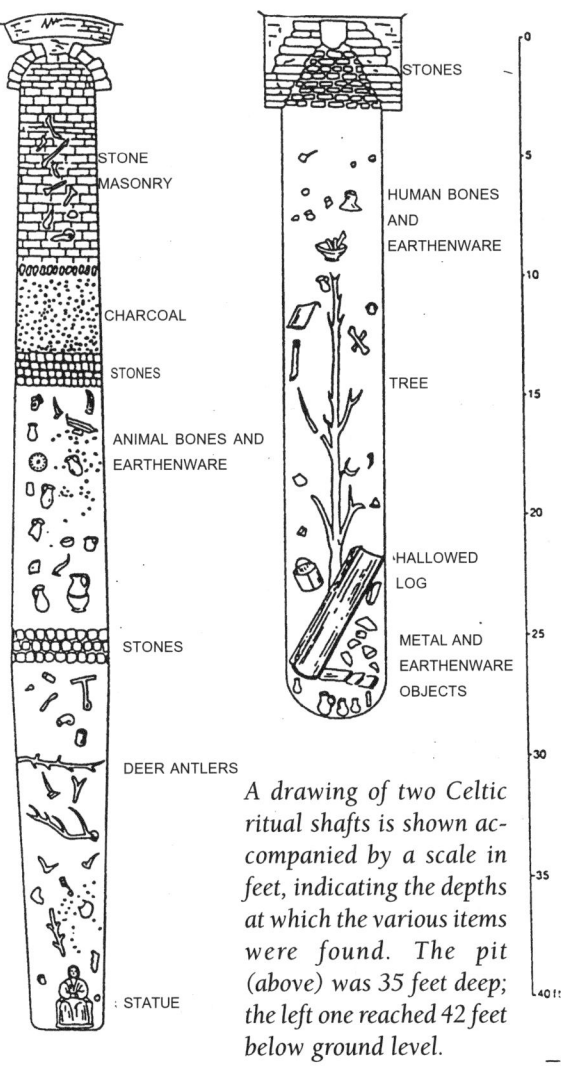

A drawing of two Celtic ritual shafts is shown accompanied by a scale in feet, indicating the depths at which the various items were found. The pit (above) was 35 feet deep; the left one reached 42 feet below ground level.

more affluent and better acquainted with the classical world, their temples became more ornate and included some of the architectural features of Greek and Roman temples. Scholars and historians concur that there are as many kinds of Celtic temples as there are clans or within areas where groups of Celts reside.

During the latter part of the fourth century B.C., Celtic temples were erected near the mouth of the Rhine River near Marseilles. Stone-built temples were reported widespread in the area; however, the outside walls of these temple structures were only ceiling high (about eight feet) with windows to let in the light. The roof construction contained a woven basket work of branches and reeds overlaid with a clay and lime mixture to keep out moisture. It was thought that the Celts, other than those in southern Gaul, adopted and patterned the idea of a permanent temple and shrine from the earlier Celts living farther east on the shore of the Danube River.

> There is a small island off the mouth of the Loire River, inhabited by the women of the Samniae, and they are possessed by Dionysus.... It is their custom, once a year, to un-roof their temple and roof it again on that same day before sunset. Each woman is to bring her load to add to the roof; but the woman whose load falls out of her arms is rent to pieces by the rest, and they carry the pieces around the temple with a cry, "Evah," and do not cease until their frenzy ceases....[39]

Reference has been made to the statuary at the source of the Seine. Here Professor Roland Martin excavated sanctuary figures of what have been determined as gods and heroes. During a later part of the first century B.C., a sanctuary built with stones from an *oppidum* (proto-city) yielded a much more sophisticated body of free-standing statuary, according to Chadwick. In addition she claims that there were schools of sculpture that were to influence the development of Celtic statuary. It might be argued that a truly Celtic feeling for pre-Christian imagery long survived the introduction of Christianity in Britain and Ireland. Stone heads form part of the decoration of a number of Irish Romanesque churches.[40]

It could also be argued that the display of such statuary was later introduced into Roman Catholic Churches in the United Kingdom in the form of saints, Christ on the cross, the Virgin Mary, and other saints of the Church.

What has been described as a typical Romano-Celtic temple has been found at Augustdunum (Autun), France. This square two-story brick and concrete structure held a central towerlike shrine-room, similar to the temple reconstructed at Beaune, France. Extending out from the main building approximately six feet was a base for short posts, holding up a roof anchored at about first-floor height. This made a kind of portico or ambulatory cloister walk. There was only one door to the building at the front of the temple structure, used as both entrance and exit to the building. The structure was white and had two windows on each side of the gabled roof to illuminate the interior.[41] The bricks for the building must have been adobe bricks since no kilns have been found in the area where such buildings were erected. These buildings were too small to house any size congregation who might gather for worship. Such buildings were a place where the Druids would gather to receive their messages and then bring them outside to the gathered congregation.

Another worship center, the Temple of Lydney, located on the banks of the Severn River in Gloustershire, was a temple of the Nordens, erected between A.D. 365 and 367.

This temple differs from the normal Romano-Celtic form (Basilican plan). Healing was found to be associated with this temple. Connected to the temple were guest houses, baths for visiting worshipers, and an *ablation* or healing center, a place, perhaps a pool, where people could make void a disease or dysfunction of their bodies. In addition, people were said to be assigned certain rooms where they would be visited by a god who would grant them healing while they were asleep. The gold coins found there suggest that this was an establishment for wealthy patrons. Other sanctuaries, rich in detail, are found in both northern and southern France.

Several shrines may be found spread across the continent from the area of the Danube and into Gaul. No shrine is as ornate as the one found in Gournay, however. This shrine was situated bordering on three Belgic tribes and seems to have had both political and religious importance. It was political because of border problems between the tribes and religious because of the influence of the shrine and the belief that their gods lived there and could oversee their every action.

From drawings, this shrine was made of wood. There was a wooden fenced enclosure high enough so outsiders could not see what was going on inside. In the center of the inner courtyard was a sacrificial altar with a square gabled-roof held up by four posts on each corner over the altar. This altar enclosure was flanked by two tall poles, twice as tall as the poles holding up the roof above the altar. In the inner courtyard to the right of the altar were three pools enclosed by a low fenced area with an entrance gate. These shallow bodies of water were thought to be for the ritual of cleansing.

Just outside the larger fence, a deep moat surrounded the fenced enclosure with a bridge as the entrance to the shrine. Inside the fenced enclosure was a shallower moat in which were found votive offerings of various types, i.e., skeletons of horses, pigs, and sheep, cattle skulls and human remains, which were thought to be for special burial rather than sacrifices. In addition, great amounts of gold in bronze urns were found here.

A similar sanctuary has been found at Ribemont-sur-Ancre (Somme) which, in addition to the one at Gournay, contained various kinds of military arms.

Diodorus Siculus (?–A.D. 394) was a historian who seemed to be intrigued with the Celts. His writings cover a wide range of Celtic interests. Here he writes of their spirituality and their mode of worship.

> And a peculiar and striking practice is found among the upper Celts, in connection within the precincts of the gods; for in the temples and precincts made consecrate in their land, a great

amount of gold has been deposited as a dedication to their gods, and not a native of this country ever touches it, because of religious scruple, although the Celts are an exceeding covetous people.[42]

One special thought needs to be understood and emphasized about the early Celtic temples. They were not built to house a congregation where the Druids could teach and share a religious message. These temples were only for the Druids or priests to prepare their message for the people. The people gathered outside, and the priest or Druid came out of the holy place to address the people. There was also no special time for worship but at the invitation of the Druids.

THE CELTIC CALENDAR (COLIGNY)

Just as the Celtic law was rooted in the notion of a divine order and was made and enforced by a priestly panel of jurists, so Celtic science was based in religion, and the Druids were its chief practitioners. As scientists, the Druids were mainly concerned with astronomy. They studied the shifting relationships of the sun, the moon, and the stars, and they used these cosmic changes to anticipate the future of earthly events. For this purpose they invented a remarkably sophisticated calendar.

> In 1887, in a vineyard in what is now the French town of Coligny, Coligny archaeologists found shattered physical remains of one version of this calendar. Pieced together, the Coligny [c]alendar forms a bronze plaque about sixty inches high and forty-two inches wide, and it dates from the early first century B.C. The notations are in Roman letters and numerals, "but in a Celtic language."[43]

The calendrical system itself preceded the Roman occupation of Gaul and owed no debt to the Julian calendar invented by the Romans.

The Coligny calendar divides the year into a system of months and seasons that coincides with the Celtic seasonal festivals (reported later). Clearly its makers and users were Celts!

The Celts, like the Hebrews, reckoned a day as from sundown to sundown. The Creation story in Genesis says:

> "God called the light Day, and the darkness he called Night. And there was evening and there was morning one day."[44]
>
> It is also repeated "And there was evening and morning . . ." for Day one through Day six.[45]
>
> Each day was counted, and is today still practiced among the Jews and Moslems, from moon-rise to moon-rise. . . .[46]

Fifteen nights made up what the Celts called "the bright half of the month" (the period of the waxing moon), and fifteen nights of "the dark half of the month" (the waning period of the moon). The bright half was the auspicious time for doing things; the dark half held gloomier prospects. This is reminiscent of *The Farmer's Almanac* for planting, fishing, investing, etc.

The Coligny calendar contains sixty-two of these lunar months plus two intercalary months. The Celts apparently adjusted their lunar year to the solar year by inserting an intercalary thirty-day month alternately at two-and-a-half year and three-year intervals. (The Julian calendar and its derivative, the modified Gregorian calendar now in use, accomplish approximately the same end by varying the lengths of the months and by adding leap-years.)

The Celtic year was divided into four seasons (not winter, summer, spring, and fall), each of which was ushered in with a liturgical period. While the laity celebrated with feasting and games, the Druids prepared for the somber duties of honoring the gods with sacrifices (animal and human). When the liturgical sacrifices were about to begin, the commoners gathered to participate in the ceremonies. The purpose of the Coligny calendar was to schedule these sacred events, rather than to simply mark the passing of time.

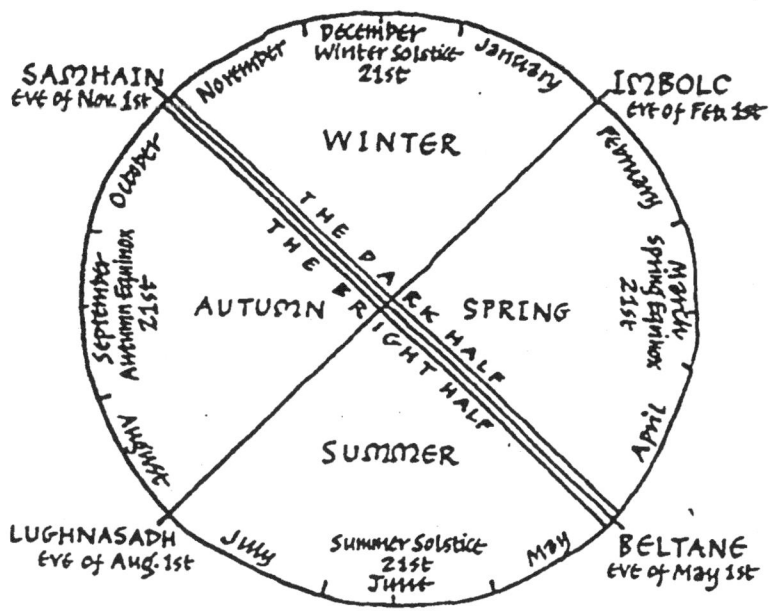

Four Festivals of the Celtic Year

It is only natural then to share the meaning of these Celtic religious festivals, which are included in the seasons of the Coligny calendar. These traditional religious festivals, it is believed, were woven into the rhythms of their daily life; their stories and mythologies as well as the evolving of their spirituality.

Irish evidence suggests that the Celts celebrated four festivals annually. Each festival marked the changing of the seasons and the role fertility played in their culture. These feasts not only played a part in their agrarian culture but also definitely were related to their evolving spiritual lives as well.

Such festivals are linked to the Celtic calendar. One will note that each quarterly section of their year opens with an explanation of each festival as follows.

Samhain

The first festival of the Celtic year was *Samhain* (Samain) and marks the beginning of the Celtic new year on November 1, as the winter season begins. The days are shorter, the trees are bare, and farming comes to a standstill. This may seem a very strange time for a beginning, yet this is a time when life rests and people look forward to the return of light and activity. This is thought to be a good time for planning, reflection, and introspection, an intermediate period between the end of one year and the beginning of the next. Samhain means "the coming together."

Mythologically speaking, this was a time when all barriers were lowered between the gods and humans; a time of reconciliation when the tribal god and Mother Earth in her tribal guise had intercourse so the fertility of the land and all creatures and people were renewed.

The festival of Samhain really began its celebration on the previous night (New Year's Eve), October 31. At this time the gates of the otherworld were opened. The spirits of the dead were believed to return from their dwelling place, roam through the land of the living, and communicate with their ancestors.

Samhain, and its mood of witchery and fear, survive on this traditional Halloween (October 31). Odd, isn't it, that this special festival celebrated by the Celts years before Christ falls on what our present churches celebrate as All Souls' Day and All Saints' Day respectively. Parts of Samhain have been actively translated into Christian parts of our present liturgical calendar.

There is a historical mythical calendar[47] published annually in our time, marking the Celtic New Year celebrations as well as historical and mythological dates, and in addition dates referring to Celtic deities.

Imbolc

The second festival of the Celtic year was *Imbolc*, which began on February 1 in the modern Gregorian calendar and ended in April. The festival ushered in the budding of trees and the beginning of spring and began the second quarter of the Celtic year. This season is under the aegis of St. Brigid. Brigid has three aspects of her nature. She is matron of healing, smithcraft, and poetry and is the mistress of inspiration and prophecy. Many healing places, such as springs, wells, and rivers, have been dedicated to her.

We know little about the ceremonies that were connected to this season with the exception that such rites were related to the time when spring lambs were born and ewes came to nursing, which underlies the meaning of Imbolc.

The patron deity of these flocks and fertility specifically was St. Brigid (Brigantia). She was known by St. Ffraid in Wales and St. Bride in Scotland and is the secondary saintly protector in Ireland after St. Patrick. Brigid is venerated in all parts of the Celtic world.

Concerning mythological memories, when the hard ground of winter becomes the softer ground of spring, we hear this story:

> As the Cailleach had hardened the earth with her hammer at the beginning of Samhain, so Brigid was believed to make it soft again with her white wand, with which she awoke growth.[48]

Brigid was the mother-goddess of childbirth.[49]

Beltaine

The third festival of the Celtic year was *Beltaine, Beltane,* or *Beltine.* (May—July).

Take your choice of the spellings. The name means "Bel's Fire." Bel is the shortened form of Belenos or Beli, "the shining one," an archaic god named "the solar healing god" whose fire was used in minting coins. The last syllable of the word "tane" means fire. Belanos is one of the oldest gods concerned with the pastoral element of his people. This festival celebrates the summer's warmth, the maturity of the growing cycle, the wonder of family gatherings in the out-of-doors.

There is much symbolism in the mythology of this season. Fire, the symbol of both heat and light, belongs to this time of year. According to mythology, fire was kindled on Beltaine Eve. Nine men, with nine different kinds of wood, made fires with a friction drill.

It was in the early part of this season that people made a thick smoke from two fires side by side, and the herdsmen drove their cattle between these fires for "purification." They followed the direction of the Druids, who believed that the cattle driven through thick smoke early in the summer would cure any disease or infection the cattle might have and protect them from disease for the remainder of the year.

Lugnasa

The fourth festival of the Celtic year was *Lugnasa,* a harvest festival. This is the beginning of the last quarter of the Celtic year, from mid-August to mid-October. The high feast day, August 1, was like a May-Day celebration.

This was the time when people were able to see the fruits of their labors and celebrate the grains standing high in the fields (August), the colorful ripeness of the fruits harvested (September), the slaughter and storage of their beasts for their eating in the winter (November).

As the autumn progressed they saw the beauty and fruit of their labors and felt the richness of their bountiful treasures, which led to a festive celebration with thanksgiving to their gods.

Their festival was named after *Lug* in Ireland; *Lugus* in Gaul, and *Lleu* in Wales. He was the chief god of the Celts. This festival marks the deeper awareness of the marriage between the land and its people.

Why does the central part of this festival fall on August 1? Because in Celtic mythology, Lug honors his foster-mother Tailtu, who is said to have died on that date. The writers of mythology note that Tailtu was an ancient goddess of agriculture who was said to have died from clearing trees for planting. It is believed that Lug and his foster-mother, though unnoticed by anyone, were always in the fields helping bring in the harvest.

> It has been reported that after the harvest, at the end of the festival of Lugnasa, many games were played. Swimming the horses across lakes, contests of strength, dancing and skills, were only

a few of the parts of the celebration, and letting off steam and the conclusion of the harvest.[50]

In all of these festival celebrations, there was present a sense of spirituality expressed or implied. Miranda Green in *The Celtic World* elegantly proclaims, "The perception of the supernatural as being present in the natural world penetrated all aspects of Celtic belief." Their gods were present, and to their gods they gave allegiance because earlier they felt responsibility to their gods for family and all gifts given to them. We can see in their spirituality an evolvement through their involvement.

It is believed that these Celtic festivals began, at least in part, in the early agrarian era of the Celts about 1700 B.C.. They possibly included some earlier gods in their activities, and these festivals evolved into greater and more exciting experiences each year. Among other activities, these Celtic festivals, as presented here, continued until shortly after the coming of Christianity in the United Kingdom through the Celtic church. (See the Celtic Year Logo on p. 93)

A shaman, known as a medicine man or priest among the early people, had the ability to invite good spirits and cast out the evil spirits. Shamans are found among Mongolians, Maoris, Polynesians, Eskimos, and most tribes of Native American Indians.

Shamans were also found among the Celts. It is certain that Druids were shamans, but we are not certain that all shamans were Druids. They were credited with casting spells, controlling the elements, causing storms and raising fog. Such functions are given in mythologies like the Welsh "Gereint and Enide" and "Tain Bo Cualange."

Another element of the shaman is centered in hunting and in the ancient belief that animals also possessed souls. In my work as a Presbyterian missionary pastor in Alaska (1950–1961), my work with Eskimos in northern Alaska, and the Indian people in Southeast Alaska, I had personal contact with shamans in five cultures. In several instances, in these encounters, I was referred to as a fellow shaman because of the priestly function of my ministry.

As I hunted with several of these shamans, they shared with me their belief that animals possessed souls, and I was privileged to be present to hear and see their rituals prior to their spearing a walrus or shooting a deer or a moose. The same belief was described by an Eskimo shaman to the Danish explorer Knud Rasmussen: "All the creatures that we have to kill and eat, all of those that we have to strike down and destroy, and make clothes for ourselves, have souls, which therefore must be pacified, lest they should avenge themselves on us for taking their bodies."[51]

It has also been reported through Ward Rutherford in his book *Celtic Lore,* saying:

> We are reasonably certain that shamans emerged in the hunting phase for they are plainly recognizable in cave paintings dated around 30,000 B.C. where they are shown among groups of hunters.[52] These shamans were present to offer incantations before and after the hunt.

To review, we have seen the evolving spirituality of these early Celts. From a most primitive culture, they began with a determination that their definition of power, found within a majority of Celtic families, was given to them by the gods. They demonstrated in a multitude of ways that they were responsible to the gods for all of their gifts.

These indelible traits, which they believed were not only for themselves but for all people, they brought with them as they migrated into the United Kingdom of the Celts.

CHAPTER 3

HISTORICAL DEVELOPMENT IN THE UNITED KINGDOM: FROM THE MIGRATION TO THE REFORMATION (1558)

> I do not have to wait until the whole world is perfect. Indeed, I can contribute right away my peace, goodness, and happiness to the entire human family.
> —Robert Muller

The ancient Celts enjoyed a new genesis in a new country. But to begin history, and to ignore prehistory, is to lose sight of a key fact. When the Celts come to this stage of history, almost every important development had already taken place. Now they face the task of putting into practice what they have learned in crossing Europe, especially using their conception of power as being a gift from the gods, centered in the family. They also have a sense of accountability to the gods for these gifts, including the use of land for tilling and their possessions. We will watch them as they proceed and make their mark in history.

The Ice Age Ends

About 8300 B.C. Wales and Britain were entirely free of glaciers. The Ice Age began to retreat about 10,000 B.C., causing Britain to become an island. The Severn Sea came into existence, and a sea rather than a strait separated Wales from Ireland.

THE CELTS

The United Kingdom Is Inhabited

We must first remember that the land into which the Celts have migrated had already been settled. Archaeologists have substantiated that in the Neolithic Age (Beginning about 2500 B.C.) traces of humans have been found in the United Kingdom of the Celts. Humans were found in Wales on the coasts of Aberystwyth, the Cliffs of Gower, and the sand dunes near Porthcawl; in Scotland on the east coast, no farther north than the Firth of Forth; and in England from the Bristol Channel on the west around to Dover. Because it was inhabited at this time, we must conclude that it remained inhabited until the Iberian Celts arrived.

STONEHENGE (2800–1400 B.C.)

Stonehenge, one of the wonders of Europe, can be seen today on the Salisbury Plain in Wiltshire, England, and is proof that the Druids were present this early in England. Stonehenge is a Druid monument to the sun.

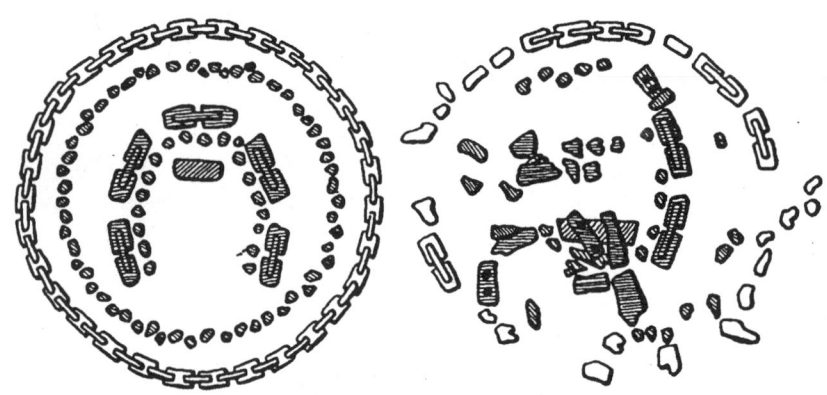

The Plan of Stonehenge, above, shows the arrangement of the stones as scholars believe it was originally built, and the position in which the remaining stones were found. The ancient monument, right, attracts many tourists to Wiltshire, England.[1]

Historical Development in the United Kingdom:
From the Migration to the Reformation (1558)

Having cited this source, I know there are others who have come to different conclusions at a later date. I refer back to Peter B. Ellis' comment on page 78. In addition let me share with you another similar quote:

> Although Stonehenge is associated in the popular mind with the Celts and their Druid priesthood, neither the Celts nor their Druids had much to do with the place. The first part of Stonehenge was built between 1900 and 1600 B.C.—long before the Celts arrived in Britain.
>
> Nevertheless, the practices of modern Druids (which have nothing to do with the Celtic religion), and their yearly meeting at Stonehenge to celebrate the summer solstice have focused popular attention on the historic Celts.[2]

It is a group of huge rough-cut stones and is believed that it took three periods of construction to complete; ranging from 2800 to 1400 B.C. The second period saw the erection of a circle of some eighty blue stones, each of them weighing four tons. They were generally considered as being quarried from rock in the Preseli Mountains. There are other hypotheses of how the rock got there, but it has been proven that they were not from the same locality.

> In 1952, archaeologists from Edinburgh University discovered two underground holes that probably served as ritual pits. They sent bits of charcoal from these pits to the University of Chicago to be analyzed by the radio-carbon method. The scientists there determined that the charcoal dates from 1848 B.C., plus or minus 275 years. Such stones are found only in western Wales and were brought about 300 miles to this site. Three hundred blocks of sandstone, each about 30 feet in length and weighing an average of 28 tons, stood in a 100-foot circle. A continuous circle of smaller blocks was laid on top of them. Inside was a circle of 60 blue stones in the shape of two horseshoes, one inside the other, and opening toward the northeast. Near the center curve of the inner horse-shoe was a flat block of sandstone, 16 feet long, which was probably the altar. Eighty yards east of the altar, a stone marker was set to cast a shadow on the altar at dawn of

the summer solstice (approximately June 21) and on the winter solstice, about December 21.[3]

Some scholars think that Stonehenge was connected to the Druid sun worship. Whatever its purpose, isn't this engineering quite an accomplishment for its time!

In addition to Stonehenge in England, there are many similar megaliths in England and Wales. Few people are aware of the Australian Standing Stones at Glen Innes, New South Wales. The inscription on the stone is written Glen Innes in 500 B.C. in ogham, an early Irish script.

Cromlech Buildings

Cromlech is an ancient monument of rough stones with one huge flat stone resting horizontally upon the others. The word comes from the Welsh *chrom* (arched) + *lech* (flat stone). To the archaeologist the cromlech is a chambered tomb. Alwyn D. Rees once remarked, "Doubtless the same term would be applied to Westminster Abbey, if that building were to be excavated. Bodies were certainly placed in them, but as they were centers of ritual for the community they were more than burial places.[4]

Mining and Materials (from 3000 B.C.)

Earlier ages were more than a mere age of wood. It was also an age of bronze, copper, and the use of tin to harden copper. Gold was made for jewelry and adornments. Manufacturing became more sophisticated. Metal wheels replaced wooden ones; metal plows took care of more than one furrow; metal axes were double-bitted; and oxen were harnessed as well as horses. Wool was carded and made into thread from which garments were woven. Land was no longer worn out by over-farming, and the practice of manuring fields enabled farmers to reap larger and more productive harvests.

The Iberian Celts Arrived (circa 2000 B.C.)

The Bronze Age settlers arrived in what we know now as the United Kingdom about the time of Saul's reign in Judea. These pre-Celtic people were of many races and small in stature. All were not dark-haired and were collectively known as Iberians.

The Iberians, who originated in the area of Spain and Portugal and were mixed with the Celts, introduced into the islands metalworking in bronze, gold, and copper. In addition to hunting, they tended herds of sheep, pigs, and goats. They were skilled archers, initiating a revolution in agriculture with balanced mixed farming and plow tillage. They were of good intelligence (according to Greek and Roman writers), having raised themselves from the primitive culture of the Stone Age to a recognizable civilization. From these folks came the poets of Ireland and Wales.

By 2000 B.C. Britain and Wales had the bulk of its original stock of people. These people intermarried, became much less nomadic, and settled. Farming became the heart of their economy.

A Bit of Linguistics (2000 B.C. or 600 B.C.)

Miles Dillon argues that it was the Beaker Folk who brought the Celtic language(s) to Britain. He claims that it was the Celts who carried the Indo-European language westward. (See *The Celtic Realms,* 18, 265). Other scholars, no names given, support the other theory that the Celtic languages and the Celtic culture were brought to Britain centuries after 600 B.C. by small groups of migrants who are also unnamed. Someone has said that a British writer set forth the second theory "to keep the Cumry Celts from claiming that their language and the language of their ancestors has been present in this land for more than 2,000 years." If this is true, the Celts of the migration at 2000 B.C. could account for this theory. Historians and others like Miles Dillon support the belief that the Cymraeg (the Welsh language) has been spoken in the land for over 2,000 years. This proved that Cymraeg is the oldest continually spoken language in the world.

The Second Wave of Celts (400 B.C.)

The second wave of Celts came about 400 B.C. The second swarm of Celts were the Brythonic Celts, among them Welsh, Cornish and Breton from around Helvetia (Switzerland). They were a group that migrated farther east than others, and at one time battled with the Hittites and the Galatians.

CAESAR'S INVASION AND BRITAIN UNDER SIEGE
(46 B.C.—A.D. 476)

Archaeologists share their findings and declare that by this period human beings existed in Wales in unbroken sequence for over 10,000 years. Britains in Sussex and Earlham have artifacts discovered that date back to 350,000 B.C. It has only been about 500,000 years that Homo sapiens have spread over a greater part of the world.

Britain at this time was a land of mystery to the classical world, and only with Caesar's expeditions of 55 and 54 B.C. do we get the first reliable look at the land where they found tribal units, a dominant warrior artillery, and a wild agrarian landscape.

Both times he landed at Kent with 10,000 men. His intent was to wage a personal retribution against Britain for the aid Britain had given to the Gauls during a previous war, thus helping the Gauls to defeat Caesar. He claims these were by no means an invasion. His strategy was to secure an appraisal for Augustus, who came to power in 27 B.C.[5]

In response to Caesar's report to Augustus, Augustus declared his doubt that Britain was a profitable addition to the Roman Empire. It seems that his followers had other ideas, however. It was then, slightly over a decade later (46 B.C.), that Caesar invaded Britain and kept the country under siege until A.D. 476.[6]

An amazing assortment of races composed the Roman legion. There were cavalry units from Gaul, archers from Numidia in North Africa, and slingers from the Balearic Islands (in the Mediterranean) east of Spain.[7]

These accounts come from the pen of Caesar himself, which makes them suspiciously slanted, like several of the Roman writings, including Tacitus Agricola:

> Ireland lying between Britain and Spain, and easily accessible from the Gallic Sea, might serve as a valuable link between the

provinces. . . . I have often heard Agricola say that Ireland could be reduced and held by a single legion with a fair-sized force of auxiliaries: and that it would be easier to hold Britain if it were completely surrounded by armies, so that liberty was banished from its sight.[8]

There seems to be little written about fighting, except in their rout of the Druids at Anglesey, and the annoyances by some independent tribes. Caesar's point of view gives the impression that they had little or no contest and that a kind of cold war existed.

What Caesar called annoyances was the Celtic manner of fighting. Caesar's tactics were mostly in the open field and head to head in which his warriors were superior. The independent Celtic tribes were not confrontational fighters (except Boudicca). Instead they relied on a resistance movement type of hit-and-run. They would come out of the mountain areas and attack and return. Tribes using hit-and-run tactics included the Silures in South Wales and the Ordovices in north and central Wales. The Romans did admit that their fight in Wales was most costly.

The Romans also had problems with the Brigantes, a federation of independent tribes that extended across Northern England. The Romans, however, formed a wedge between the tribes, divided and conquered, but with a huge loss of life for the Romans.

In the meantime (A.D. 43), another Roman contingent poked its martial nose into Britain. This time it was Aulus Plautius, who crossed the channel from Boulougne with four legions of 3,000 to 24,000 men from the second, ninth, fourteenth, and twentieth legions, plus a host of auxiliary soldiers—40,000 men in all. After landing, and capturing a sizable strip of land in three months, the second and the twentieth legions marched west and established themselves in Chester. Then the second legion marched south into Wales and set up its encampment at Caerleon. Then Aulus Plautius felt a secure enough hold on southeastern Britain to invite Emperor Claudius to come for a ceremonial visit. By A.D. 47, at the end of his term as imperial governor, Aulus Plautius felt he had fulfilled the purpose of his invasion and returned home.[9] Then came A.D. 60 and the Iceni. Tacitus provides a dramatic description of the anguish of the Roman soldiers as they saw across the Menai Straits and viewed the Druids in awesome panoply on Mona (Anglesey).

In A.D. 61, under Seutonius Paulinus, they cast aside their clothes, swam across the straits, massacred the Druids, and destroyed their sacred groves and shrines.[10]

This report from Caesar seems rather far-fetched. There had been no earlier accounts of Roman soldiers swimming anywhere else, and Menai Strait must have been wider at this point in time.

Even today the narrowest place where they are purported to have crossed is about a mile wide. The question is, did they swim wearing their armor?[11]

The Romans failed to consolidate their forces and keep any hold on the Iceni. Embittered by the treatment meted out by the Roman army, the Iceni revolted, led by their queen Boudicca. She had good cause to revolt! The Romans were particularly brutal to her and her daughters!

> Dio Cassius' portrait of Boudicca, queen of the Iceni, a Celtic tribe in eastern Britain in the first century A.D., would fill anyone's heart with terror, and a woman warrior too: "She was huge of frame, terrifying of aspect, and with a harsh voice. A great mass of bright red hair fell to her knees; she wore a great twisted golden torque, and a tunic of many colors, over which was a thick mantle fastened by a brooch. Now she grasped a spear, to strike fear into all who would watch her."[12]
>
> "Thousands of Romans and their allies were slaughtered by her," was all that Caesar's pen wrote."[13] But Caesar's pen made much of the retribution for that massive slaughter, and in most colorful language. He lists the numbers in the tens of thousands of Britains killed at Norfolk alone, and that the town was left desolate for many generations![14]

It is believed that these Celts who fought Caesar were those who believed that power certainly should not be gained by amassing land, taking away another's possessions and people, but power should be thought as being in the family, their land and possessions given to them by the gods. How would you feel if an invader stole your land and raped the women in your family? To get even is human—not spiritual!

Ireland itself was never conquered by the Romans, according to Chadwick,[15] or as previously boasted by Tacitus' account of Agricola. Not even one soldier set foot on Irish soil. Also, the

Empire's intention of conquering the entirety of Britain was never fulfilled, probably because of the fighting ability of the Picts of Northern Scotland.

In consequence, for the remainder of their stay, the Romans were obliged to maintain troublesome borders between their province and Britannia. The distinction between Romans and Britains was meaningless after A.D. 214. About that time Britannia was divided between Britannia Inferior and Britannia Superior. No one knows what the exact boundaries between the two provinces were, but it was believed that Wales was a part of Britannia Superior. The Bretons at this time, at least those of the upper-class, were considered Romans. Rome was their country, and the memory of that fact remained for generations. From 244 to 284 the legions of Rome elevated fifty-five emperors, and from 286 to 296 Britannia was assigned its own emperors.

The last vestiges of the old social structure were disappearing by A.D. 300. Then in 367 came the Barbarica Conspirito (a conspiracy of the Barbarians), when Britannia was attacked from the north, east, and west. It was believed that this was the final disaster, but the authorities succeeded in reasserting control. The Roman Empire was under increasing threat in 369. By 383, there was little evidence that Roman style and comfort existed. In 405, the western coasts of Britain were plundered by the Irish from the channel.

> Britain slipped from the hold of Rome and became estranged from its organization and culture. The estrangement was a long process; it took a century or more, and during those years the nation of the Welsh was born.[16]

For 350 years, the Romans were in supreme authority in South Britain, but the Celts in the United Kingdom, who fought Caesar and Paulinus, were neither exterminated nor quite absorbed. They remained in their mountain glens in Wales and in Cornwall and in Cumberland, living a simple life in their tribal communities. Probably they paid tribute to the Romans but otherwise were left to carry on with their harmless religion and customs.

During the Roman occupation Wales had as fair and incorrupt an administration as that country had ever seen. For the Welsh who destroyed the rules and regulations there was fierce punishment, though not much more cruel than the Roman gallows or the transportation to sea that awaited the ones who stole the squires' sheep.

For those who cared to leave the hill-forts and work in the centers of Roman urban and country life, there was a chance to prosper and to make good; to travel as a legionary or train as a craftsman. Wales in the Roman era was probably as civilized a place as it is now. For them there was security, transport, entertainment, and culture.

Aftermath of the Roman Demise and the Formation of the Historical Celtic Kingdoms (A.D. 400–800)

By the fifth century Roman power was on the decline, and in 407, the Emperor Honorius sent a letter to the principal cities of Britain, telling them to defend themselves. In 409, the last detachment of Roman legions left the country, never to return.

Once they reached the United Kingdom, the Celts thought they were finished with the Greeks and Romans who gained power by amassing territory, but here were Romans again! They came back to conquer still more land. The Romans found, however, that in spite of the loss of their men and property, they could not hold the land as their own.

During his time in the Celtic kingdom, Caesar seemed to do everything in his power to make this Celtic land a part of Rome. He had a vision of completely destroying every vestige of Celtic culture and language, and to completely Romanize the land. The readers of Celtic history perceive that he believed that he had accomplished the Romanization of the Britains.

The whole of Britain was never as thoroughly Romanized as the Romans thought, but Britain (England) was much more Romanized than Ireland, Scotland, or Wales. So a larger resurgence of the Celtic culture came through the Irish and Welsh. There is more written material and cultural growth in Wales and Ireland in these 300 years than in any previous period. This is probably true because the Druids and the Bards (the base of the Celtic culture) waned in Britain (England) but remained prominent in both Wales and Ireland at this time. Shortly after the Christian movement, the Druids and Bards reappeared.

No doubt some Celts were assimilated into and lost to Romanization; however, the Celtic social structure and Celtic languages survived quite well! Cymraeg (the Welsh language), a prominent Celtic language, is still spoken to this very day and has been purported to be the oldest living language still spoken.

Looking back, the Celts must have been elated to see that they were justified in their belief that the gods cared for them in their definition of power.

This is a quote from an author who depicts the crisis facing Wales in 1936 and that facing Gorman and the Britains in 429. During the Roman dominance in Britain all the Celts would have claimed this as their belief in power and the obligation to their gods.

> Wales, Wales my country is a vineyard given to my care, to be handed on to my children and to my children's children as an eternal inheritance; and see these pigs rushing to defile it. I now call on my friends, commoners and scholars, come with me to the gap, stand with me in the breach, so that the beauty that was may be kept for the ages to come. And there, my lord, is the vineyard of your beloved, the clearing field with faith . . .[17]

It seems that the Celts may have lost the battle and won the war.

THE ROMAN POWERS GONE—WHAT THEN?

With the Romans gone, we find clans and tribes within small kingdoms being ruled again by native Celtic leaders. Most of these leaders were the very people who defended their land. Some of them gave a certain allegiance to the Romans in exchange for certain concessions that kept their people from vindictive harm and protected their land from being ravaged. Within these mountains, plains, industrial areas, and farmlands—the place once called the United Kingdom of the Celts—these great people could again proudly claim that name!

They are still congregated together as a host of conglomerate people—including now the Picts from the highlands of Scotland; the Gaelic peoples of Ireland; the scattered Cymru; people from the Isle of Man, where both Manx and Gaelic were spoken; as well as the Bretons from around the area of London and Armorica (the Cornwall Peninsula). How this part of the world will evolve will be on the shoulders of the Celtic leadership within these boundaries.

The prestige of birth and heredity were always paramount in the nature of the Celts while they were in Europe, where they massed together to fight a common enemy. In the United Kingdom, the Celtic spirit of individualism that pervaded their society prevented them from banding together in a common cause. There was no state, civic, or national government to unite the Celts. Once the Romans were gone there was infighting among the clans and tribes in a struggle to determine which brother or cousin would be a tribal leader.

It is believed that the Celts did learn something during the Roman incursion; if not organized wartime tactics and the importance of a strong central government, at least they learned the necessity of unity with all other Celts in accomplishing any project large or small. In the invasions of the Irish from the west, the Picts from the north, and the Saxons from the east, it was necessary for them to seek and to maintain their own identity.

Until this time, the entire north and west of Britain had maintained its Celtic population virtually unchanged. Scotland, northwestern England, Wales and Cornwall, and the islands to the west, were entirely Celtic. Of these areas, the Lowlands of Scotland and northern England spoke Gaelic; Wales and the Cornish peninsula spoke Cymraeg (Welsh). North of this periphery were the Picts, who were at least half-Celtic.

Had the Picts succeeded in permanently occupying southern Scotland, and even penetrating further south; had the Irish succeeded in establishing a kingdom for themselves on the west coast of Scotland and the smaller territories on the western peninsula of Wales, this area would be nonetheless Celtic.

In 420, Vortigern (the Gwrtheyrn of Welsh tradition), a Celtic prince adopted and trained by the Romans, was the military leader of eastern Britain who called in Saxon mercenaries to fight against the Picts. When the Saxons gained strength in eastern Britain, Vortigern was hated. But the deed was done, and the Saxons infiltrated the Breton Celts.

The Goths Invade Eastern Britain

In 430, the Goths invaded eastern Britain. During this time the Bretons became estranged from their organization and culture. This estrangement was a long process, and during these years Wales was born.

The Fall of Britain (De Excidi Britanniae), written by monk Gildas (540), was thought to be a very influential document. But rather than writing as a historian, he wrote as an "irate sermonic cleric," reviling the leaders of Britain. For more revealing documents about this period, the *Anglo-Saxon Chronicle* (898) is composed of events from the year 635 forward and includes narratives of the English kingdoms. The writings of Owain Hywel Dda are important to the understanding of the English history of the Welsh kingdoms.

Another Wave of Migration

This wave of migration began about 530 and reached its peak in years 550–580, but did not conclude until about 700. These migrants were thought to be a series of remaining Celts from northern France.

The Welsh Language

The Welsh language began to be written down in about 600, and it was this new medium that Taliesin and Aneirin, the early Welsh poets, used. They proved that this language was a new medium for great literature. Previous to this time, throughout the territories of the Western Empire, Latin had been the sole written language.

Dykes and Walls

Dykes and walls played an important place in this era of Celtic history.

Offa's Dyke

Offa, a Breton, was king of Mercia, who fought the Welsh in A.D. 778 and 784. Mercia, on the English border with Wales, was one of the last English kingdoms to come into existence. Offa's intention was to build a dyke as a well-defined boundary between England and Wales. It was unfinished when Offa was killed in the battle of Rhuddlan in A.D. 796.

Wat's Dyke

With the capture of Pengwern, the Saxons had reached the fringe area of upland Wales. The border not only took away good agricultural land, which the hill people wanted to reclaim, but the boundary was unstable. Mercia reacted by building Wat's Dyke. It was the work of Aethebald, king of Mercia from A.D. 716–757.

Hadrian's Wall

This is a barrier of a much earlier time. It was during the Roman invasion of Scotland. In A.D. 117, a powerful uprising of the Celts in Scotland and northern England took place, serious enough to bring Emperor Hadrian to England. Between A.D. 122 and 128 the great stone wall was built, between what is now parallel to the Cheviot Mountains—from Solway Firth to Berwick-on-Tweed.[18]

Ferment and Promise (A.D. 800–1200)

This is an up-and-down time for the Celts, more than ever. We have watched the Celts respond to Roman domination and later seen them rising, like Phoenix, from their ashes. We have seen their sturdy strides upward, only to see them attacked, lose strength, and fall only to rise again.

This ninth century begins with the Celts seemingly riding an apex, only according to Nora Chadwick "to see the Irish Sea lose its importance for Britain as Scotland and England gradually turned eastward and became a maritime kingdom no longer, but a landlord power."

Ireland

Ireland was known back in the eighth century as "the Gaelic Island of the Celts." Early on it had the Gaelic name "Eire." The Romans, who never set foot on the land, called it Hibernia or Ibernia.

The early settlers probably arrived about 6000 B.C. Between 400 and 600 B.C. the Celts arrived from France and Spain. Ireland split into many small kingdoms, ruled by tribes and controlled by families who fought against each other for leadership supremacy as did the Welsh, but later they combined when kings were appointed to rule.

Through the eighth century, Ireland was left alone. Their island was a sanctuary where they were able to be at peace with themselves, develop their country, and farm their land.

The first attackers were the Norsemen (Vikings and Normans). Their first priorities were the headlands and the small islands surrounding the country. This penetration lasted through the ninth and tenth centuries. No place seemed to escape their incursions. They left few caves unexplored.

Manuscripts, art works, etc. usually were stolen rather than destroyed. Many of the items taken are now housed in Scandinavian art galleries; however, Ireland also benefitted from the invaders. The Vikings built Ireland's coastal harbors, making the Irish proud of their coastline and improving their defense against invaders and helped establish a proud nation from a number of smaller states. Through intermarriage with the Celts, the Vikings made the country strong.

At first, the Vikings destroyed Celtic sanctuaries, but after mild protests, helped put the Celtic sanctuaries back in order. In addition, many people adopted Celtic ways.

The invaders remained a part of Ireland for almost two centuries. No one knows when they left Ireland.

Most of Wales was saved from Viking invasions, except Anglesey. This area was known as "the granary of Wales." It was too valuable to the Danes and too inviting not to strip. In A.D. 853, it was devastated by these "black foreigners," as the Danes were called.

Rhodri Mawr—Rhodri the Great (816?–877)

The small kingdoms of Wales gradually became unified. They start with the house of Merfyn Frych and his son Rhodri Mawr in the ninth century, and Hwyl Dda (Hywel the Good) in the tenth century. Rhodri Mawr came to fame because of his ability as a warrior and his skill as a leader. He became ruler of Gwynedd in 844 on the death of his father; Powys on the death of his uncle.

According to Miles Dillon and Nora Chadwick in *The Celtic Realms*, we can trace the Welsh dynasties and their descendants (see p. 117) as well as follow some measure of the political history of Wales from the sixth century; the period of Gildas' princes, and the early phase of the establishment of the Saxon dynasties in Britain, until the South Welsh prince Hywel Dda submitted to Edward the Elder in the tenth century.[19]

Many small kingdoms in post-Roman Wales of the fifth and sixth centuries present the same state of affairs as in Ireland. They were gradually brought under control of a single dynasty descended from Cunedda. In the ninth century, Rhodri Mawr became king of approximately all of Wales, which remained Welsh during the Norman period. At his death in 877, his kingdom was shared among his three sons: Mervyn, Anarawd, and Cadell. From Anarawd, the line of Gwynedd in the north is his rule; and from Howell the Good, son of Cadell, came the lines of Powys and Deheubarth. This division into three kingdoms is the state of Wales reflected in the laws.

Hywel Dda (910–950)

Like Rhodri, his grandfather, Hywel became known as Hywel the Good by a later generation. This title was added to his name and did not imply that he was always right or could do no wrong. It was necessary that as a state builder must be true to his word, strong and forthright in his vision. "Good" was a title given to him not because of his actions but because of his accomplishment of strengthening the kingdom and keeping it together.

Hywel was responsible for the law of the land. This law was not a state law that kept order through vindictive punishment; rather it was a folk law that used common sense and, though not mentioned, resembled the old Celtic belief that power lay in the family, its possessions and land, all gifts from the gods. This kind of common sense power is thought to be implicit in this case.

The manner in which Hywel Dda handled matters led to peaceful growth. One of the most interesting phases of Welsh history led to the control of North Wales by Rhodri Mawr, whose grandson Hywel Dda (d. 950) was first to submit to an English king.

In a gradual process, the various Welsh kingdoms were affected within a few generations by a series of royal marriage alliances. The defeat of the Danish army, and the death of their King Gomer at the hands of Rhodri Mawr, ended Welsh isolation. The Welsh joined with Wessex and became a part of a wider continental sphere. It was in this atmosphere that great Welsh poetry had its beginning.

Of particular importance to the Celtic lands and the Celtic culture is the armed Norman invasion into the United Kingdom of the Celts.

The Norman Conquest

In 1066, Norman warriors under the leadership of William, Duke of Normandy, successfully conquered England, and the Norman influence spread throughout the United Kingdom. The

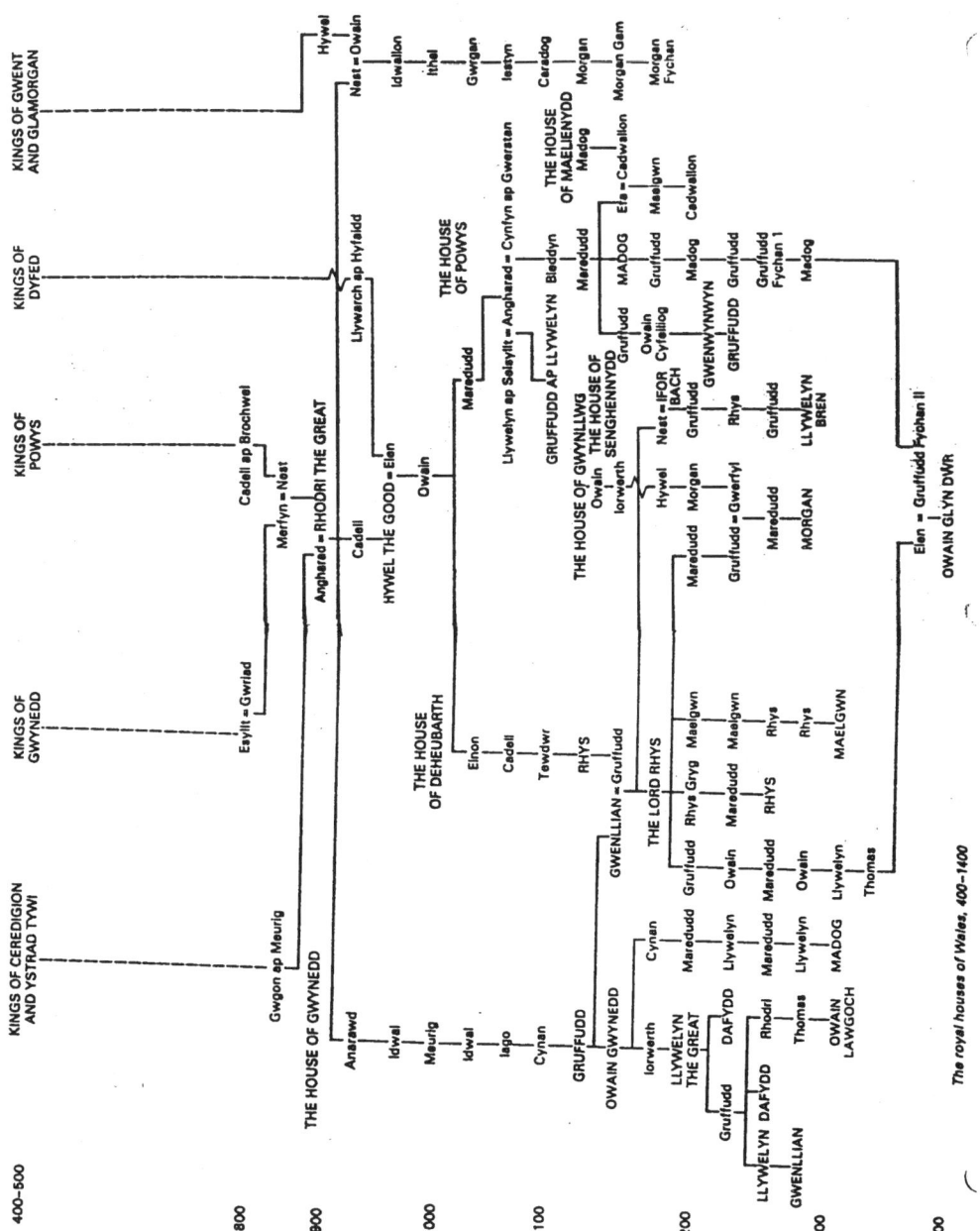

The royal houses of Wales, 400–1400

Duke, known as William the Conqueror, led a Norman army across the English Channel into England.

William was a proud and ruthless ruler and a vassal of the king of France. He hoped to follow his cousin, King Edward the Confessor, as King of England. William claimed that Edward I named him as his successor. The chief contender for the throne was Harold, Earl of Wessex. But William also claimed that Harold, who had been shipwrecked on the Norman coast in 1064, had sworn a solemn oath to support William's claim to the throne. In 1066, King Edward died. The Anglo Saxon Witan (the Great Council) elected Harold king. (See Harold II.)

William at once declared his right to the throne. He secured the support of the pope and gathered an army of 5,000 men. William landed without opposition near Hastings on the coast of Sussex because Harold had gone north to defend against and defeated the Norsemen. Harold then returned and attacked the Norman army at Hastings, where he was slain. This was known as the Battle of Hastings. William then marched on to London, where he was crowned King of England on Christmas Day, 1066.

William established Norman rule in England and prepared *The Domesday Book* (from the Latin *domus*, meaning home or residence). There were two volumes of the first official census (one 760 pages, the other 900 pages). The listings included the names of the landlords and the value and extent of their holdings. The survey was ordered in 1085 and 1086.

He ordered territory taken from the nobility and the large landowners and divided among the unfree. Many English families trace their names to the entries in this book.

The kings of Scotland and England and their ruling classes are listed separately in the addendum as are the kings or the rulers of Ireland and Wales.

The Early History of Scotland

Early Scottish history is particularly difficult to trace because at the dawn of this period our contemporary written records, from as far back as the early seventh century, are, to say the least, nonexistent. This is due to the fact that Scotland was once divided among four nations, differing widely from one another in origin and all speaking different languages.

There were the Picts to the north, the kingdom of Dal Riata (Argyl) to the west, the Britons to the south, and the area from which the Romans had departed.

The final union of the Scots and the great Pictish nation is traditionally said to have happened in the Scottish Highlands in A.D. 843, the early home of the Picts. Not long afterward, the Picts seemed to become a people of the past. Some early writers claim the Scots simply wiped them out; more believable historians claim they were assimilated in a short time. This assimilation took place somewhere in the middle of the ninth century, under Kenneth McAlpin.

Kenneth McAlpin, king of the Scots, claimed the throne of the Picts in 844 and established the first united kingdom in Scotland. He and his successors waged many wars against the British and the Norsemen, who continually raided the Scottish coasts. Kenneth McAlpin died about A.D. 860, and the kings that followed retained Pictish customs. Their chief place of authority became Scone, where early kings were crowned, until the Stone of Scone was stolen by the Britons.

The northern British people whose lands adjoined southern Scotland have left no subsequent written records. For our information about them we rely on Britons from Celtic Cymraeg (the Welsh Celts), who always recognized a kinship with the people of Southern Scotland, whom they called in neighborly terms *Gwyr y Gogledd* (men of the north). They called their neighbors in South Wales *Gwyr y Des* (men of the south).

Early Wales

According to Davies, by the time of Rhodri Mawr (circa 870), there were about 2,048 kings in Gwynedd. Considering the size of Wales, these kings were thought fortunate to be sovereign over even small land holdings. Rhodri Mawr succeeded in uniting most of Wales before he was killed and before he received any recognition for such an accomplishment. Gryffudd ap Llewellyn became the only king to rule the entire territory of Wales, and his method of uniting Wales was brutal. He hunted down his two brothers and imprisoned them.

Three years after Harold of England defeated and killed Gruffud ap Llewellyn (August 5, 1063), and because of his defeat of the Welsh king, Harold was named ruler of England. Strangely overlooked were the lineages of Edward the Confessor and William, Duke of Normandy. On his accession to the throne, of all things, Harold married Ealdgyth, the widow of Gruffudd ap Llewellyn.

By 1081, however, it seemed impossible to believe that any kingdom in Wales had any future at all. Not wishing to try to annex Wales, but to place a buffer between Britain and Wales, William gave pieces of land (Hereford, Shrewsbury, and Chester) along the border to many of his faithful followers. These border barons were malevolent men from Normandy who built the first earth and timber castles. By 1100, most castles were built more securely of stone. These Normans were not kind to Gruffudd ap Cynan and the Welsh.

William I died in 1087, and his territories were divided among his sons, who were unable to gain much of patronage. William II was much less masterful than his father. The Normans, after barely four years of campaigning, subdued England by 1090, and it seemed that Wales would be subject to them after just a fourth of a century of campaigning.

Surprisingly, this never came true! Small kingdoms outside Norman control were spunky enough to challenge the Normans at every turn. After William II died, Wales was restored to its former status.

Then Henry I came to the throne (1100–1135). As long as the Welsh rule endured, the boundary line between these areas were generally set by 1105. Between 1130 and 1300, eighty towns were established in Wales. According to John Davies, some twenty of them had come into existence before 1135, with Cardiff as the largest, having about 25,000 inhabitants. Shortly after, these towns sprang up all over Wales, such as Cardiff, Carmarthen, and Haverfordwest; and in the uplands Glamorgan, Afan, and Glynrhondda.

By 1130, the literature of Wales, in both Welsh and Latin, developed extensively. The Welsh referred to this time of literature as *Cymraeg coeth* (refined Welsh) and *Cymraeg hardd* (beautiful Welsh).

With Henry II (1154–1189), the first rulers of England from the Plantagenet family came to the throne. (See Addendum for the listing of kings of England.) During Henry II's reign, the Welsh regained the territory they lost during the reign of Henry I.

A Little Interlude

In Europe at this time the Roman Catholic archbishops controlled most governments, and the kings came and went by their behest. This had not happened in England yet; however, Thomas a'Becket (1118?–1170), the Roman Catholic archbishop of Canterbury, began to test the waters.

Becket,[21] proved to be a thorn in the side of King Henry II. King Henry II disagreed and argued with the archbishop of Canterbury, over basically two things: (1) The archbishop's extravagant living, using the Church's money; (2) His beginning to usurp many of the rights that belonged only to the king. King Henry II declared, "The archbishop, in his ordination vows, had both the duty and the function to truthfully censor the king, but 'never to act in his stead, unless the king gave him lease to do so.'" Not long after, Henry II made a cryptic remark, which several of his knights took as a cue to "do away with the archbishop." He was murdered by the knights of King Henry II while he was at vespers in the cathedral on December 29, 1170. Because of this insidious crime, the pope did not wait the limit usually imposed for canonization. He declared the archbishop a saint two years later.[22]

By 1200, England had the beginnings of a feudal kingdom of sorts with writs of law and a royal court. The barons who were appointed were given several restrictions, none of which were too severe. They were given the freedom to indulge in private warfare. Along with the Marcher Lords, they also were given the liberty to build strong stone castles to protect themselves when they waged war against their neighbors, when it was thought profitable.

Since England formed the largest political unit in the United Kingdom, its kings attempted to annex others. The first king to succeed partly in this task was Henry II. His legal mind believed that he had enacted laws that would encourage other parts of the kingdom to annex and make a United Kingdom. He had already extended his rule over Ireland. If anyone could put words in his mouth, they would be "It's about time the kings should be centered in England!"

Until this time kings of Scotland had been crowned at Scone Palace on the Stone of Scone, a stone crowning the mound of Moot Hill. Later, the Stone of Scone was removed to England in Westminster Cathedral.

Geoffrey of Monmouth, a pope (1100?–1154?) and a Breton Welsh historian, wrote his first book on the history of British kings in various places, entitled *Historia Regum Britanniae*. Welsh scholars claim that when his word was translated into English, several mistranslations appeared. One sentence in particular brought to light reads, "In the early times, the whole of Britain once belonged to the Britains." It should read, "In the early times, the whole of Britain once belonged to the Bretons."

THE MAGNA CARTA (A.D. 1215)

This legal move has been called the "cornerstone of English liberty." English barons forced King John to approve this document in 1215. It marked the first time that anyone had ever limited the absolute power of a king in England or anywhere else. It was also the first document that promised certain rights to all freemen in the kingdom.

The charter resulted from a long struggle between the king and the barons. The barons ruled large estates and had to pay exorbitant taxes on them. They wanted to limit the king's power over them and to define his right to tax them as intrusive overlords. In the late 1100s, King Richard I taxed the barons heavily to pay for his foreign wars, including the Third Crusade.

When King John was crowned in 1199, the barons hoped that he would not tax them as heavily, but he demanded more, and for his own purposes. Finally, in 1213, a group of barons and high-ranking church leaders met at St. Albans near London. They drew up a list of rights they wanted the king to acknowledge, but each time the barons presented their request, King John refused to grant them. At last, John saw that he could not defeat the army of barons and high-ranking church leaders and agreed to meet the barons at Runnymede on June 15, 1215. There the king finally agreed to place his seal on the document known as the Great Charter. This document later became as relevant to Scotland and Wales as it did for the English barons.

King John was determined to change or negate the charter when he died in 1216. He was followed as ruler by his son, Henry III, who was only a child but made the same promise when he came of age in 1225. It was known earlier as the Magna Charta, but in 1946, the British government adopted the Latin spelling Magna Carta.[23]

THE BIG TURN OF EVENTS BEGAN CIRCA 1200

The Event of 1277 was to forever change the configuration of the United Kingdom of the Celts. It would also mark, to this very day, the manner in which this land will be governed.

Before we proceed any further, in order to get a clearer picture of the history of this era, we need to understand that in most history texts from 1200 forward, the Celts were increasingly being left out except to glorify the Britons. It can be clearly seen from A.D. 1200 forward that much of the published history of England was being written "with a British accent."

This is not just the belief of this author. Brian Davies, curator of the Pontypridd Historical and Cultural Centre in Wales, details how the Celts were "deliberately robbed of their early history." He claims, "The English stole our heritage! In order to create the Dark Ages required by Saxon triumphalism, the witness of the continual history of the Welsh Church back to Roman times, preceding the foundation of the national Church of England by several centuries, had to be pushed to the margins of consciousness and if possible to be literally buried." Davies concludes, "Concerning early British history which they still innocently use is not the product of calm, objective collection and assessment of data. It is a politically motivated construct, a falsification of history for the purpose of English nationalism."[24]

In addition to the English not being true to history, they also have shown little love or concern for those residing within the Commonwealth at this time.

First, King Edward I ordered all Bards killed. This was to stop the promulgation of Celtic lore and Celtic history, since the Bards were mostly responsible for what we know as Celtic lore and Celtic history. Second, the feeling of the Britains seemed to be, "If the Celts are not written about, they will fade away."

When we read the early history of this land, we have to remember that the historians who wrote this section of history wrote in the names Britain and England. Such names did not exist during the time about which they wrote: These names were in use at the time the historians lived.

The name Brittany was given by the Gauls to a peninsula across the English Channel south from Cornwall in 474. Britains could be used in reference to the folks who migrated from Brittany, but this doesn't seem plausible because migrations from here seemed to be very few in number. Britain could be a corrupted name for Breton, that group who migrated from France or Spain, but they were Celts. Possibly the best explanation can be dated to about 1273, when the Bretons changed their name into the Britons, and the spelling change into Britains came to pass. But what about England? It seems that when Britain and England are mentioned, historians just re-used them, and so does this writer.

Dillon-Chadwick, Davies, and James seem to assume that those called Britains were that group of people who were already living here before the invasions of Vikings, Saxons, etc. They were mostly Celts of one kind or another, diluted by intermarriage and assimilated by these invaders.

At this juncture we approach one of the mighty events that changed the entire perspective of this part of the country forever.

Shortly after the Celts migrated here, this land became known as the United Kingdom of the Celts. They brought with them a special belief in power, which they had practiced all across Europe. Their belief in power was the exact opposite of the belief in a power that was practiced by the Greeks and the Romans.

The Celts believed that amassing land or people for power were actions against the gods. This is why they went to battle against the Greeks and Romans and many times annihilated them. This is the kind of belief in power that the Celts brought into their new land.

Prior to the coronation in 1296 of King Edward I (1239–1307), he was known as the Confessor and also as the English Justinian because of his fame as a lawgiver. He could also have been called the Enforcer, as you will see. He followed his father Henry III, who in 1267, formally called the nation the United Kingdom. He believed that this could happen, and in 1267 Henry III formed the Treaty of Montgomery[25] with Llewellyn ap Gruffudd, whom he had named Prince of Wales. Llewellyn was the first and *only* prince of Wales from Wales. Ever since King Edward I stripped him of his title, all princes of Wales were heirs apparent to the English throne!

Henry III who followed, though a fickle king, believed there would be a United Kingdom. This treaty was a great achievement for Welsh Celts, but it is not found described in any English history. We will find omission of Welsh Celts consistent in both the spiritual history and the national history of England.

The Treaty of Montgomery (1267) came just before King Edward was crowned and began warring against the Celts. The treaty was a recognition that Llewellyn ap Gruffudd had established a definite and acceptable Welsh polity. Between 1267 and 1272, everything that was necessary for that part of the United Kingdom to grow into statehood was found within the boundaries of Wales.

In 1275, under his title Prince of Wales, Llewellyn requested King Edward I that he be allowed to build a castle in the area of the Severn at Dolforwyn to fortify the area for the crown. This request was denied! Edward I feared LLewellyn would acquire too much power and ruin his plan to conquer the Celts.

Llewellyn pressed King Edward I with the fact that the Treaty of Montgomery gave him the right as the Prince of Wales, and all he was obliged to do was to report to the king and his right would be granted. Edward disregarded Llewellyn's request, denying the validity of the treaty. In addition, Edward took away Llewellyn's title, Prince of Wales, which was the right under which Llewellyn made the request, and gave the title to his son who later became King Edward II. All other princes of Wales hereafter were named from England's hierarchy. Llewellyn ap Gruffydd was the only Welshman to ever be named "Prince of Wales"!

Between November 1276 and February 1277, Llewellyn wrote letters to the king declaring his desire to meet with him and discuss their differences. Edward I refused, noting that he had made up his mind, and informed Llewellyn that he would "attack his possessions with an army larger than he had ever seen, making these possessions of yours, mine!"[26]

Edward I then made a public statement: "It would be more fitting and suitable at this time to burden myself and the inhabitants of this kingdom with the cost of wholly overthrowing the malice of the Welsh Celts, rather than facing the future, as in the present, the inflictions of the conflict they have caused."[27]

As a result of this vindictive statement from Edward, and that Edward would soon seek to capture Wales, Llewellyn led a portion of his army toward Builth, where he had strong support. Here he could count on legions to assist him in a defense. By 1280, however, King Edward was in control of all of the boundaries of Wales.

But the war was not yet over. The missing Llwellyn ap Gruffudd was yet to be found. On the banks of the River Irfon, on December 11, 1282, Llewellyn was killed in ambush. His head was sent back to London and displayed in public as proof of the success of King Edward I! But in Wales, Llewellyn ap Gruffudd was hailed as the only true Prince of Wales!

After many continued battles and skirmishes, the Welsh Celts were defeated and became a part of Britain. It all ended when Dafydd had taken the lance from Llewellyn, his brother, and was killed at Shrewsbury!

King Edward was so anxious to inform the pope that Wales no longer had a ruler worthy of papal patronage, that his messenger crossed the wintry Alps, reaching Rome in five weeks.[28] The Welsh Celts were forced to live under the ruthless English political system, but the Welsh Celts vowed that their life and culture would not die even though they were betrayed by part of their Celtic family.

At this time, a mass denial was broadcast from roof-tops by the Britons that Celts didn't exist anymore, probably to inflate the egotism of King Edward. Some historians, however, corroborated the fact that Celts were everywhere in the country. There were Gaelic Celts in Scotland and Ireland, Cornish Celts in Cornwall, Welsh Celts in Wales, and Mancs Celts from the Isle of Man, to say nothing about Celtic Bretons in Cornwall and in the area of London. In addition, there were Druid Celts and Bardic Celts throughout the kingdom.

These Celts mixed with the invaders and others, and thus diluted the pure Celtic stock. But they were Celts nevertheless! Also, because of their location, the Breton Celts became more a part of the ruling class in their area. They probably felt more superior and more organized, while the other Celts were more loosely organized, but the Breton Celts were Celts nevertheless!

About two years after the coronation of Edward I, the Bretons betrayed their Celtic brethren, the Gaelic Scots and Irish, the Mancs, the Cornish, and the Welsh. The Bretons changed their name to Britons and allied themselves with King Edward I as he invaded Wales, then Scotland, and Northern Ireland. Edward assimilated the Cornish and the Mancs, taking their people captive and robbing them of their lands and goods and future as a nation. The new Britons called their home the British Isles, and after that Great Britain. Recently they seem bent on calling the whole area England.

By selling out to Edward, the former Bretons denied their Celtic heritage and turned their backs on everything Celts held dear: the power given by their gods and their right to their land through the gods' favor.

Then, like the Greeks and the Romans, these Britains began to pillage and amass territories, making themselves the largest feudal system in the world. Under its protection they gathered over the years as many as seventy-three countries, making them protectorates.

And, lest we forget, they almost managed to take another protectorate. "The land of the free and home of the brave" almost became "the land of the conquered" rather than "the land of concord"! You need not be reminded who started that war, and who it was that was determined to add another protectorate to its warchest. But the Revolutionary War was won by thirteen colonies to become "One nation under God, indivisible, with liberty and justice for all,"[29] with sovereign states rather than one of Britain's protectorates.[30]

The Britons didn't have to expand their country by fighting their neighbors and annexing territories through aggression. In time Scotland, Ireland, Wales, Cornwall, and the Isle of Man could have peaceably been persuaded to form a United Kingdom, or possibly a union of states with a central government. Such could have been worked out, but that wasn't tried![31]

During this period King Edward I wasn't satisfied with only invading the remaining Celtic countries; he issued an edict decreeing, "All the Celtic Bards are to be slain to a man."[32]

He claimed that the Bards in their singing and in their entertainment were telling tales that ridiculed Edward; and that by doing so, they were defaming the nation over which he was king. Edward added that the Bards sang and spoke in a language that he did not understand. Note that this will not be the last sovereign or public voice to speak against the Celtic Bards or demand their lives.

Edward's Incursion into Scotland

Living in Northern Ireland were a tribe of Celts called Scotti. Many of them migrated to the western coasts of what became Scotland and also North Wales about A.D. 500. It is believed that this tribe of Scotti Celts gave Scotland its name.

Edward I's forces, depleted from his wars in Wales, the Hundred Years War, and war waged in attempt to protect British territories in France where there were several Celtic communities, struggled in futility through Edward's remaining reign trying to conquer Scotland.

Among several men who claimed the Scottish throne, Edward chose John de Baliol as king in 1290, but he insisted that John pay a heavy homage to him. The Scottish people, humiliated and infuriated by this demand, revolted. In 1296, de Baliol joined the Scottish rebel forces, which were defeated by Edward's English troops stationed in the country.

Shortly after in that same year, William Wallace (1272–1305), a Scottish patriot known for his strength and courage, took over the leadership in Scotland. He led several bands of patriots, waging a bitter war against the invaders from Britain.

The British forces raised a large army against Wallace, and Wallace soundly defeated them at Stirling Bridge. At this point, King Edward I hurriedly returned from France with heavily armed soldiers and defeated Wallace at Falkirk. Wallace escaped, continuing his fight from the hills. This "guardian of Scotland" was captured by treachery (like Llewellyn ap Gruffudd) and was tortured by the British before being executed for treason, ordered by Edward Plantagnet.

But the Scots were not finished fighting for their freedom. Robert the Bruce (1274–1329) spent most of his life trying to free his countrymen from British rule. Bruce's military life began as Earl of Carrick. In the beginning he swore allegiance to Edward I. Later, he changed sides and allied himself with William Wallace.

When Bruce was crowned king, Edward's anger forced Bruce to become a fugitive. His brother Nigel was hanged, disemboweled, and beheaded. His daughter was imprisoned in a cage in the Tower of London. That year Red Comym betrayed Bruce to Edward. Bruce stabbed Conym in anger in front of an altar in a church. Kirkpatrick of Closeburn finished Comyn. Then Bruce had himself crowned king, but the English defeated him. He dismissed his troops, went to Ireland, and let his enemies think him dead.

The next spring he landed in Carrick and defeated the English. Within two years he had gained control of almost all of Scotland. He then advanced in Scotland, destroying everything as he went, and defeated the English under Edward II at the Battle of Bannockburn in 1314. Shortly thereafter, under Edward III of Britain, Britain recognized the independence of Scotland and the right of Bruce to the throne of Scotland, this time as King Robert I. He died eighteen months later.

Edward I had stated earlier that some kings of Scotland had been crowned in Britain. This seemed to be a stretch of King Edward's imagination because at this time the kings of Scotland were crowned in Scotland. Scotland was still independent!

Among these kings of Scotland who came to the throne in Scotland were:

- Angus mac Fergus, southern Pictish king.
- Kenneth mac Alpin, the Pictish king.
- John de Baliol, appointed by King Edward I.
- Robert the Bruce, later King Robert I.

In 574, Columba ordained Aiden as king of Dalraiada at Iona almost certainly on the Stone of Destiny.[33]

Whether the Stone of Destiny was definitely used in any or all of these coronations, some writers claim it cannot be substantiated through history. However, Nigel Tranter argues that Bruce would certainly have been crowned on the Stone of Destiny, refuting Edward's claim that Bruce's crowning was invalid. What has been substantiated is that earlier King Henry II made a wish to have kings and queens coronated in Britain.

King Edward I thought he stole the Stone of Destiny. The Stone of Destiny was in front of Scone Abbey. He took the false stone to London, where it was placed beneath the coronation chair of Edward I. He had been duped, however, taking a false one made of sandstone. Edward must have known it was fake because two years later he had returned to Scone Abbey and demolished the Abbey looking stone.[34]

David II, son of Robert the Bruce, died in 1371 without having an heir, and several families competed for the Scottish throne. The Stuarts won the struggle, and Robert II was crowned in 1371. Later Stuart kings still had to handle the issue of feuds with the Scottish barons, and Scotland was not yet a part of Britain and would not be until 1707!

In 1524, the English ruling class in Wales began to govern the country in an increasingly oppressive manner. The Welsh Celts then appealed to Cromwell, even though they thought it was a situation impossible to remedy. They wanted to be granted the same privileges enjoyed by the rest of his subjects. They hoped to rid Wales of the officious English overlords and be allowed to run the country as his subjects.

A step in this direction was taken with the Act of February 1536, which allowed appointments of justices of the peace in counties of the principality, with such appointments entrusted to the Welsh gentry.[35] Central to this act, to the Welsh and the Celts, was the "abolition of any legal distinction between the Welsh and the English." This meant that the penal code would be abandoned and not just formally appealed. Thereafter, in the eyes of the law, the Welsh were English, but everyone living in Wales would be Welsh.

Central to this incorporation was the abolition of any distinctions between the Welsh and the English.[36] In the wake of this kind of incorporation, the Welsh received representation in the English Parliament, a right not previously granted them.

In 1536, twenty-six members of Parliament were granted to Wales. The number rose to twenty-seven in 1543.[37]

"There were about 7,500 words in the Act of Union; of these, 150 words deal with the Welsh language. But that two percent has caused more discussion than the other ninety-eight percent,"[38] and has remained so down through the years. The problem was, Wales was not granted the exact English pattern of representation, which was two members for each county and two members for each borough. The Welsh pattern was one apiece for every county and borough. According to the English, some counties were not considered worthy of representation because they could speak only Welsh, and no translators were allowed in Parliament. It was necessary, therefore, that people of these areas must plead their problems through an already appointed representative. Parliament has put it to the Welsh, not only in this document but in other documents as well: "English is to be the only language in the courts of Wales, and those using the Welsh language were not to be elected to any public office in the territories of the king."[39] The language clause was not only discriminatory but the clearest statement that would impoverish the Welsh. It would prove totally inconsistent with Cromwell's expressed intentions to strengthen the distinctiveness of Wales. In 1543, Parliament made a change, taking away the language barrier and allowing translators for Welsh speaking representatives.

This is not to say that all the Celts did, after settling in the United Kingdom of the Celts, was fight and skirmish and make war. They did more than continually look over their shoulder for approaching trouble and meet it head-on.

They had to make a living and did so by using the skills they acquired prior to their coming to this new land. They used ingenious ways to farm, mine and manufacture, weave, and make pottery. They never lost their ability to transport and trade. In addition, the Druids kept their heritage alive, and the Bards sang and told their stories over and over.

Celtic Legend—Mythology

From time immemorial, folks have always been curious about things that surround them. Why does the sun always rise in the east, make its way across the sky, and set in the west? Why is some land hilly and moist while other land is low and arid? What makes things grow? What makes an echo? Then the more personal questions: Why am I here? Who created my world? Where does my strength come from?

People down through the ages, before there were books with some answers, made up their own explanations. Beautiful, fanciful, intriguing ideas have been passed down by word of mouth to our present time. Their innate sense made them focus on the fact that something greater than themselves existed in their universe, and so their gods were woven into myths and legends. The stories that people made up were called myths, and the system of such stories is called mythology.

Mythology is defined as "the collected body or system of the traditions or legends of a people in which are embodied their beliefs concerning their origin, gods, heroes, etc.; the science of myths; a treatise of myths."[40]

Greek, Roman, and Norse mythologies have been recorded and described, but few Celtic mythologies, which are probably earlier, have been recorded only recently. Celtic myths also contain ideas reflecting spirituality.

The subjects of mythology are diverse. It tells us, for example, about the genesis of the gods, the creation of the universe and of our world and, often, how it will end. Sometimes, though not always, it gives hints of how we must act to ensure divine goodwill. . . . Mythology is history told in other terms.[41]

> Celtic mythology is a great study in itself, and would take volumes to share types and examples found in each Celtic culture. Here I will introduce to you this author's favorite author in the area of Celtic mythology and encourage the reader to explore further Ward Rutherford, who states "The mythology of the Celts can justly be claimed as one of the jewels of the European cultural heritage."[42]

It is a shame that many view myths as heathenism, paganism, and even idolatrous. Mythology is the response of a questioning mind through storytelling to describe evolutionary stages in the development of a people's faith. There is a strong possibility that we, had we lived in that early time, would have developed a like mythology.

Only in Ireland and Wales did the language and literature survive that sprang directly from the ancient Celts of Europe, uncontaminated by Imperial Rome. Such was true, especially in Ireland, because no Roman Legion entered that country. Much the same could also be said of the Welsh language and literature, even though Rome did invade Wales. The Welsh language was never given up, and no other language was ever accepted. As for the Welsh literature, any contamination was not by the Roman legions but by the loss of some credence and content by being handed down by word-of-mouth until the words of the Bards were later transcribed.

Most of the transcribers were monks. To them, the documents they were translating were blatantly pagan, and the documents were probably transcribed in a cleaner form. However, many of the transcriptions came through to us with what some might call down-to-earth words or earthy descriptions. What the Celts euphemistically referred to as "the friendship of the thighs" remained loud and clear.

One can find such earthy descriptions in one of the Irish myths entitled "Bricriu's Feast." Such comments were either written down by a monk who believed that what he was writing must be true to the author or translated by one other than a monk. This one was probably transcribed by the latter. Later, however, especially in Ireland, many myths, because of the teachings of the monks, were purified and sanitized in language but not in content.

The Bardic Druids, during times of entertainment were not above describing a battle scene with all the bloody details just to see the women cringe and hear them scream. They could also sing lilting love stories with the lyre that would cause anyone to swoon. Their elocution on any national theme was said to even bring a stone to attention. These were the kind of stories of which myths were made. It was probably the national theme, in a language they couldn't understand, that roused King Henry III and King Edward I to ask for the heads of the Bards!

In addition to reciting folk stories of otherworld hunts, magic islands, underwater cities, and abduction by other-world beings, the Bards weren't above lampooning the gods. Whatever the recorded myth, most myths were intended to be sung, chanted, or to be presented with the background music of the harp or lyre. This is something that made Celtic myths unique.

When one reads Celtic mythology, especially Welsh mythology, one will often run across the word *Mabinogian*, referring to a collection of Welsh myths. *Mabinogion* is not a Welsh word! *Mabinogi* is a Welsh word meaning "story" or "tale." Lady Charlotte Guest is said to have added *ion,* seeking to make the word *Mabinogi* plural. The word *Mabinogion* was later accepted and has been loosely translated as children's stories.

There are actually only four children's stories in the Mabinogion, and they are about people called Pwyll, Branwen, LLyr and Math. Other myths are included, so the title should read *The Mabinogion and Other Myths.*

One of the other myths is "Bran the Blessed." A summary of the myth might read like this: Bran lost his life in a fierce battle with an Irish king. As he lay dying, he ordered seven survivors to cut off his head and carry it with them. They take the head to the underworld and live happily there with Bran as his guest for about fourscore years. Then these seven disobey Bran's order and find themselves back on earth. They still possess Bran's head and, according to Bran's instruction, bury it under London so it will guard Britain forever. This might have happened, but some culprit dug it up, presumably hoping to possess its magic.

Early Celts believed, for example, that no god could pull the sun across the sky and make it disappear in the evening and make it appear again in the morning! So the legends gave the god a chariot and a white horse to do the job. Even this seemed impossible. So ardent was their belief that many gods must be responsible that they built Stonehenge to worship these gods of the sun.

It was such stories as these that were written into legends, which became the cores of mythology. The stars came to be known as the good people that the gods placed in the heavens, etc.

Celtic Art and Technology

Like Celtic mythology, Celtic art is also a study in itself. Every time you salt your food; observe a wheel of any kind; eat bread made from wheat ground in a mill; watch a plow operating in a field; use a handsaw; wash with soap; wear a bracelet, necklace, or earrings; look in a mirror; weave a blanket, shawl, or pair of socks; watch fruits, nuts, and vegetables grow; store food; make pottery or use a kiln, you see and use the technology of the early Celts! Some of these arts were begun and used before 1000 B.C.

More has been written about verified Celtic art and technology on the continent of Europe than any other art forms still in use. In early trade markets in the then-known world, items made by the Celts were in great demand. Hot items for sale or trade were wagons, chariots, woven materials, metal tools, clothing, and looms, plus other utilitarian items.

These same Celts brought their ingenuity, workmanship, and technical skills with them into the United Kingdom of the Celts.

Early Christian architecture became widespread in Ireland. Saint Columba's house, built of stone and mortar in 814 on the site of a wooden structure, is among the best preserved ruins near St. Columba Monastery at Kells. The walls are more than a meter thick.

In addition to houses and buildings for cattle and storing tools and wagons, the Celts were very adept in the construction of ringforts, ramparts, storage pits, and temples.

Art forms created and scribed by the early Celtic monks also need to be mentioned. Their meticulous writing of texts, and the intricate development of ornamental pages in color, blow one's mind. Their accomplishment was done without such pens and inks that are available to us today! To catch the beauty of such art see plates of *The Lindisfarne Gospels, The Book of Kells, The Book of*

Durrow, and *The St. Teilo Gosples* on pages 305–310.[43] They are literally graphic spiritual statements to the world. In the light of such intricate copywork penned by dedicated hands, to get the best view one needs to use a magnifying glass.

> My hand is weak with writing; my sharp great point is not thick; my slender-beaked pen juts forth a beatle-hued draught of bright blue ink. A steady stream of wisdom springs from my well-colored neat fair hand; on the pages it pours its draught of ink of the green-skinned holly. I sent my little dripping pen unceasingly over an assemblage of books of great beauty, to enrich the possessions of men of art . . . whence my hand is weary with writing.[44]

Sculptures were also a part of Celtic art form. Intricate carvings of Celtic gods have been found inside temples. There were household gods, crosses, pillars, human forms in full stature, heads and busts, both military and civilian.

Many people of the twentieth century have been intrigued by a multiformed design of Celtic art without realizing either its meaning or historical background. This ancient pattern is known as *the Celtic knot*. These designs composed of twisting spirals, intertwining ribbons of line, form different patterns that lack any definable beginning or ending.

Configurations of this Celtic knot can be found on all pages of the illuminated Celtic Gospels presented in this volume; if not on the "carpet" or on the "Initial" pages, they can be seen as borders or in divisions of chapters. This Celtic knot has also been carved on many Celtic crosses.

The early Celts were known for their highly developed sense of the spiritual and their religious beliefs concerning the survival

Moone
Celtic Cross

Trinity Celtic Cross

Papal or 12th Century
Celtic Cross

Latin

Celtic Grave Marker

Greek

St. Anthony's

St. Andrew's

Calvary

Celtic Cross of Scriptures

Patriarchal

of the soul and the immanence of their gods. One of the strongest and most elusive symbols is the Celtic knot.

Do we find any explanations of the Celtic knot from the pre-Christian era where it was found, either at Hallstatt or La Tene? The following explanation is found in early histories and usually follows variances of this story:

> The early Druids, who were the early teachers of their faith and keepers of the Celtic history, believed in a being who would thwart the Celts' desire to follow their gods and deter them from becoming better people. This figure was later called the devil or Satan. The early Celts, it was thought, used this Celtic knot as a device to ward off such evil influences. The Celts believed that this evil power was frustrated by anything that was without either a beginning or an ending. It is said that this is why the Druids venerated rivers, streams, and running waters. So this Celtic knot, without either a beginning or an end, could have been used as protection against anything that would alienate them from the gods or from their becoming better people.[47] (Some believe that the Celtic knot had its beginning as early as 1200 B.C.)

Some scholars believe that the Celtic knot was imported from the eastern Mediterranean area, where drawings of intertwined serpents have been found. However, none of these drawings are as intricate as those of the Celts.

Another form of art not found among the Celts of Europe are simple grave memorial stones, various forms of carved crosses, known as *the Celtic cross*. (See pp. 138–139).

Again early Welsh and Celtic history was deliberately falsified by nineteenth century historians and archaeologists in order to present Christian civilization as an achievement of the English. According to a fresh investigation, Celtic cross evidence has been found at Llantwit Major/Llanilltud Fawr parish church in the Vale of Glamorgan. In this area was found a sculptors' school circa 1033.

Writing in the latest issue of *New Welsh Review,* (1997) Bryan Davies, curator of the Pontypridd Historical and Cultural Centre in Wales, gives a detailed account of how some distinguished Celtic crosses came to be dismissed as rather poor examples of tenth and eleventh century memorial masonry rather than to be seen as the most ancient crosses of their kind anywhere in the United Kingdom of Ireland.

The superb surviving examples of early Welsh monumental art are found at LLanilltud Fawr, Margam, Coychurch, and Mether Mawr in Glamorgan, etc. In the light of this available evidence an unnecessary gap in Celtic history is filled.[48]

Someone is bound to ask the following questions:

1. *Who were the craftsmen?*

    There really were no craftsmen among the early Celts that one can list by name. Each person who had such inborn ability took to the task. Later on, when the societal structure was formed (p. 49–50), craftsmen were listed and probably included women and youth.

2. *How were they trained?*

    No mention is made of training in the early years of the Celts, but likenesses are seen in different carvings, and it is imagined that some copying must have been in vogue. It is only later, when craft societies were formed, that training was a high probability.[49]

3. *What and who identifies the art as Celtic?*

    The answer here is found after the fact. In excavations in and during such periods as Hallstatt and La Tene, for example, because of certain marks and likenesses, items were especially and collectively deemed Celtic.

4. *What were their favorite materials?*

    There seems to be no specific favorite materials. They used whatever kind of clays were at hand and the best for certain potteries. Both gold and silver were used for jewelry, sometimes adorned with gemstones. Iron and other metals were used for weapons, wheel tires, and plowshares. Special pens and inks were used in their calligraphy. (See *The*

Lindesfarne Gospels, The Book of Kells, Book of Durrow, and *The St. Teilo Gospels* on pp. 305–310)

5. Where can such art forms be found?

In the Hallstatt and La Tene collections in what is now Germany and France respectively. A copy of *The Book of Kells* has been on display in libraries throughout the United States and as recently as 1997 in the state library in Salem, Oregon. A true copy of *The Book of Kells* may be found in Dublin, Ireland with *The Book of Durrow.* The first copy of *The Lindesfarne Gospels* can be seen in the British Museum in London. There is also a recent Celtic display on the fourth floor of the British Museum in London. Other such Celtic artifacts can be seen in French and English museums. Contacts for specific items should be made through the British Tourist Centre, the Welsh Tourist Centre, the Irish Tourist Centre, or the Scottish Tourist Centre for further directions.

The following chapter will weave back through this history and trace the events and people relating and noting how Celtic spirituality evolved during these years leading to the Reformation period in the United Kingdom.

CHAPTER 4

CELTIC SPIRITUALITY IN THE UNITED KINGDOM: FROM THE MIGRATION TO THE REFORMATION (1558)

> The Maker of all things,
> The Lord God worship we:
> Heaven white with angel wings,
> Earth and white-waved sea.
>
> —*early Irish poem*

The Christian journey for the Celts needs to be understood and looked at, not as an arrival at any point, but a step-by-step journey marked by gradual progression and small pinnacles of achievement along the way. The end of this journey is not yet in sight and will only be concluded at God's end of time when eternal judgments will be made. For the present we can only enjoy and learn from their achievements and mistakes.

Their earlier Christian journey was by no means smooth, or without its periods of frustration, or its ups-and-downs. The Celts, at times, worked hard for what they gained, and at other times they worked against themselves. This was especially so in the case of the misconception and misuse of power by some Celts. Their early faith certainly did not just drop down to them from the clouds, either as something to work on or as a complete package.

We are searching for something about the Celts that has not appeared in any church history text; something concerning either their history or their spirituality, beyond a single sentence that there was a Keltic Church in Britain. Yet it is believed by many Celtic people living today that their ancestors were participants in history that led up to the pre-Reformation, the Reformation itself, and the post-Reformation period.

The Reformation began with Martin Luther in Germany, and it was no happenstance that this was also the geographical area in which the Celts had their beginning. Of course, the Reformation was aided and clarified by John Calvin, Ulrich Zwingli, John Hus, and other Reformation luminaries.

But, lest we forget, the Reformation reformed and still reforming had its real effect on those Celts who brought their faith with them to the United Kingdom. Look at this history again, through the eyes of a Scottish Celt by the name of John Knox, whose followers fought and pleaded for the reformed faith in a land called the United Kingdom of the Celts. Read this church history again, through the eyes and ears of the Celts, in the way their faith evolved not only through to the Reformation but down through the present day! It will not only give you a more complete view of the Reformation but will grant you a clearer picture of your Christian heritage.

Take a picture of these Celts as they came ashore in the United Kingdom, their new homeland. All histories refer to their landing as a migration rather than an invasion. There was no reported fighting, or the clashing of any spears, until the incursion of the Roman army under Caesar; however, we must take cognizance of the infighting among themselves for positions of leadership of the tribes and clans.

The Celts brought into this new homeland many thoughts and experiences treasured in their minds and passed down through them over the years such as the love of family. They bore the scars and memories from those who would use power to amass lands at the expense of others. They kept the memory of things they planted, that grew and budded and bloomed and bore fruit. They remembered their ability to invent and re-invent wheels, wagons, plows, as well as instruments to make life easier. In spite of all these talents and abilities, they never forgot from whence they came; those pristine groves, their silent times by sparkling waters, the words of the Druids and the songs of the Bards.

Reading various histories, these Celts, understanding that their gods call them to be responsible for their beliefs, continued with them when they set their feet ashore on this new land. They began their trek with sanctity, stewardship, saintliness, and ecology, and with their science of the sun, and the awe of the world in which they lived. These qualities of sanctity and saintliness seemed to draw them closer to the early saints and later into Christianity. Notice later in this chapter the manner in which they listened and followed the early saints, such as Patrick, David, Columba, and others.

Christianity had not yet existed when these Celts came ashore; however, they existed as beings with feeling and understanding of their faith in many gods—pagan gods they created—gods they believed in—gods to whom they felt responsible and acted accordingly. Note the gods of the Celts in chapter one.

These Celts are now ashore, and we know from hindsight that Christianity came to them; however, we do not know either when or how Christianity arrived into the hills, valleys, and shores of the United Kingdom of the Celts. For some reason, it seemed always to have been there.

No doubt the first missionaries were from no sect or denomination but from those early Celts themselves, whose general primal faith evolved into a specific personal faith, which made their conversion into Christianity almost an immediate response and their alliance with the Church possible.

In the sixth century, the great Welsh bard Taliesin claimed with perhaps a little poetic license:

> Christ, the Word from the beginning, was from the beginning, our Teacher, and we never lost His teaching. Christianity in Asia was a new thing, but there never was a time when the Druids of Britain held not these doctrines.[1]

Here is another example reported from early history of the United Kingdom concerning Christianity. The poet and author W. B. Yeats reports it this way:

> A similar story in which on the Day of Crucifixion King Conchubar and Bucrach the Leinster Druid are sitting together. Conchubar notices "the unusual changes of the creation and the eclipse of the sun and the moon at its full"; he asks the Druid about the cause of these signs, and Bucrach replies, "Jesus Christ, the Son of God, who is now being crucified by the Jews."[2]

After the Celts arrived, the Druids still practiced their rites under oak trees and by streams of water. We find their worship places in such areas as Cornwall, London, Powys, and Menai (Anglesey). They still settled grievances and lined out property, with deep religious overtones, as they did when they were in Europe. At first all of their worship was outdoors. Their temples came later.

THE ROMAN INVASION AND OCCUPATION OF BRITAIN (46 B.C.–A.D. 409)

During the Roman occupation of Britain, the empire permitted a variety of faiths to exist but with the proviso that there be no anti-Roman preachments allowed under penalty of death.

Some Celtic Druids did not abide by the Roman proviso, and several Druids were killed by various means. They were hanged from a scaffold, skewered by a sword, decapitated, and pulled apart by chariots. As a result, the Druids changed their style of promoting their faith. The Romans continued to watch them, however, begrudging Druidic practices. It was during these years that the mystery religions flourished.

Tertullian wrote (c. 200) that shortly following the arrival of the Romans, that Roman Christianity arrived in Britain. Oreign wrote (c. 240) and claimed that the Christian faith was a unifying force among the Britains. Both Tertullian and Oreign had not set foot in the United Kingdom. How could this be? The Romans were still promoting their gods, and Caesar claimed that Celts were worshiping Roman gods by other names. So it would be stretching the truth to say that the Christian message arrived that quickly.

It is more plausible that Roman Christianity arrived in Britain as early as A.D. 260. Tertullian also wrote (circa A.D. 200) that "a form of the gospel was being preached in parts of the island not yet occupied by the Roman armies." In spite of this, he believed that the Roman armies brought Christianity to Britain. Could Tertullian have been hearing about the work of the Celtic church in the kingdom? It seems that we can calibrate that Roman Christianity arrived in Britain sometime shortly after A.D. 300. This calibration is supported by a well-known artifact, a square or piece of plaster taken from a house in Cirencester on which were scratched "Pater Noster." Pater Noster was said to have been scribed on a cross.[3]

In A.D. 67, in Lydney, near the coast of Caerwent was built what was called the first Celtic temple. From this point Celtic temples became more prominent than previously were known. The temples, however, were still not a building in which they could congregate and listen to the Druids to be edified and taught. Temples housed the gods and provided a portico from which the Druids could address their Celtic listeners.

The emphasis at the Lydney Temple was on healing, complete with baths, chapels, and places to stay. Later writers referred to this as "sort of a Celtic Lourdes." History records that several Romans participated in the rituals, but it was probably more for the relaxation of the baths than for their participation in Celtic worship, although we really do not know.

By A.D. 300, with the Romans still in occupation but their hold on Britain slackening, Celtic Christianity was beginning. Concerning the rural parts of south-east Wales as the only regions for which no evidence exists that they were overwhelmed by invaders from outside the empire, John Davies, in his book *A History of Wales*, says: "The uniqueness of south-east Wales in this respect may explain the key importance of those regions as the cradle of the Celtic

Church and the starting point of a movement which was to revitalize Europe."

This was perceived more to be an evolution of their faith. These Celts were no doubt practicing their faith, which was looked upon as a form of Christianity.

Some sentiments of both Tertullian and Oreign seemed to express: Now that Roman Christianity had arrived, it would find more appeal, and Celtic Christianity would lose its power and pass into oblivion. This did not happen! The Celtic Church neither lost power nor became extinct.

As we will notice, the Celts later found Christianity more appealing when they came to believe that One God made more sense than being accountable to many gods. In addition, their belief in the afterlife was very similar. Although ecology, as a word, was not yet in anyone's vocabulary, such Celtic practices made sense to Christians.

In early A.D. 409, the last of the Roman legions departed from Britain, and in autumn of that year almost all of the vestiges of a Roman presence and influence had vanished, save what had been absorbed in the population.

The absence of Roman martial presence left a void of any type of authority over either the church or local governments. Fortunately both the Celtic Church and the Roman Catholic Church were organized sufficiently on the local level to act as authorities until governmental laws were written down. This was very slow in coming, but laws of morality and accountability were deeply ingrained in the minds of those who believed in one God or in many gods.

It is probable that at first both churches willingly shared in administrating justice. Later those who were leaders in the Roman Catholic Church took advantage of the situation, claiming that they were "the only true church." They pointed out that they were already organized, with a pope as head of the church and leadership at all levels down to local priests, and they already had experience in Europe of naming kings and rulers who would give allegiance to the church.

At this time, the Celtic Church was more active in the islands than historians later led people to believe. In addition to temples (holy places that housed the gods) from whence the Druids delivered their messages and led their people in worship, there were also Celtic churches. These were larger in structure, allowing people to gather in inclement weather, and where at other times they could meet for instruction and learning, retreat and contemplation, much like monasteries. These larger churches could be found in Britain, Ireland, Wales, Scotland, Cornwall, and the Isle of Man.

The Celtic Church held to a monastic system, which was based on a long-established usage and the highest prestige of their continental church. The Celts practiced their faith without any influence of the Roman Church. In fact, their monastic worship was practiced long before the Roman Church came in existence. They had a communal system. They did so without a tight administrative organized system as in the Roman Catholic Church. Simon James, in his book *The World of the Celts,* on page 163 writes, "The development of the Irish Celtic Church followed a unique pattern, revolving around monasteries rather than bishoprics . . ." Above all, the Celtic Church had a common spirituality and a deeply rooted love of silent contemplation.

The Celts were characterized by their great missionary zeal and outreach through their pastoral ministry to the people. The primary characteristics of these Celtic Christians are best explained by Sellner in his book *Wisdom of the Celtic Saints.*

1. Their love and respect for their physical environment.
2. Love for learning inherited from their Druid ancestors.
3. Their innate yearning to explore the unknown.
4. Their love for silence and solitude.
5. Their understanding of time—every minute counts.
6. Their appreciation of the ordinary life.
7. Their spiritual ties as soul friends.
8. The stories and sayings of the Celtic saints, with their monitoring and spiritual guidance, were an essential part of Celtic spiritual Christianity.[4]

Pope Gregory I, who sent Augustine to Britain with a band of monks to convert England, is purported to have written that these Celtic temples were really Roman Catholic monasteries where the Roman Catholic faith was taught. The hagiagraphies of several of the later saints also seem to support this thought. It was imagined that they did this to declare how strong the Roman Catholic Church was on the islands. The writers seemed to also insist that the Celtic Church was nearing the end of its ministry.

It needs to be emphatically stressed that these Celtic churches were structurally unlike the Roman Catholic churches. They were not built to accommodate large congregations. They had no altar or pews. The Celtic Church, however, did have saints of whom they were proud and from whom they received much encouragement in their faith.

THE EARLY CELTIC SAINTS

Of the early Celtic saints, there were many, both male and female, i.e., St. Brigit, St. Canair, St. Findbarr, St. Ita, St. Kevin, and others. (See Sellner, *Wisdom of the Celtic Saints*.) Here we will only deal with the patron saints of the United Kingdom.

A Patron Saint

A patron saint is a saint who, by his or her intercession with God, protects those who pray for help. The saint is always considered a mediator, dependent on Jesus Christ. When a person is declared a saint, his or her memory is honored on a particular day each year, usually on the anniversary of his or her death. Nations and countries that are predominantly Roman Catholic have a special patron saint. More recently, patron saints of people and needs have been named; i.e., St. Jude is the patron saint of those suffering from desperate cases of illness, such as cancer, AIDS, etc. St. Elmo is the patron saint of sailors; St. Francis of Assisi is the patron saint of the poor and destitute. There are still others.

When we talk about some of the early Celtic saints, we must understand that they were first called saints by the *people!* They were not called saints by the *church* until much later. These early Celtic saints, prior to being canonized by the Catholic Church, were named saints by the people because they brought the gospel to the people, won converts, and extended the faith of many.

The early Roman Church historians, however, looking back over several hundred years, incorrectly picture these early saints conducting Mass, hearing confessions, and granting absolutions when none of these functions were yet a part of the ministry of these early saints!

As the acts of heathenism in the Celtic mythologies were changed (edited) by monk transcriptionists, so some parts of early Christianity have been given a highly Catholic slant. That bias also excluded religious thought outside the monks' perceptions, namely the beliefs of the early Celts.

> Almost all of what we know of Celtic mythology comes to us second-handed through Christian monks who copied the myths from local *filids* (story-tellers). It seems likely that these Christian brothers sanitized the myths as they wrote them down.[5]

> The attitude of the monks to archaic records is amusingly summed up by a twelfth century scribe who, having copied *Tain-Bo-Cualnge*, could not resist adding a personal view: "But I, who have written this history, or rather fable, am doubtful about many things in this history or fable. For some of them are figments of demons, some are poetic imagings, some true, some not, and some for a delight of fools."[6]

> Celtic mythology . . . survived only after passing through the sieve of Christian scribes who wrote down these tales but sometimes removed offensive pagan elements.[7]

> Examples of such sanitizing can be found in . . . Cernunnos, the Celtic god of the underworld, who is pictured in Celtic myths to be equal to, but not as powerful as, Lugh, the most high god. The words of a monk copyist, "These two characters are always pictured as 'Satan' and 'God.'" In early Celtic life and literature, there was an absence of sin, punishment, and atonement. Yet

copyists wrote these into their transcribing of some myths. Yet, when read critically, this often beautiful literature may reveal much that is relevant to a modern appreciation of early Celtic religion. Concessions to Christianity were slight, and in the main consisted in obscuring were necessary the divinity of the principal characters in the myths.[8]

Could this be a mistake in reporting from Ms. Chadwick, or is there another history regarding Cernunnos? Both Peter Ellis and Miranda Green report that the name Cernunnos means "the antlered or horned one," and that he was probably a fertility god.

Much of the history of the early Celtic faith, and other beliefs of this time, are noted as older Christianity. Augustine has been quoted on this matter in church history texts: "Augustine tried to reconcile the 'older Christianity,' which he found established here, with a more up-to-date form which he brought from Rome."[9]

What seems to strike the modern observer about the Celtic Church, in contrast to the Church of Rome, was its pastoral way of life, its uncomplicated Christian fervor, and its faith over form. This is what the men of Rome disliked and repudiated. The Roman bishops were forced to accept that there were at times more converted from Iona, the home of the Celtic Church in Britain, than there were from Canterbury, the Roman Church center.

An example of this contrast happened at Lindisfarne. The official church had a short-lived success before Oswald occupied the Northumbrian throne and wished to evangelize his people. He sent to Iona for a missionary. The first monk to arrive at Lindisfarne was Corman, who proved too rigid and austere for the challenge. It was in 635 that Aidan volunteered to replace him.

Aiden set up a new monastic community on Lindisfarne, now Holy Island, with the result that there were two ecclesiastical orders in Northumbria; one centered in Iona (the Celtic Church), and the other in Canterbury (the Roman Church). It was at this juncture that the champions of Rome began a battle in another area. They believed that the Celtic Church did not celebrate Easter on the proper date. (See "Easter," pp. 160–161, 254 and "The Synod of Whitby," pp. 160–161).

Saint Patrick (390–461)

Some folks find it hard to believe that Saint Patrick, the patron saint of Ireland, was not born in Ireland. According to history, he was born in Bannavem Taburniae. You will not find this place on any present-day map. It was thought to be a Roman army encampment, existent during the Roman invasion into the United Kingdom.

Neither historians nor archaeologists can pinpoint the exact location. An early encyclopedia places the area somewhere between Fflint and Wrexham in North Wales, but this cannot be true, for St. Patrick in his own words says, "on the west coast of Britain." In his own words he was captured and taken to Ireland by Irish pirates, and Irish pirates did not penetrate this far inland. Bannavem Taburniae had to be a Roman encampment near the sea, much farther west, somewhere in the neighborhood of Anglesey, or further south along the west coast of Wales.

The *Confessio* written by Patrick near the end of his life gives much information about his birth and early life. He was kidnapped by Irish raiders and carried off to Ireland to tend sheep. Guided by a voice from heaven, he made the 200-mile trek back to the coast where he found a merchant ship that took him to France. He then somehow made it back to his family. Again he heard "the voice of God, beckoning him back to Ireland, through the voice of the people."[10]

The first firm date in Irish history is A.D. 431, when Pope Celestine sent Palladius "to minister to those of the Irish who believe in Christ." It wasn't until the following year that Patrick (no indication of ordination or priesthood) arrived in Ireland. This mention of existing Christians is a cause for speculation.

If Palladius was sent to minister to "those of the Irish who believe in Christ," someone had been called by God to go to Ireland to form a Christian community before Palladius arrived. The other possibility is that a Christian community had been formed there by the existing Celtic Church. The latter reason is more believable.

This explanation does not detract one iota from Patrick's calling as a missionary from Wales to Ireland, nor does it take away from him any reason for the church to later canonize him as a saint.

Patrick wasn't named a saint because he drove the snakes out of Ireland but because of the witness for his faith in Jesus Christ and his ministry to the world against all odds. Saint Patrick's special day, March 17, is celebrated in many places around the world. He deserves the honor!

Holy Patrick Full of Grace

> Holy Patrick, full of grace,
> Suffered on Cruach, that blessed place,
> In grief and gloom enduring then
> For Eire's women, Eire's men.[11]

Saint Columba (521–597)

The patron saint of Scotland, who was known as "Colum-Cille" or "Columcille," was born on December 7, 521, into a Celtic royal clan in Donegal, Ireland. He was a student of Finnian of Clonard, who was well-known as a "Father" to many young priests. Some histories report him as "the early patron saint of Scotland." Before the Reformation in the United Kingdom, he was reported replaced by St. Andrew, the disciple of our Lord, who became "the present patron saint of Scotland."

The early history of Scotland is a particularly difficult one to trace, owing to the fact that Scotland was divided among four nations, all speaking different languages.

Columba was a notable and talented storyteller, writer, and poet as well as one of the great Celtic leaders from Ireland.

A tale is told of his birth. His mother had a dream that she received a cloak, like Joseph's coat of many colors. In the dream, a young lad stole the cloak from her, which caused her to be very sad. The same young lad returned to her in a dream and said, "Woman, you have no need to be sad, but rather you should be filled with joy! The meaning of this dream is that you will bear a son, and Ireland and Scotland will be full of his teachings." Columcille was born and later offered himself to "the Lord of the Elements."[12]

Columba made his rounds in Ireland, ministering to the needs of the people, baptizing many, erecting churches and some monasteries, and leaving people with a nearness to God that they had never known. Then Columba became involved in a war that erupted between the Christians and Pagans in the Irish kingdom. A battle took place in which many died, and after that Columba's conscience troubled him greatly. His journey to Scotland was a self-imposed penance. Columba landed on the isle of Iona in 563 at the age of forty-two. At Iona, he developed a flourishing monastery, which became the chief center of the Irish Celtic Church. Two years later he went on a missionary journey to the Picts. By the work and prayers of Columba and his fellow missionaries, the kingdom of the Picts was won for the gospel's sake.

St. Columba was a Celtic priest and an abbot but never became a bishop in the Celtic Church, and he always deferred to a bishop in celebration of the sacrament. He remained as head of the Irish Church in Iona until his death in 597.

SAINT DAVID, PATRON SAINT OF WALES (520?–589)

The Welsh call him Dewi Sant. He is one of the most influential monks of the sixth century Celtic Church. He was the founder and bishop-abbot of the see of St. David's, earlier called Menevia (the Latinized form of Gwynedd.) His mother was Non, who became a missionary, founded monasteries, and was later named a saint. His father was Ceredig, king of Cardigan.

In his early years, David gathered around him a few pious folks who lived with him in a kind of commune. They studied Scripture together, worked together in harmony, planted gardens for feeding both themselves and their neighbors, prayed daily for each other, and worked for the betterment of the community. They did this with a high regard for God, the message of Jesus, and acting out their faith before the local people. All this time the burden on their hearts was for the salvation of Wales. They also called him "Dyfrwr" (the waterman), suggesting that he patterned himself after an early monastic sect that rejoiced in hardship, never speaking without necessity, never ceasing to pray mentally, and that shied away from strong drink, drinking only water and milk.

He could have continued his solitary life in the comfort of his community with his followers, planting his gardens, sharing the fruit of his labors with his neighbors, and being fairly content with his life. He could have been buried and had a memorial service honoring his piety and his love of his neighbors and then be forgotten.

Instead he studied with Henfynyw (Aberaeron) in Cardigan and ruled the diocese of St. David's. In a manuscript of the early tenth century, he is declared to be "the primate of the Welsh." Another manuscript in the following century states that from ancient records at St. David's, some of which are in the saint's own hand, David founded many monasteries, performed various miracles and healed the sick, made a journey to Jerusalem, was an excellent preacher, and led a hard life with his fellow monks. These manuscripts are kept in the archives of St. David's Cathedral.

Looking over the life of St. David one must see him as: (1) A *planner*, strategizing his message and designing his approach; (2) A *convincer*, a salesman for God if you will; (3) A *radical*, as one who was willing to go to extremes, willing to do more than usual; and (4) A *revolutionary*. Such a venture had never been done before!

The author believes these attributes of Dewi Sant is what made the change for the better in Wales. But there is still a big question in the mind of the author: What did Dewi do to be *sainted by the people* yet missed being *sainted by the church*? Certainly there were people sainted (canonized) by popes before that time! The Church was first to canonize Matthew, Mark, Luke, and John, as well as Peter.

Was the pope petitioned to canonize David? Again, there is no record. Did the pope think that David did not merit such an acclamation? We'll never know. Why did the Church wait until 1120 to make David a saint? It was Callistus (better known as Pope Calixtus II) who canonized him 531 years after his death. Dewi Sant's Day of Celebration is marked as March 1.

The Illuminated Gospels

It is said that the intricate and illuminated manuscripts took time to be developed by saints and missionaries to portray the Word of the Lord. Giraldus Cambriensis, the Welsh patriot and historian, has this to say about such manuscripts:

> If you take the trouble to look very closely, and penetrate with your eyes to the secrets of the artistry, you will notice such intricacies, so delicate and subtle, so close together and well-knitted, so involved and bound together, so fresh and still in their colorings that you will not hesitate to declare that all those things must have been the result of the work, not of men, but of angels.[13]

The Book of Kells is an illuminated, or decorated, manuscript of the four Gospels. The calligraphy and penmanship have earned a reputation as the most beautiful book in the world.

It was begun at the island monastery at Iona and completed at Kells, Ireland, following the Viking invasion of Iona in 805. The manuscript was stolen in 1007. It was later discovered and remained at Kells until the seventeenth century when Henry Jones, Cornwalls' chief of intelligence, gave it to Trinity College, Dublin, where it still may be seen.

The text is Jerome's Vulgate with Old Latin readings and features. Over the years many monks must have been employed copying the text in calligraphic Irish hand and compressed script for the passages of the Gospels.

The famous illuminations of the book, the work of four illustrators, enhance most of the text with rich tracery. Not a single page is without decoration. The margins and blanks are filled with human and animal figures. Full page decorations include canon tables (concordances of the Gospels), pages, and important passages of the Gospels are presented in ornamental script.

These elements combine to make *The Book of Kells* a supreme artistic expression of the Middle Ages. Another such expression is *The Book of Durrow,* from the same era.[14]

The Lindisfarne Gospels, which include the four Gospels, are the earliest, and best documented of the illuminated Scriptures (dated between 600–695). They have been named as "The world's greatest masterpieces of manuscript painting."

These illuminated Gospels were created at Lindisfarne now known as Holy Island in Northumbria southwest of Berwick-on-Tweed, and scribed "For God and St. Cuthbert." The presenters of these Gospels have been named in the early history of the island as being "Eadfrith, Ethelwald, Billfrith, and Aldred.

Copies of these Gospels are now open to view in The British Museum in London.

The *Teilo Gospels* (now called the *Chad* or *Lichfield Gospels* because they are on display at Lichfield Cathedral) are illuminated art created by Welsh monks in the early part of the eighth century. They have been identified as "Insular Miniscule Script," which had become widely known in *The Book of Kells, The Book of Durrow* and *The Lindisfarne Gospels*. Wales now also has a part in the formation of Celtic Christian art, but their existence has been denied since the Edwardian conquest of Wales in 1282.

That the *Teilo Gospels* were written in Wales is beyond a doubt, proven by connoisseurs of art and noted historians. If the *Teilo Gospels* were not considered in existence or important pieces of Welsh Celtic art, why did the English lie that such a heritage existed and then rob Wales of its illuminated Gospels, house them in Lichfield Cathedral, and claim them as their own? Why does not the dean of Lichfield Cathedral return these pieces of Celtic art to Wales where they rightly belong? No better place is being created for their display than Llandeillo, the center of St. Teilo tradition. (See copies of these Illuminated Gospels on pp. 305–310)

THE NICENE AGE (325–590)

We are now at the conclusion of the Nicene Age, a period of 265 years. You have been brought through the Nicene Age without mentioning it. What you have read in this chapter thus far has been church history (Celtic spirituality), which has never been recorded in any church history text to date with the exception of a small quote in Zenos' *Compendium,* referred to previously. (See p. xv)

The events of the Nicene Age, written in church history texts, focused on incidents that transpired outside the United Kingdom and which you will see soon being enforced in the United Kingdom. Please take note of the following:

- Constantine, being the sole Emperor (330), had definitely made up his mind, not only to leave Roman Christianity unmolested, but to favor it, and make it the *only true church* and *the state church.* Note that this has been presented in the United Kingdom even before it has been enacted by the Roman Church.[15]
- *The Suppression of Heathenism.* The Roman Church now began to assume more of an aggressive attitude and role against paganism, even making it a penal offense. Note further, the Church was making the law, rather than the State, and that the Law is being defined as illegal any means of worship, which conflicts with the Roman Church's definition of worship.[16]
- *Privileges of all clergy are defined.* The clergy were to be exempt from public service; from taxation; given the power to decide all disputes, with their decision being final. Such prerogatives sound like a phrases from the laws of the Druids. Again, we will see the Roman Church's action against the Druids in the United Kingdom.[17]
- *Qualifications for entering clerical life.* There was to be no military, nor dancers, actors, or slaves. Above all things celibacy was required.[18]
- The Council of Nicea became a main turning point of faith in the United Kingdom, and the Nicene Creed was being used in worship in many of the Celtic congregations.[19]

It was at the end of this Nicene Age that only one church history text has been found that mentions that:

> A Christian Church existed in Britain during this period (the Nicene Age). Very little is known about it. The population was Keltic. From later data it is to be inferred that this Church had an independence and character of its own.[20]

The prime points of difference between the Celtic Church and the Roman Catholic Church were at this time:

1. *The time of observing Easter.* The Roman Catholic Church did instigate several meetings with the Celtic Church to merge with the Catholic Church; however, since the invitation seemed to be one-sided, the Celtic Church declined. On their last meeting, the Roman Catholic Church sought the Celtic Church's response to some trivial points of discussion: "How should we conduct baptism?" *We* was stated as if both churches were already merged. Or "What is the correct style of tonsure?" (Tonsure was shaving the head prior to entering the priesthood.) The Celtic Church could have cared less!

    Later in this meeting came the question: "What about this longstanding problem on setting the date for Easter?" The celebration of Easter was not the problem but a uniform date for its celebration was.

    It must be noted here that the Roman Catholic Church had already officially adopted the precise date for Easter, as fixed in 547 by Victorius of Aquitaine. If we look at the former discussions called by the Roman Church, it would appear that the outcome would not change from the Roman Church's previous adoption.

    This was a long and hard-fought struggle, and the controversy was not about superficial details. It was something that was much deeper than that, and was nothing less than the struggle of the Church of Rome to establish unity and supremacy, which would safeguard the survival of Catholic Christianity in the west. The struggle of the Celtic Church, on the other hand, was to maintain the spiritual independence and a right to adhere to its own ancient and honorable traditional usages.

The dispute was finally referred to the Synod of Whitby in 663,[21] where only the Easter question was discussed. The Roman case won by having a preponderance of voters (voting with a stacked-deck), or Easter would be celebrated on the Sunday after the full moon or following the vernal equinox (after March 21). It cannot come before March 22 or after April 25. The manner of celebrating Easter was more important to the Celtic Church than designating a uniform date of celebration. From the time of the Synod of Whitby, Easter has been celebrated on this special date.

2. *The form of tonsure.* There was no tonsure among the Celtic Church, but among those in the Roman Catholic Church there was much discussion. How should tonsure for the Roman clergy be cut? Should the hair on their head be cut resembling a cross, or should it be in the form of a circle resembling a halo? The latter was favored, and to the present time some Roman Catholic orders still prefer this form of tonsure.

3. *Government by councils,* and ignorance of or refusal to recognize the authority of the bishop of Rome (the pope), caused much consternation. Ireland at this time, thought to be a Roman Catholic stronghold, was inhabited by many adherents to the Celtic Church, which remained adamant about such a demand. It may have been all right to require such an obeisance from the followers of that church, but to demand it from any other people was out of the question. One can see here the initial beginnings leading to the Reformation in the United Kingdom.

From this point on, we will continue to present the Celts in the life of the Church, to give you a complete church history picture to the present day.

In 596, Pope Gregory determined to send a mission to the United Kingdom. Augustine was designated by the pope, but he was rather reluctant to lead that delegation. He did arrive in Kent the following year, however. He lived and taught in Canterbury and shortly thereafter was confirmed as Canterbury's archbishop.

Now, as one reads history, it seems the two most powerful churches at that time were the Celtic churches and the Roman churches, each containing Celts. It was prominent at this time that the Roman Church appeared to be in competition for the most powerful church, not only in asking all people to recognize the authority of the bishop of Rome. But now we find Pope Gregory commissioning Augustine concerning the Celtic Church and all other non-Catholics.

Several historians, among them Nora Chadwick and John Davies, have pictured Pope Gregory the Great (Pope Gregory I) as being highly autocratic and dominant in his appointment of Augustine. He seemed to them to be obsessed with the belief that The Roman Catholic Church at all costs would be dominant over all people in the United Kingdom.

In Gregory's commission charge to Augustine, he has been quoted by some as saying: "We commit them all to your charge. . . . that the unlearned may be taught. . . . the weak strengthened by persuasion, and the perverse corrected by authority."[22] Whether these were the exact words that came from the mouth of Pope Gregory, we cannot be certain, but with the temperament of the pope they seem natural.

Davies goes a step farther and seems to infer that Augustine desired to follow the pope's charge to the letter. As a result Davies claims, that when Augustine rather arrogantly sought to give substance to that authority, he was rebuffed by the Welsh bishops.

The age of the saints was a memory. It was long-cherished and of infinite value in the spiritual history, especially with the folks of Ireland, with their intellectual influence abroad. The presence of any form of central organization in the Celtic Church would certainly be a plus. It was suggested that since the work and missionary zeal of St. Patrick on the island, Armagh should be the place. It was for a brief while, but before long it was voted that Iona, with the constructive statesmanship and the spiritual and intellectual integrity of Columba, with the powerful monastic sanctuary at Iona, that Iona be designated as head of the Celtic Church.

IONA

Iona, that small rocky island off the west coast of Scotland, was never under the aegis of the Roman Catholic Church! Many wanted that rocky island to be the center of the entire Celtic Church; however, historian Bede states that (circa A.D. 690):

> The Roman Catholic Northumbrian monk Ecgberht (Ecgberct) from Ireland brought almost all that were not under the domination of Iona (the Celtic Church) into Catholic unity.[23] Then, in 716, Iona celebrated Easter by the Roman dating. In that same year, a Northumbrian abbot, Coelfrith of Jarrow, expelled all the Columban clergy (followers of St. Columba) from his kingdom. The supremacy of the Irish Church (Roman Catholic) now passed again to Armagh and was complete.[24]

The Celtic Church in Iona was thought by the Roman Church to soon disappear as the center of their faith, but the Church of Rome underestimated the strength of the Celtic Church. Iona stands even today as a landmark of the Celtic Church and has become a place where Christians come to renew their faith.

The fact remains that the Celtic Church designated Iona to be its official center of Celtic spirituality. It appears to have been done not because they saw the Roman Catholic Church with its power in one place (Rome), with the pope as its head. Instead the Celtic power was not in a pope but in its zeal in ministering to the person of Jesus Christ. Here again we see the early Celtic definition of power coming through. The Celtic Church seemed to believe that if this church was to continue, it must have a central place of identity as well as to say to the world, "If the center of the Catholic Church is in far-off Rome, ours is right here in the United Kingdom at Iona!"

Now is the time to look back and see the people's thinking on Celtic spirituality to date. Six areas of Celtic spirituality have been presented by various Celtic historians, and I do not know to whom to give primary credit. The six areas are:

1. *Spirituality of the tribe, not the city.* The tribe is a collection of families and clans. It is in these individuals where spirituality is calibrated rather than in specific places. i.e., I am a Celt rather than I am from Dublin. Celtic bishops were over a group rather than a place. Spiritual leaders lived and worked with people rather than over a prescribed area.
2. *Spirituality of the story, not the law.* There were laws, but stories were directives for one's life. These stories of the saints, who worked, forgave, and prayed, told how there is needed a life to be lived. Stories of angels and saints needed to be taken more seriously. Spirituality was not calibrated by how people kept the law but by how their spirituality kept them within the law.
3. *Spirituality of the out-of-doors, not the indoors.* Worship needs to be in the first setting the gods gave you—the out-of-doors. See the mountains, rivers and streams, and things out-of-doors as places to worship, and give thanks for them. Don't just pass by. Worship can also be thought of as being in a building, for it was out of a building that the Druids came with their words of hope and direction.
4. Spirituality of the circle, not the square. The Celtic monastery of the seventh century and a stone structure was built in a circle, with the bones of the saints in the center, resembling a bee-hive. One may be seen in Kildare, Iceland and on Skellig Rock in the Atlantic off the southwest coast of Ireland. In Celtic spirituality, a square did not signify eternity, but a circle did. (See Celtic knot, p. 137, 140)

5. *Spirituality is particular and unique rather than abstract and general.* To the Celts general spirituality was no spirituality at all. The basis of one's spirituality is why does one believe and what does one believe. These constitute one's spirituality. They used this example: The nature of the sparrow's singing is not what it takes to be a bird but "why" and "how" the song? Every design is a new creation.
6. *Spirituality of inclusion not exclusion.* In relation to the Celtic pre-Christian cultural tradition, the Celts' movement into Christianity was smooth. The Celtic Christians had no martyrs. They were eager to keep their stories "Christianized." Everything needed to be included and affirmed. The Celtic Church was inclusive. Anyone who desired to worship God in the manner they wished were welcomed. In contrast, both the Church of England and the Roman Catholic churches demanded "worship there or else"; the Church of England because it was the state church, and the Roman Catholic Church because they believed it was "the true and only church."

SOUL FRIENDSHIP

Anamchara, signifying "soul friendship," predates Christianity. Where did it came from? Who or what was responsible for its beginning? No one knows except that the soul was thought to be the seat of the emotions, so it had to be more than just a loose kind of friendship.

We have mentioned earlier that one of the characteristics of Celtic spirituality was "soul friends." This thought was developed around A.D. 900, and each step of the way became ingrained into the spiritual life of the Celts and continued down through the years to the present day.

In early Celtic mythology writers noted that the fairies had some influence over humans, mostly keeping them on a moral track. There was also the belief in the Little People, especially in Irish lore, who were later called Leprechauns. This is a deep and extended subject to probe. The suggestion here would be to introduce you to "A. E." (An anonymous Irish mystic named Rodiant), who has written *Visions of the Old Gods of Ireland,* and to William Butler Yeats, who are authorities regarding these Little People. In addition there is W. Y. Evans Wentz's book, *Fairy Faith in Celtic Countries,* which is commended for further study. There has also been the talk of guardian angels and their responsibilities. But here we begin to see the Celts and talk about what they called soul friends, people who they knew and chose to be a special part of their spiritual life and growth.

The soul friendship that we are talking about here was basic to the Celts as early as A.D. 900. Soul friendship is more than one heart and one mind in a togetherness relationship. It is even more close than what people refer to as "my best and closest friend."

Soul friends first began between the early saints. One can read about it in their lives, but until people experience it themselves, it may seem only a blur. It is a kind of deep spiritual enrichment between two persons, or as one of the early saints said: "It goes so deep between two people that one can confess to the other, and deep enough to grant penance, and to receive it as well." It is as if the other person is like God, because each of these people desire a spiritual best for each other. It is the highest spirituality that one can probably reach on earth!

It wasn't long before soul friendship was being practiced among Christian lay people. In the early Celtic Church, this practice was not only clergy with clergy, or clergy with lay people, often it was lay people with lay people. This practice was not always segregated, men with men and women with women either. It could be a man and a woman, or a woman and a woman, or a woman and a man.

As the author himself states, "In my personal life, the best thing I ever did was choose a soul friend! I did not discover what soul friendship meant until I was more than halfway through my ministry. Since then I have been recommending it to my clergy and lay friends, not for any other reason than for the great blessing it can be personally to them and also for the Church!"

Edward Sellner, who wrote the book *Wisdom of the Celtic Saints*, shared these seven aspects of soul friendship with Dr. Arthur Holder, who in turn shared them with a group of people in a seminar on Celtic spirituality attended by the author. They are as follows:[25]

1. *It takes real friendship.* Not a set of personal relationships. No one is like an academic adviser to the other. It is a deep and mutual friendship that wants the "absolute best" for the other.
2. *Mutuality and respect for each other's wisdom.* Meet each other where they are. Difference in age should not matter. Sometimes a token given to the other on impulse might be considered. Not as a gift for gift's sake or the feeling allowed that the receiver must give a gift in return.
3. *Common vision and intuition.* Both may even have the same dreams. Both think alike. If so, it appears to be for the other one's benefit. Grow together.
4. *Not only affirmation for the other but the ability to challenge.* Neither is so holy that they don't need to be challenged.
5. *Subordinated with God, who is the "soul friend" of all.* God knows who our soul friend should be and nourishes each. Doctrine of Election. We are not always aware who our soul friend should be. God will provide if we are desirous of one.
6. *Survivors elapse their time.* Even if the other soul friend moves away, you may choose another, if you are not in talking distance. That soul friend can still operate. If your soul friend dies, they still may be operable and function even though you may choose another.
7. *Helping each other to discern a proper balance and change.* When a problem is posed, don't say "Do this!" but rather "Why don't you try this?" or "Why don't you do this for a while?"

Lest we misunderstand confession in the early Celtic Church during the Nicene Period, we need to realize that for the Celtic

Christian Church at this time there is no comprehension of *sin* against God, or *God's grace through Jesus Christ, offering forgiveness* except between persons who were wronged and who say "I'm sorry!"

Christian repentance is a word that they did not understand.

What they did realize at this point is that through their lives the gods gave them gifts, and they believed that the gods held them responsible for these gifts, and they realized what these gifts were. In recent times, Celts have come to believe in One God, who was the kind of a God who could do everything that they believed "their gods" accomplished. This One Creator God also holds them just as responsible for these gifts.

Misusing the gifts that God has given them, and for which they believe God holds them responsible for their proper use, requires that they should at least say "I'm sorry!" as they would to a friend. They, as yet, do not see what they have done is a *sin*, because they have not been confronted that certain things they have done are sin.

So when soul friends talk about confession to a soul brother or a soul sister, they are still seeking to erase from their lives the things that slow them down from being a better person.

Thus we are able to see how, when they were presented "salvation by grace through faith in Jesus Christ," at the time just preceding the Reformation in the United Kingdom, Celts could easily understand what this God has planned for them. The Celtic people, who are a part of the Celtic Church now would, without much persuasion, become either a part of the Catholic or the Reformed Church! A majority of the Celts became a part of the early Reformed Church, but it is still thought to be the Celtic Church.

THE RISE OF THE REFORMATION IN THE UNITED KINGDOM
(1000–1557)

Not much has been written about a Reformation happening in the United Kingdom until the return of John Knox from his escape to Geneva. He then challenged the Catholic churches head-on. The reason for his return was that the Church of England (Anglican) controlled the history that was written, and such history at this time was alien to the Church of England. It was only when the Church of England had a king sympathetic to the Protestant tradition was any history written about the Celtic Church.

Here historians seemed to have had a hey-day with their pens. But, in and around 900, no one even had an inkling of any such upheaval. In fact it was little known that the Reformation had begun in Germany in 1517. It was forty years later before the Reformation began in Scotland.

It's a good thing the Celtic Church spent time reviewing and crystallizing their beliefs around A.D. 1000, because they were soon to be hit with a desertion from their ranks. This catastrophe among the Celts would set them back to regroup about 1272.

Between A.D. 1000 and 1200, there seems to have been very little written about the Celts in the United Kingdom, either in matters of civics or spirituality, because the English royalty controlled the press. If an overview were taken, it would seem that the islands were still in a kind of pre-feudal system, each living unto themselves, each in their own geographical location, give or take some dilution through intermarriage.[26]

The situation seems somewhat like this: The Gaelic Celts were situated in what later would be called Scotland and Ireland. It could be said that the Gaelic (Irish) Celts and the Mancs Celts (the Isle of Man) were probably more pure Celt than the others because of their island isolation. The Cymry (Welsh) were not as isolated as either the Irish or the Mancs but seemed to be fighting among themselves, hoping to unite Wales into a self-sufficient unit to rule themselves in the United Kingdom and hoping all others would do the same. With the Welsh, they were united in the idea to make one Wales, but the question was who would the leader or leaders be? The Cornish were becoming a kind of admixture but with a narrow Celtic majority. The Bretons were still in the area of what we now call England. Although they were probably not in the majority, they were numerous and powerful enough to be heard.[27]

Picture the United Kingdom of the Celts, each group spread over the area, still segregated and without much organization.

Now picture the situation at hand about 1220. The area where the Bretons resided had the best military and civic organization of all the Celtic lands. Add to the Bretons, the Angles, Saxons, Vikings, and the Gauls, etc. to give a kind of melting pot with different kinds of people.

Edward I (1239–1307) sat on the throne. In present history, some are called kings of England, although England per se was not yet a historical name for this area. Be that as it may, Edward I had a dream and a desire to expand and control these islands but recognized that he alone did not have the ability to make such a conquest.

It was at this point, about 1270 because in 1272 Edward I desired to set out and conquer Wales, Ireland and Scotland, but he did not feel he had sufficient manpower to make such a foray. It was at this juncture that the Bretons changed their name to Britons, offered their services to King Edward I, and aided him in his conquest. This was the first time the word *Britain* was ever used! Yet historians, writing from their vantage point, have confused history by earlier calling all inhabitants of this area Britains!

The other Celts determined this act to be "the most despicable event in the lives of the Celtic people" because (1) the Bretons were thought to have adopted a power to plunder, pillage, and proffer, which was against main Celtic thought; (2) the Bretons, in doing so, would be held accountable for their actions against the gods or against the One God; and (3) the Bretons made their own Celtic people their enemy.[28]

Turncoats, these Celts were! These Bretons who changed their name to Britons became overlords to their fellow Celts. They were responsible for their actions in holding dominion over their own people to the present time! All because of their reneging on their belief in power defined by their forefathers and their foremothers over the years!

The wars ended, and the Celts are still paying allegiance today to their captors. Over the years they have individually asked for their freedom, but the only answer has been a deaf ear.

The Celtic Rites

The Celtic rites were Latin formularies used in Scotland and Ireland through the eleventh century. These rites were in custody of Celtic missionaries who roamed the continent at the opening of the Middle Ages (circa A.D. 500). Being ardent lovers of liturgy, they collected ceremonies and forms from many, not the least of which were eastern. Although this tradition was eclectic and viable, it produced a number of books, notably *the Stowe Missal*, which offers an example of Celtic worship from the eighth to the tenth centuries. *The Gallican liturgy* was employed by the Frankish kingdom until the era of Charlemagne, when it was deliberately suppressed in deference to *the Roman rite*. It was rather fully delineated in the notation of Gregory of Tours (A.D. 594) and several liturgical texts of the seventh century.

The Latin Mass, a rite of the Roman Church, was not really uniform for all areas; many had other versions until the thirteenth century.

Being eager to establish preaching as a part of the Mass in his domain, Charlemagne enjoined that a sermon must be delivered in all churches every Sunday and that every Christian know the Credo and the Pater Noster. In the Celtic Catholic churches, in connection with the sermon, the service included a "bidding prayer," the Lord's Prayer, the creed, the general confession of sins, as well as the church announcements.

The Roman Catholic Mass, in this early time, was mandated to be held even without any communicants present. Liturgically speaking, the gospel was to be read from the right side of the chancel, the epistle from the left, their positions to be reckoned from the standpoint of the altar toward the congregation. No Old Testament book was to be read. Unleavened wafer brought to an end, the symbolism of the loaf. For some reason not given at this time, only the wafer was given to members of the congregation. The wine was only to be drunk by the celebrant of the Mass. The Mass as noted here was celebrated circa 1100 in Europe and other places but was not celebrated in the Roman Church in the United Kingdom until the early part of 1200. There seemed to be no problem elsewhere concerning the Mass. The thirteenth century was especially important in the history of the Latin rite.

According to the new conception of liturgical uniformity, in which the head of the Church conformed rather to its members, there was a prolific growth of diocesan and monastic usages. While these did not presume upon the fixed character of the Mass, they did admit a bewildering variety in ceremonial and silent devotions of the priest.

A singular Mass, or a "Mass-only" service, was adopted in the *Missale Romanum,* a simplified mass-book prepared by the papal curia during the age of Innocent III. During this same time, Innocent III gave precise definition to the liturgical colors. White was selected to be reminiscent of the clouds of ascension. Red honored the blood of the martyrs and the holy fire of Pentecost. Black was appropriate for seasons of penance and masses for the dead. Green was used on occasions that were without any special significance. It was much later that purple was used, and its use was begun during Lent.[29]

The Catholic doctrine of the Mass, at this time it was explained, was not intended to be a mere historical recollection of a bygone event. It was maintained to be the Lord's passion continually being made present and actual in the liturgy. The bread and the wine were not to be thought of as symbols but as the "real body" and "real blood" of Christ (transubstantiation), immediately following the prayer of consecration.[30]

During the wars with Edward II and others, very little is said about Celtic spirituality in any depth, except through the Roman Catholic Church. There was no one to report Celtic spirituality from any other side!

This appears to be a rather sterile historical period except for the Roman Catholic presentation. Later we will see that Celtic spirituality grew into two divergent groups—the Roman Catholic and the non-Roman Catholic faiths.

The people of faith in the United Kingdom portrayed a marked division. The Roman Catholics were described as administratively organized (pope, bishop, down to the local priest) and blatantly pontifical, "the only true and real Church," and their faith in the process of articulation to the public. Contrary to the fact stated by the Roman Catholic Church, the non-Roman Catholic churches were organized in both structure and theology during this period of time.

To set a background, and to explain the actions and events that would soon transpire in the pre-Reformation period in the United Kingdom, we need to understand the actions of the Roman Catholic Church in Europe. In 1520, at the Diet of Speyer, the Roman Catholic Church excommunicated Martin Luther. In 1526, at the Diet of Speyer in the city of Speyer, the Roman Catholic Church granted no tolerance to Lutheran believers. Here they were called "Protestants," that is protesting against the true Church. Those not following the true Church could be burned at the stake. Those Protestants in turn accepted the title but used the Latin root form for protest, *protestare*, meaning to stand up for something; namely their faith.

The growth of Protestantism in the United Kingdom of the Celts owes its rise to many factors already presented. It took a course somewhat different from that followed by Lutheranism in Germany and Calvinism in other countries. In the beginning, Protestantism was a way of seeking compromise with Roman Catholicism. In doing so, Protestantism received indirect support from Henry VIII (1509–1547), who had a dispute with the pope over his attempted divorce, which the pope would not grant. For that reason Henry VIII refused to recognize the pope any longer as head of the Christian Church and made himself head of the Church of England. Seeing that many people objected to monasticism, he took advantage of the situation and dissolved all the Roman Catholic monasteries in the United Kingdom. But this did not make him a Protestant at all, for in 1521 he defended the Roman Catholic faith against Lutheranism, and the pope officially named him "The Defender of The Faith." Henry VIII kept this title to the end of his life. All later monarchs, though nearly all of them were Protestant, continued to use this title. Such a title is still used by the present Queen Mother, as head of the Church of England.

The Welsh Roman Catholics and non-Roman Catholics seemed to continue in a mode of compromise. They didn't seem to be as confrontational, to the same extent that existed in England and Scotland, where the Roman Catholic Church with its position and power forced its theology and practices on non-Catholics. It was in this pre-Reformation time in the United Kingdom that people began to take sides either accepting or rejecting the Roman Catholic tradition, as had already taken place in Germany and across Europe.

Since the invention of the printing press in 1445, only 108 books were published in Welsh, which was an infinitesimal number compared with the numbers printed in English and French. But that number compares favorably with only four books being published in Scottish Gaelic and only eleven in Irish Gaelic.

One of the books that received the inordinate attention of the Roman Catholic Church was that of the Welshman John Prys, who had accepted the Protestant belief in "justification by faith."

> Prys' book contained the Credo, the Lord's Prayer, and the Ten Commandments. It was an attempt to introduce the Scriptures to the people in their mother tongue. Rome frowned on such attempts, for "only the true Church could interpret Scripture," argued Pope Gregory VII, "and if Scriptures were available to everyone, ... Scripture will be misinterpreted by those of little learning, ... who will be led into perdition."[31]

As a rejoinder, other church leaders urged priests to "explain to the people in their language the essentials of the faith."

Unknown to the Roman Catholic Church, some key passages from the Bible had already been translated into Welsh by Dewi Sant, the Welsh patron saint. Twenty-two manuscripts—*Y Bibyl Ynghymraec*—had already been published. Such translations may have contributed to the belief that the Bible had been translated into Welsh centuries before the Reformation elevated the mother tongue to a central position in worship.

In 1549, the first edition of the *English Prayer Book* appeared. Henry VIII had died in 1547, and the book was the work of the advisers to his son Edward VI, an avowed Protestant. The Roman Catholic Church also became indignant because "only the priests could pray, and anything not published by the Church was anathema."

Another Welsh book, *Ban Wedi Ei Dynnu o Gyfraith Hywel Dda,* (The Lofty Has Been Removed from the Law of Howell the Good), noted clerics had already been allowed to marry. That right was granted in 1549 in Hywl Dda's law, by a clergy consensus, a change with far-reaching implications for the lives of all clergy. Again the Roman Catholic Church proclaimed that people outside the Church were interfering!

A more far-reaching revision of the Protestant version of *The Prayer Book* in 1553 infuriated the Roman Church. *The Prayer Book* abandoned transubstantiation, a belief that the bread and wine of the sacrament immediately turned the real body and blood of our Lord at the conclusion of the prayer of consecration. This doctrine became a marked difference between the Mass of the Celtic Roman Catholic Church and the Sacrament of the Celtic Protestant congregations.

Edward VI died in 1553. He was succeeded by his sister, Mary, who had inherited the unyielding and unrelenting belief in Roman Catholicism. She was determined to reestablish Roman Catholicism as the Church! During her reign, Mary had burned about 300 so-called heretics because they did not recant their faith and follow her into Roman Catholicism.

The English Church (Anglican) had not yet come to one mind to give respect to all religious forms. Because of the spiritual power exerted by John Calvin in Geneva, Switzerland, plus his spiritual and scriptural work in the *Institutes of the Christian Religion,* powerful reverberations were being felt in the United Kingdom, not only through the Scottish Presbyterians but also through the Puritans, or nonconformists, as they were publicly known. The beliefs of Calvin were dramatically felt even though he never set foot on their soil or met the people he influenced.

In Scotland the attempts at church reform prior to 1557 could be considered as a series of sporadic, but continual, outbreaks in opposition to Roman Catholic incursions into their territory. Patrick

Hamilton began preaching reform in 1528 and was seized and burned during one of these incursions by the Roman Catholic Church. George Wishart appeared fifteen years later and met with better reception on the part of the nobles, but he was also seized by the order of Archbishop Beaton and burned. Beaton paid the penalty for his persecutions by being assassinated in his own castle in 1546.

John Knox (1505–1572) was also seized and imprisoned for complicity against the Roman Church. After a short while he was freed and fled to Geneva in 1554 to escape the furor of "Bloody" Mary. John Knox claimed to be an avid Celt who would fight like the Celts of old, if necessary, to hold this land that God had given to his people. It was he who became the leader and genius in forming the Church of Scotland.

Mary Queen of Scots came to the throne planning to restore the Roman Catholic Church and make it the state church. It wasn't as easy as she thought. She met an implacable enemy in John Knox, who met her at every turn. He had an answer to her every question, and to her face he called her an idolater. He had her imprisoned, allowing her to practice her faith but in the privacy of her cell.

It can be said that, if John Knox laid the foundation of Presbyterianism from the knowledge and tenacity he found in Geneva, Andrew Melville (1545–1622) built the superstructure. This man combined hard work, serious zeal, noted learning, and a strong inward faith! Step by step he gained on the opposition, when in 1592 the second *Book of Discipline* was written, which became known as *The Charter of the Kirk*. This gave Melville written proof of his proclamations.

THE SCOTS CONFESSION
(1560)

The date is 1560. The place is Scotland. The cast of characters are the Reformers, which were mostly later Presbyterians. The backdrop depicts complete religious freedom at all odds!

If one does not understand the background of these Celtic Scots, then he will not be able to understand the words of the Confession either! For on this Scots Confession hangs the Reformation in the United Kingdom!

The Scottish Christians were besieged on every side. They were hemmed in on one side by the hierarchy of the Roman Catholic Church with an edict: "Death to all unbelievers!", meaning all non-Roman Catholics. There had already been many who were burned at the stake for their faith! Up to this time, the Roman Catholic Church had controlled the emperors, and it was just the opposite with the Church of England, where the monarchy controlled the Church.

They were also hemmed in on another side by the hierarchy of the state church, the Church of England, which demanded "Either worship in our churches, or face death or imprisonment!" Both lay members and clergy who were not of the Church of England lost their lives by burning, imprisonment, or were pilloried in the public square. There was also another category—people who adamantly believed that what was happening wasn't worth the suffering.

The only other side left was flanked by the British army, which insisted, "Everyone in the United Kingdom must speak English or be fined or imprisoned. The Scots faced the same odds as did King David, when God gave him a choice: 'Which is it to be? Three years of famine in your land, or three months of running away from your enemies, or three days of epidemic in your land?'"[32]

These Scottish Celts believed that these groups were using power as did the Hittites, Galatians, Romans, and Greeks before them. These groups also believed that power was amassing land and making other people subservient to them and their cause. The forefathers of the Scottish Celts fought against such people, because they believed it was still against the gods to do so. The Scots were not so much fighting for land and to get people to be subservient to them; as they were striving because of their faith in God and for a freedom to worship without interference from a king or a church!

What in the Scots Confession fueled this radical independence? First the Confession rejected any mediator than Jesus

Christ. Each worshiper could pray directly to God without any intermediary and without fear. Second no further sacrifice was necessary for salvation—not even the sacrifice of the Mass. Christ had fully atoned for human sin. Third worshipers could recognize the true Kirk (church) not by its hierarchy but by the true preaching of the Word, and rightly administering the sacraments, and ecclesiastical discipline.

The Confession allowed the worshiper to resort directly to Scripture as a check on what they heard in the Kirk. It was Christ who was head over the king and the pope! The Confession defied both the government and the Church for usurping such power. This Confession also asserted that no power of any earthly hierarchy could or should get in the way of the mission of Jesus Christ!

The Welsh Calvinistic Methodist Church, the Presbyterian Church, and the Reformed churches of Scotland, joined by other Celtic churches, were on their way to the Reformation in the United Kingdom of the Celts! Led by the Celts! Was it a pure strain of Celts? No, but Celts nevertheless! Note how their faith evolved!

Our discussion will now take up the history of the Celts from this time to the year 1950.

CHAPTER 5

HISTORICAL DEVELOPMENT IN THE UNITED KINGDOM (1558–1950)

> We swear by peace and love to stand
> Heart to heart and hand to hand.
> Mark, O Spirit and hear us now,
> Confirming this our Sacred Vow.
> —*an early Druid blessing*

What comprises the history of the Celts now that the Reformation in the United Kingdom has begun? How did they build on such a foundation?

One would imagine that the historians would have a hey-day with their pens, reporting the influences this new beginning was starting to accomplish or the manner in which they felt it missed the mark.

Certainly, like many news reporters, they picked up the "blood and guts" items, such as burning people to death, hangings, and the public pillorying of people in the town square in the pre-Reformation period, but nothing on spirituality—Celtic or otherwise! Historians made much of such sensational news; however, they wrote nothing more than what appears in the annals of church history texts.

Did this type of historian die? Was there nothing more sensational to write about? Was the press controlled by the church or the commonwealth? Or, as some historians concluded, the Celts were no more! They had somehow vanished!

Social evils, governmental goofs, civic circumstances, and the ups-and-downs of politics are mentioned by historians but only as happenstances of the time. Nothing was written regarding the influence or lack of influence of the Celtic churches in the post-Reformation period. Whatever they believed to be the outcome, several Celtic historians were convinced that the Celtic strain lived through this period of time from the Reformation through 1950.

Through hindsight we might view how they handled themselves by our standards and make our comments. But again, we need to look through their eyes and get a feel through their hearts. In order to do this, why don't we travel again with the author, trying to possess Celtic eyes and hearts as we take in this history following the Reformation. How shall we do this? We shall take the historical events of royalty over this period and add instances from the perspective of Celtic historians. This will show the conditions under which they lived and the circumstances to which they responded.

Elizabeth I
(1533–1603)

As Queen of England from 1558–1603, Elizabeth ruled one of the most glorious periods of English history. Born in London, Elizabeth was the daughter of King Henry VIII and Anne Boleyn. When her mother lost favor with the king and was beheaded, Elizabeth at three years was declared illegitimate. But she was later given her place in the succession to the throne. When her half-sister Mary, a Roman Catholic, became Queen, she was suspicious of Elizabeth, the Protestant heir to the throne. For a time, Elizabeth's life was in great danger.

Problems of Her Reign

When Mary died in 1558, she left Elizabeth with many serious problems. These included a war with France, a bankrupt treasury, and the difficult question of Britain's religion. Elizabeth ended the war and placed Britain's finances on a sound basis. She then tried to find a solution to the religious question that would satisfy the majority of her subjects. She reestablished the Anglican Church, freeing it from Roman Catholic control, but the church was not completely Protestant.[1]

Elizabeth's reign was called one of the most glorious periods of English history, or the Golden Age, for several reasons. Mary, the center of discontent, was removed. Elizabeth kept two foreign suitors, Philip II of Spain and the French Duke of Anjou. When she took sterner measures against the Roman Catholic Church, she drew the wrath of Philip II of Spain. Spain, which at that time was the most powerful state in Europe, sent an armada against Britain, but superior English sailors destroyed the Spanish fleet.

Elizabeth's actions against the Roman Catholic Church added fuel to the fire at the beginning of the Celtic post-Reformation age and brought a sense of well-being to Celtic Protestants. Although Elizabeth was not an avid church person, it was believed her choice was made on practical grounds against the vindictive manner of her half-sister Mary and her plots against Elizabeth.

Elizabeth, in the process, became a living legend. She brought self-confidence and pride to the kingdom. Some think she became the living legend in early English literature in "The Virgin Queen," the "Gloriana" of Edmund Spenser, and in the title "Good Queen Bess." During her years, Shakespeare began his writings and England developed a colonial empire.

Celtic Events During the Reign of Queen Elizabeth

It was during the years of Elizabeth's reign that the Celts came into prominence in several areas. One of oddest of these events was the excommunication of Queen Elizabeth by Pope Gregory XIII. What made this excommunication odd was that Queen Elizabeth was not a Roman Catholic. How could a pope excommunicate someone who was not a Roman Catholic? This situation has never been explained by the Roman Catholic Church. This excommunication brought further division among the Celts who included both Roman Catholics and those of the Reformed faith.

The Renaissance was said to have begun as early as the 1200s and came to fruition about the time of the Reformation in the United Kingdom. Renaissance by name is probably a misnomer. Renaissance is really marking a shifting of emphasis from medieval society to a rebirth of culture. Historians writing on this period substituted a worldly point of view with reference to literature and the state. This could possibly be the main reason that historians neglected writing about the Celts.[2]

The literature of the Celts composed a great part of the Elizabethan Age. Other writings of this time were:

- First edition of *The English Prayer Book*—1555
- *Apologia*—Bishop Jewel's doctrine defined—1562
- *The Welsh New Testament*—1567
- *Catholic Christian Doctrine*—1568
- William Morgan's *Welsh Bible*, 1588
- *The Counter Reformation*, written in Welsh—1596[3]

The Agriculture of the Celts

The Celts brought with them improved farming and growing methods from the mainland of Europe to the United Kingdom. Farming was productive in the United Kingdom, more than enough produce was harvested to supply their own needs and sufficient left over to sell and trade goods to the general public. Economic growth facilitated population growth. The number of farms was increasing as landowners formed consolidated units, cleared stones, and fertilized with lime. In the richer lowlands, the new arable land was suited for growing corn. In favorable times a surplus was produced, which was exported to Bristol and Ireland.

The Education of the Celts

Aristotle (384–322 B.C.) was a pupil of Plato (427–347 B.C.), and they made much progress in education. Formerly the state had provided only physical and military instruction or training, but children of free parent, sometimes girls as well as boys, received instruction in reading and writing, literature, and music.[4]

Plato had an academy and used some of his own money for teaching. Aristotle had a gymnasium only for children of Greek culture.

> The education of the young and the intellectual lives of all classes was carried out by two classes of men known as Druids and seers, who taught entirely by means of poetry orally transmitted. Their subject matter was saved by use of metrical form from the inevitable disintegration which it would otherwise have suffered, since their courses were said to have continued sometimes for as long as twenty years. Despite the absence of books their teaching was on a lofty plane and included such subjects as the stars and their motions, the nature and greatness of our earth, the power and majesty of the immortal gods, and other matters which comprise natural and moral philosophy. Among the most important of their tenets was that of the immortality of the soul.[5]

Following the Druid's teaching, several pupils were taught by the early saints. Now about 1500 they were being taught by the church in a parochial and catechetical manner, which did not take root in England until 1530.

> In the matter of education—William Herbert—scholar, planter in Ireland, the first Welshman (a Celt) known to have addressed the House of Commons, and a pioneer of education, in 1590, sought to established a college for the Welsh in the ruins of Tintern Abbey. Herbert's hopes were not fulfilled, but years earlier, in 1571, Jesus College, Oxford's First Protestant Foundation, was established.[6]

> Shrewsbury School, founded in 1552, was especially popular, but Welsh pupils were also to be found at Westminster, Eaton,

Winchester, Bedford, and St. Paul's. They were all grammar schools.[7]

These samples of Celtic histories were during the reign of Queen Elizabeth I. The following are the kings under whose reign the Celts continued to live, to act and react, according to rules and pronouncements of their authority.

JAMES I
(1556–1625)

James I was the son of Mary, Queen of Scots, and Lord Darnley. When his mother abdicated in 1567, he became King James VI of Scotland. When his cousin Queen Elizabeth I of England died in 1603, he became King of England.

> James was impractical and impolite. King Henry IV of France is said to have called him "the wisest fool in Christendom." James believed strongly in his own divine right to rule and quarreled with Parliament. He was intolerant of Protestant dissenters.[8]

The first permanent English colony in America was established in Virginia in 1607. It was named Jamestown in honor of James I. The Puritans, Protestant dissenters, migrated to New England later in his reign. The major achievement of James' reign was the translation of the Bible by a commission of churchmen, published in 1611. It became known as the King James Version.

James married Princess Anne of Denmark in 1589. Their daughter Elizabeth married the German elector of the Palatinate, and one of their great-grandsons became King George I of England in 1715. James was succeeded by his son Charles I.

But King James I got into trouble with the Puritans and Parliament.

> The new king could not get along very well with the many Puritans who were living in England during his reign, because they

wanted a more democratic church government than was to be found in the Anglican Church, and the king wanted to remain head of the church and maintain the bishops. He also became angry when the Puritans said that they did not want *The Prayer Book* any longer, which was used in the Anglican Church during the services. He annoyed the leading members of Parliament because he wanted too much power in the government. So they complained bitterly about this proud king from Scotland. The situation became so unpleasant for a time; from 1614 to 1621 there were no meetings of Parliament at all.[9]

Under James I, things seemed to functioned on their own, without too much concern about the matter of law, sickness and disease, mining claims, or economic growth. It was almost a place of anarchy, but not quite!

The Celts in Europe, years before they migrated into the United Kingdom, had metallurgical skills. They mined ores—copper, tin, and iron and for precious metals, gold and silver. In the United Kingdom they mined in the same manner; however:

> The owners of the land owned the coal, iron and other ores beneath their land, and they could profit from mineral exploitation either directly or through leases. The precious metals—gold and silver belonged to the Crown, as did other metals used in coinage of copper and tin. Elizabeth I, near the end of her term, was anxious to exploit the resources of her kingdom.[10]

The first Welsh venture of the Company of Mines Royal was the works established in Neath in 1584 to smelt copper ore from Cornwall. As the supply of ore was not reliable, the enterprise came to an end about 1602.[11]

In 1617, Hugh Myddelton of Denbigh leased a work at the rent of £400 a year. . . . the annual return on the venture could be as much as £24,000. He sent 3,000 ounces of silver to the royal mint in 1624.[12]

The economic growth that occurred in the southern part of the kingdom after the union of Ireland, Scotland, and Wales with

England did not lead to a high standard of living for the people as a whole.

This period saw the highest rate of inflation, more than anything experienced until this century. After generations of comparative stability, there was between 1530 and 1640 a four-fold increase in the price of ordinary goods.[13]

Sickness and disease were tremendous problems during this time in all areas of the United Kingdom. It was predominantly found in the lower class of people who were deficient in vitamins A, C, and D. Some had faith in herbal remedies, others in magic potions resurrected from the Druid past. These folks could not afford the services of a doctor, even if they could find one. In addition, doctors were very crude and careless.

The only educated person in many villages was the clergyman; however, he had little or no education in medicine. The only means at his disposal was educating the people in methods of public health and in making them amenable to social disciplines. This was the aim of the Puritans, since government under James apparently wasn't too concerned about health or welfare. In addition, James I persecuted the Puritans so strongly for their effort that many of those most helpful and most knowledgeable in the area of sanitation migrated to America.

Under James the laws of this period were not a problem, but matters of enforcement were! There were too few magistrates to do the job. Many of the Celts and others, for their own safety, took the law into their own hands. This brought many culprits to the attention of the available magistrates, and punishment was inflicted. Then a greater problem reared its head. Magistrates encouraged those who took the laws into their own hands and vigilantes were organized.

The conditions under which the Celts existed at this time were, for the most part most unfavorable to our present-day standards but were also apparently inadequate when we consider the standards during their time.

CHARLES I
(1625–1649)

Charles I was born in 1600 and became king in 1625. During the next four years, he called three Parliaments and dissolved each one because its members would not submit to his demands. (So much for those who believed in "the right of kings.") In 1628, he accepted the Petition of Right drawn up by the third Parliament. But he violated it by raising money through unlawful taxes and loans.

From 1629 to 1640, Charles ruled without Parliament. In 1639, he tried to force Scotland to use English forms of worship, and the Scots rebelled. Charles had to call Parliament to obtain the money he needed to fight the rebels. He dismissed one Parliament after three weeks but had to summon another, the Long Parliament. It met from 1640 to 1653 and held its last session in 1660. When the king tried to seize five parliamentary leaders in 1642, civil war broke out. Charles had the support of most of the nobility, gentry, and clergy. The Puritans and the merchant class supported Parliament. Cromwell became the leader of the parliamentary army. His victories at Marston Moor in 1644 and at Naseby in 1645 brought the civil war to an end. Charles fled Scotland, but the Scottish leaders turned him over to Parliament. In 1649, Charles was convicted of treason and was beheaded. He met his death bravely. England became a commonwealth and later a protectorate.[14]

Those who look at the government in that stage of history may have believed they had the answers to its dilemmas, but they did not possess the knowledge, the temperament, the royalty, or the Parliament needed at this time period. The situation at that time pitted the "divine right of kings" against the Parliament, the representatives of the people.

During the last four years of his reign (1621–1625), James I was not very active and let much of his work as king be done by his son and a certain nobleman whom we call the Duke of Buckingham. These two young men were hostile to the Puritans and friendly to the Catholics.

Finally the new King of England, Charles I, succeeded his father James I. He made life so unpleasant for the Puritans and other Protestants outside the Anglican Church or the Church of England that some 20,000 of them came to America, where they founded New England. Among them were the Pilgrim fathers, who in 1620 landed at Plymouth Rock. Several thousand English Protestants lived for years in the Dutch Republic, where they fought for religious liberty after they went from England to Holland.

In 1640, the Puritans rebelled against King Charles I. They were assisted by the Independents, who received that name because their congregations were independent units in their church. Greatest among the Independents was Oliver Cromwell, who fought against the king, had him imprisoned, and finally had him executed. Then Cromwell took over the reigns of government.

Before long under Cromwell, the "persecuting" side became the "persecuted" side. If these well-meaning folks had been more moderate in their attempted reforms, they might have succeeded, but they overplayed their hand.

This section of history under Charles portrays to the public insights into the divine right of kings in the United Kingdom. This belief holds that monarchs get their right to rule directly from God rather than from the consent and wishes of their subjects. According to this belief, it is up to God to punish a wicked king. So far as the people are concerned, the king can do no wrong. The first blow against divine right of kings came under Charles I, showing that such a philosophy leads to confusion. Such was the lesson displayed in all parts of the kingdom of which the Celts were a part.

The Long Parliament
(1640–1653)

The Long Parliament lasted without break from 1640 to 1653. It was not formally dissolved until 1660. The Long Parliament opened with a direct conflict with King Charles I. It met during the two civil wars, ordered the king's execution, tried to rule in the uneasy years after the wars, and was finally dissolved to make way for a new parliament under King Charles II.[15]

With a number of Celts in the Long Parliament, several lasting reforms were made. It abolished the Star Chamber, where men were tortured for confessions and tried without a jury. It declared that the king could not collect money without its consent. It also brought about the execution of King Charles' advisers, the Earl of Stratford and Archbishop William Laud. On religious questions, the Long Parliament was seriously divided between Puritans and Presbyterians, and neither side would give in to the other, which almost always ended in a tie vote. In 1648, a detachment under Colonel Thomas Pride kept any group from entering the house as a majority. This Long Parliament was the Parliament that made England a commonwealth. It was dissolved in 1660 and reconvened only to call elections as the first order of business.

Charles II
(1630–1685)

Charles II, the son of Charles I, was the first of the restored House of Stuart. In 1561, the Scots proclaimed him king, but Cromwell defeated his army and he fled to France. After Cromwell died in 1658, the English people became dissatisfied with the protectorate. They invited Charles to return, and he was crowned in 1660. His first Parliament granted him wide powers.

The important events of his reign included two wars with the Dutch, the great plague, the Great Fire of London, the Rye House Plot, and the passing of the Habeas Corpus Act. The court of Charles II was considered the most immoral in English history.[16]

One would think that a king personally called to return from France to serve the people, and given a new Parliament that restored both the monarchy and the Church of England, would have had clear sailing! But Charles II turned shrewd. Charles allied with the French against the Dutch Republic during two wars, but in 1674, the Protestant leaders in Parliament forced the king to make peace with the Dutch. Then, to gain Protestant favor, he presented the Test Act of 1673, which provided that no Catholic could hold position in the government and further caused embroilment in the Church. Then when support waned, even among the opposing members of Parliament, and he could not get his way, Charles found ways by bribing members of Parliament with French gold paid by Louis XIV. During his regime the Commonwealth captured New Netherlands and named it New York (1664). It also gained a foothold in India, making more definite progress in the colonization.[17]

JAMES II
(1685–1688)

James II, born in 1663, was a younger son of King Charles I. As Duke of York, he had a distinguished career as admiral and head of the navy. In 1664, New Amsterdam, captured from the Dutch, was named New York in his honor.

James succeeded his brother Charles II as king in 1685. He tried immediately to carry out two major aims—to rule without Parliament and to make England Roman Catholic. But his efforts aroused so much opposition that he was forced to flee the country. In the "Glorious Revolution" of 1688, Mary, his Protestant daughter, and her husband William of Orange, were proclaimed joint-rulers in his place. James spent the rest of his life in exile.

Why was the reign of James II so short?

> England was becoming a first-rate power at last, and if a prudent king had succeeded Charles II in 1685, the English government would have remained nearly autocratic for a long time to come. But James II differed from his brother in that he was stubborn and conceited. He was at once opposed by parliamentary leaders, for they did not wish to have a Catholic king rule over them, nor could they tolerate his undisguised practice of autocracy. So they invited his son-in-law William III to accept the English throne. The Revolution of 1688 was called the Bloodless Revolution since it was not followed by a civil

war. James quietly left England and William ruled in his place until his death in 1702.[18]

WILLIAM III
(1650–1702)
AND
MARY II
(1662–1694)

William III, known as William of Orange, was King of England, Scotland, and Ireland. He was born in the Hague, the son of the prince of Orange and Mary, the daughter of Charles I of England. He gained fame by his opposition to King Louis XIV of France. William III ruled 1689–1702; Mary II from 1689–1694.

William hoped to gain England's support, so he became friendly with those who were opposed to King James II, who was Roman Catholic. When James' son was baptized Catholic, the Protestants turned to William and Mary. Both were related to the royal family, and both were Protestant. The rules of both political parties asked them to rule England. Although they were to rule jointly, William insisted on making the decisions.

Although William was one of the ablest kings of England, he was not popular. The people did not understand his ways, and he did not understand the English political system. Mary II died from smallpox in 1694.[19]

> One of the first things that William did in England was to provide religious toleration for the large number of Protestants who did not belong to the Church of England. But still more important was the Bill of Rights of 1689, which ranks with the Magna Charta and the Petition of Right in giving Englishmen valuable political rights.[20]

Among the privileges granted by the monarch to the people were the right to present petitions in Parliament, to receive proper treatment when accused of a crime or misdemeanor, to elect members of Parliament regardless of the king's wishes, and to be more fully represented in Parliament. The king could no longer levy any taxes for his own benefit but was to receive a regular apportionment from Parliament.

What a glorious revolution was accomplished for England! This does not imply that William III and his wife Mary became monarchs of England because Parliament made them monarchs. On the contrary, Parliament continued to do what even the nobles did in England before the Norman Conquest in 1066. They could only remove one monarch or appoint or elect another from the same family. It is still assumed by Parliament, as it is still done today, that God alone could decide who was to be King of England. For that reason the coins of Great Britain and Canada continue to state that the monarch is "King by the Grace of God." All that the revolution did was to restore ancient customs and to end absolutism.

During the reign of William and Mary much was done to prepare the way for the rise of the cabinet system and democratic government. Two political parties originated, the Whigs and the Tories.

ANNE
(1665–1714)

Anne was the first queen of the joint kingdom of Great Britain and Ireland. Her title was the result of the union of England and Scotland into Great Britain in 1707, the most important event of her reign (1702–1714). She was the last monarch of the House of Stuart. Though she had fourteen children, none survived her, so she was succeeded by her cousin George.

Anne was born in Twickenham, near London. She was the second daughter of King James II and married Prince George of Denmark in 1683. She became queen in 1702, after the death of her brother-in-law William III.

Although her health was never good, Anne took part in public affairs. She often attended debates in the House of Lords and was particularly concerned with religious legislation. Anne's reign is often called the Augustan Age because the leaders of the times tried to reproduce in England the political stability and classical art of Rome under the Emperor Augustus.[21]

Queen Anne succeeded William III, since she was his wife's sister, and since he left no heir. And, because she left no heir to the throne, a new house (of Hanover) acquired it in the person of George I, who was the son of the elector of Hanover.

GEORGE I
(1660–1727)

The following kings are now considered rulers of Great Britain. George I came to the throne when Queen Anne died in 1714. He was the great-grandson of King James I of England. Born and brought up in Germany, George had succeeded his father as elector of Hanover in 1698.

George was a shy, obstinate, and lazy man who neither aroused loyalty nor concerned himself with English affairs. He knew that he had become King of England through a series of coincidences. But he did keep in close touch with his ministers, of whom the most famous was Sir Robert Walpole. The two most dramatic events in George's reign were the Jacobite Rebellion in 1715, which attempted to restore the Stuarts as rulers of Great Britain, and the bursting of the "South Sea Bubble."

This was the time Sir Robert was both Lord of the Treasury and Chancellor of the Exchequer. His primary purpose was to govern Britain with as little excitement as possible. Then came his undoing. He had profited much in the great financial scandal in 1720, when the South Sea Company collapsed, and he was disgraced.[22]

> At this time, a little "democracy" appeared in the governing process of England. George I spoke German proudly, he never learned to speak English fluently, and left the parliamentary leaders to their own plans.
>
> It gradually became customary to form a "cabinet," which was made up of men in control of the majority party in Parliament. The

chief of these leaders became the prime minister, who would retain his office only as long as his followers commanded a majority of the members in the House of Commons, while the members of the House of Lords sat for life and received their seats by inheritance or by appointment.[23]

GEORGE II
(1683–1760)

George II succeeded his father, George I, in 1727. Born in Hanover, he was almost as German as his father. A brave man and ambitious for military prestige, he was the last British ruler to lead troops on the battlefield. This increased his popularity enormously.

Although George II was a stubborn and rather stupid man, he usually took advice, especially if he was persuaded that he had really originated the idea. During the first part of his reign, he depended chiefly on Walpole and upon his wife, Queen Caroline, who took an active part in politics. Later, his chief ministers, Henry Pelham and the elder William Pitt, helped him greatly.

Great changes marked the reign of George II. Triumphs, especially during the Seven Years War (1756–1763), laid the foundations of an empire in India and Canada and increased British prestige throughout the European world. The failure of the second Jacobite Rebellion in 1745 proved the stability of the Hanoverian regime. Agricultural and industrial advances changed the political and social structure of the country.[24]

At home the British were nobly served by their capable prime minister, William Pitt the Elder, who subsidized the armies of the Prussians against the French in order to keep the French busy in Europe. He also inspired parliamentary leaders to take a strong action against France, so when peace was signed at Paris in 1763, the French surrendered all their land on the North American continent and the right to fortify any region in India. Great Britain received Canada and the region east of the Mississippi.

During this time, the English merchants and manufacturers compelled their king and Parliament to recognize their class interest and so direct the foreign policy to secure more markets for their manufactured goods and more raw materials for the domestic industries. Where the English merchants made the mistake was that they looked upon the colonies as mere dependencies of Great Britain, which could be freely exploited.[25]

What wasn't counted on was that the colonists in America were former English subjects who fled to America. They had already experienced the exploitation of the British and thought they were free. But things would change!

GEORGE III
(1738–1820)

George III governed Great Britain during one of the most critical periods in his country's history. He succeeded his grandfather George II in 1760.

During the following sixty years, several revolutions modified every aspect of British life. The French Revolution threatened Britain's existence. The American Revolution cost Britain its American colonies, and the continuing Industrial Revolution created a new society and more than doubled the British population during his reign.

New territories (protectorates) were acquired in the place of those in America, however. In 1800, the Act of Union brought Ireland into the kingdom, which became known as the kingdom of Great Britain and Ireland.

George III took a far greater part in governing England than George I or George II. Hard-working and proud of being English, he tried to destroy the power of the Whig aristocrats who had held control for many years under Walpole, Pelham, and the elder Pitt. George chose his ministers, especially Lord North and the younger William Pitt, with this in mind. Unfortunately George was emotionally unbalanced and became hopelessly insane in 1811.[26]

British historians said little, if anything, about what observers would see concerning Parliament's adoption of new measures to annoy the colonies and made barely a cursory mention of the American Revolution.

What was worse, King George III was for the time being almost an absolute monarch and used many members of Parliament as his tools. That's why he was able to get the Stamp Act passed. This act stated that the English colonies in North America would have taxes levied on newspapers and magazines to the English government. Then the Boston Tea Party is followed by British penal laws, demanding that the Boston harbor be closed until the "tea tax" was paid.

It was then the American Revolution began in earnest. The twelve colonies were joined by Massachusetts in the rebellion that followed in 1775. The Continental Congress was called together that year and took quick action. If they hadn't issued the Declaration of Independence in 1776, our nation could have become "another English protectorate"!

GEORGE IV
(1762–1830)

The son of George III became king in 1820. He had served as regent for his father from 1811 to 1820. He lacked his father's ambition to govern and, with his brothers, he lowered the prestige of the royal family.

His private life was scandalous, and he had no share in the important reforms of his brief reign. Of these were the reform of the criminal law and of the police, the freeing of trade, and the grant of increased toleration of both Protestant dissenters from the Church of England and Roman Catholics. Nevertheless George IV was a man of taste, and he commissioned some of England's most beautiful buildings.[27]

The English Industrial Revolution greatly changed the lives of the British people in the 1700s. This made Great Britain the world's first important industrial nation. New machines in factories produced more goods than hand methods could produce in homes. Inventions, such as the steam engine in 1769, made better machines possible. Coal mines expanded to provide fuel for factories. Steamships and steam railways began to operate, and industrial cities such as Birmingham and Manchester grew rapidly.

Things began to fall apart, however. The French Revolution broke out in 1789, and Great Britain went to war with France in 1793, because France had taken over the area that is now Belgium and threatened to conquer other areas. Then after thirteen months of peace (1802–1803), war broke out again, and Lord Nelson won a victory over the French fleet at Trafalgar off the southern coast of Spain. Such expeditions proved costly.

At home came the Irish Revolt. The British monarchs had held the title King of Ireland since the 1200s. But the Irish never accepted the English rule, which the British never seemed to understand, and the British never did lend a hand in helping in their affairs. Then in 1800, without consultation with the Irish leadership, Parliament passed an Act of Union seemingly to make all things right. But most of the Irish were Roman Catholics, and British laws at that time kept the Catholics from voting or holding office. Again, without a vote as to what the Irish as a whole desired, Parliament changed the laws to give Catholics equal political rights. Such would prove the right thing to do in our time, but this was 1800.

To put it bluntly, everything seemed to have been forgotten during the wars with France. Depression followed and made things worse! Unemployment spread, particularly in factory towns. Earnings fell, and many farmers could not pay their rents. Prices rose, and many poor workers faced starvation.

WILLIAM IV
(1765–1837)

Great Britain faced revolution, when William IV took the throne in 1830 and served until his death in 1837. The Whigs saw reform as a way to break the power of the Tories. They prepared a bill that gave the middle class people with certain property qualifications to vote. Lord John Russell, leader of the Whigs, introduced a reform bill in 1831. The House of Commons finally passed the third version of the bill in 1832. The House of Lords planned to reject the bill, and the Whigs resigned. But the Tories could not form a cabinet that Parliament would support. Pressed by the Whigs, William IV threatened to name enough new lords to provide a majority for the bill, and the House of Lords finally passed it.

The first Parliament elected under the reform bill made slavery illegal in Great Britain's colonies (protectorates) in all parts of the world. It also improved child labor laws and set up safety inspection in all factories.[28]

Queen Victoria
(1819–1901)

Victoria was considered one of the greatest rulers in English history. She was queen of the United Kingdom of Great Britain and Ireland and empress of India. The Victorian Era, named for her, included the greater part of the 1800s. It was an era in which Great Britain reached the height of its power. The Victorian Age featured the greatest expansion at home and imperial expansion abroad. A period of sentiment and self-indulgence ended as Victoria came to the throne. The English people became high-minded, modest, self-righteous, and enterprising.

Victoria ruled for sixty-three years, from 1837 to 1901, the longest reign of any British monarch. She became queen at a time when the people neither liked nor respected the throne. But by being above reproach, she raised the throne to a position of respect and veneration. In her later years she became the symbol of Great Britain's greatness. Victoria was a wise and capable monarch, but the greatness of her country was due more to such ministers as Sir Robert Peel, Lord Palmerson, Benjamin Disraeli, William Gladstone, and Lord Salisbury than to her. Great Britain was a constitutional monarchy, and Victoria believed that she could only warn, advise, or encourage the prime minister.

Many great events took place during her reign. In 1837, small rebellions broke out in Canada. Upper and lower Canada were united in 1840 and given self-government. Britain fought the Opium War in China in 1840, the Crimaen War in 1854, the South African War in 1899, and various small wars with the Chinese, Abyssinians, Afghans, and Zulus.

A mutiny broke out in India in 1857, and the following year India was transferred from the East India Company to government control. Victoria was proclaimed empress of India in 1877. The British seized control of Egypt and many other areas. In Ireland, the Anglican Church was disestablished and the land system reformed. Parliament passed acts improving labor conditions, making education more affordable.

In February 1840, the queen married her cousin, Prince Albert of Saxe-Coburg-Gotha. It was a happy marriage. Victoria and Albert had four sons and five daughters. The eldest child, Princess Victoria, married the crown prince of Germany.

In 1861, Prince Albert died. Victoria never recovered from her grief. She withdrew from social activities and dressed in mourning for many years. Avoiding London, she lived for the most part at Osborne on the Isle of Wight and at Balmoral in Scotland. After the death of her husband, the only adviser to whom she showed affection was Benjamin Disraeli, whom she called "Dizzy." In 1887, the people of the empire celebrated the golden jubilee of her reign with great rejoicing. Ten years later, her diamond jubilee was celebrated as a great festival of the empire. Immense crowds greeted the queen as the royal procession made its way to St. Paul's Cathedral to give thanks.

Victoria died in her winter home on the Isle of Wight on January 22, 1901. Her eldest son then became Edward VII.[29]

It should be noted that between 1878 and 1900, the British showed little interest in the European continent. In the nineteenth century, Great Britain had developed a policy that was officially called "splendid isolation." The British were so concerned with their colonies and their commercial pursuits that they followed with little interest the course of European democracy.

It could have been that the Boer War made the British most unpopular on the continent. But during the Boer War (1899–1902), the British saw with alarm how much adverse criticism their actions in South Africa had produced in the great nations on the continent. Moreover, it was just at this time that Germany began to build a huge navy and to demand a larger share in the world markets. When the British sought to foster friendship with Germany, the Germans didn't seem to appreciate the cordial approach. Germany realized that England needed an ally on the continent. So the British turned to France and formed the Entente Cordiale (friendly understanding) in 1904.

In this connection it is well to note that Queen Victoria had been succeeded in 1901 by King Edward VII, who was more friendly to France than the queen had been.[30]

Edward VII
(1841–1910)

Edward became the only king of Great Britain and Ireland from the House of Saxony (Saxe-Coburg) in 1601. He was the oldest son of Queen Victoria and Prince Albert, and was made Prince of Wales. He studied in Edinburgh, Oxford, and Cambridge Universities and traveled extensively. In 1863, he married Princess Alexandra (1844–1925), daughter of King Christian IX of Denmark.

During Queen Victoria's widowhood, Edward represented her at public gatherings. He was a patron of the arts and sciences and helped found the Royal College of Music. He was also one of England's leading sportsmen. Horses from his stables won the English Derby three times.

Edward was greatly interested in international affairs. On a visit to India in 1875 and 1876, he improved relations between his own country and the princes of India. His official visits to Ireland in 1885 and 1903 helped postpone a conflict that had seemed inevitable for centuries. He became the first reigning British monarch to visit Russia, and his presence there in 1908 strengthened the Anglo-Russian Agreement of 1907. His son,

George Frederick, who became King George V, succeeded him on his father's death in 1910.[31]

George V
(1865–1936)

The second son of Edward VII became heir to the throne when his older brother died in 1892. Meanwhile he had been trained for the navy and became a vice-admiral in 1903. He was married in 1893 to Princess Victoria Mary of Teck. They had six children.

George toured the world after his father became king in 1901. When he succeeded his father in 1910, his subjects knew little about him. But he and his queen gained immediate and lasting popularity by their courage and devotion during the greatest event of their reign, World War I. This popularity was increased by George's attention to his duties. A silver jubilee lasting three months celebrated twenty-five years of his reign in 1935. George was succeeded by his oldest son Edward VIII.[32]

At the conclusion of the war, Lloyd George, chief of the Liberals, was still prime minister. But the Conservatives came back into power in 1922. In 1923, however, the Conservatives were defeated by a combination of Liberals and the members of a new party, the Labor Party. J. Ramsey MacDonald became prime minister, and now the old system of having two political parties was gone. For a time there were three parties, the Liberals, the Conservatives, and the Labor Party. Gradually the Liberals lost members to the Labor Party until finally they disappeared as a great party.

The Irish question returned to plague the Parliament. Ireland was given a home rule bill, but before the bill went into effect, World War I broke out. After the war Ireland was divided into two entirely different parts, the Protestant north called Ulster, which wanted to remain united to Great Britain, and the rest, which was much larger and was called the Irish Free State. For a few years civil war was spread over the island, but finally the new state was set up under the leadership of De Valera. He tried to separate Ireland completely from Great Britain, but before he was able to accomplish this work, the British replied with a tariff on imported goods from Ireland.

In 1931, the Statute of Westminster decreed that all the dominions were exempt from the regulations of the British Parliament and had complete control over their own legislation. The term British Empire has been gradually replaced by the British Commonwealth of Nations. The British king remained, however, as a tie that bound all the dominions together.[33] Thus began the House of Windsor.

EWARD VIII
(1894–1956)

Edward was the oldest son of King George V and Queen Mary of Great Britain. He became king upon his father's death on January 20, 1936.

Edward was made Prince of Wales in 1911 in Canaervon Castle, Wales. He was educated in the Royal Naval College and at Oxford University. He served in World War I as aide-de-camp to Sir John French, one of England's most famous soldiers.

The prince became a great traveler and was often called the "empire's salesman." After World War I, he made several trips to Canada, the United States, South America, Africa, India, Australia, and New Zealand in the interest of world peace and British trade. His democratic spirit, charm, and diplomacy made him popular. King Edward showed a deep interest in the welfare of his people, especially the underprivileged and the working classes.

Edward fell in love with Wallace Warfield Simpson, an American divorcee. Because his government was opposed to accepting her as queen, Edward abdicated his throne on December 11, 1936, after serving only one year. His brother, George VI, succeeded him, giving him the title Duke of Windsor. The duke and Mrs. Simpson were married in June 1937.

Edward served as governor of the Bahama Islands from 1940–1945, and tried to improve economic conditions there. After leaving the Bahamas, he visited England for the first time after his abdication. One of Elizabeth II's first acts was to welcome him back to the inner circle of the royal family.³⁴

George VI
(1895–1952)

This George was the second son of George V. He became king in December 1936, after his elder brother, Edward VIII, abdicated. George VI reigned during one of the most troubled periods in the history of Great Britain. He was a popular monarch because of his untiring devotion to royal duty.

George studied under private tutors, then went to Osborne and Dartmouth naval schools. He became a midshipman on H.M.S. Collingwood in 1915, and served in World War I. He was with the Grand Fleet in the Battle of Jutland. In 1918, he joined the Royal Flying Corps and became a wing commander. He studied in Cambridge University in 1919. In 1920, he was named Duke of York. In 1923, George married Lady Elizabeth Bowes-Lyon, a daughter of the Scottish Earl of Strathmore and Kinghorne. They had two daughters, Elizabeth and Margaret Rose.³⁵

King George and Queen Elizabeth made tours of Canada and South Africa and became the first British monarchs to visit the United States. During World War II, the royal family endeared itself to the people by sharing dangers and hardships with them. Under the Labor governments of the years following the war, socialistic measures included socialized medicine and nationalization of the Bank of England, the coal and steel industries, and the railroads.

India became an independent dominion in 1947, and the words "Emperor of India" were dropped from the king's title. George was succeeded by his elder daughter Elizabeth II.[36]

A social security system from the cradle to the grave became law in 1948. It provided medical and dental insurance benefits for all.

Great changes took place in the commonwealth after World War II. India and Pakistan became independent countries within the commonwealth in 1947, and Ceylon in 1948. Burma became an independent nation outside the commonwealth the same year. Ireland left the commonwealth in 1949.

Great Britain became a leader of the free world in the fight to stem communism. It helped form the North Atlantic Treaty Organization (NATO) in 1949, and the South East Asia Treaty Organization (SEATO) in 1954.

Notice how parochial the history of the United Kingdom appears. From the Reformation, begun in Scotland in 1558, until 1950, very little is mentioned about other parts of the United Kingdom, except England and its Parliament. A majority of the history is what England has done outside the parameters of the United Kingdom—wars to amass territories and to gain protectorates. Note how many protectorates are under the yoke of the United Kingdom. During this time Scotland, Ireland, and Wales just seem to be protectorates in name only. Where is the "United" Kingdom? Notice the use of power similar to that of the Greeks and the Romans but contrary to the power as understood by the Celts; the early founders of the United Kingdom of the Celts.

In the following chapter, there will be a sharing of Celtic history and Celtic spirituality and how the Celtic people acted and reacted to "English" history during these periods, many times in spite of English rule.

CHAPTER 6

CELTIC SPIRITUALITY IN THE UNITED KINGDOM (1558–1950)

> The Church is reformed, and still reforming! We seek God from the inmost affection of our hearts and willingly surrender our lives to God in response to God's graciousness. If we are led to Jesus Christ so that he might offer us access to God, then our relationship with God does not command cowering prostration before the power and might of a distant omnipotent God; but rather it invites trust, joy, and thankfulness in the presence of the fountain of every good thing.
>
> —John Calvin

What is not usually understood, at this point in time, is that the Reformation in the United Kingdom included not only Protestants but Roman Catholics as well, and that there were Celts on both sides of the Reformation.

The Roman Catholic Church did not long remain unaffected by the great movement that swept so many out of its communion. The influence of Protestantism upon it was two-fold—direct and reactionary. As a direct influence it acted as a sort of contagion, which began to produce a more intelligent piety in the hearts of Roman Catholics and Protestants. As a reactionary, people outside these two communions seemed to take a closer look at their morality, and many of them were Celts. These responses to the Reformation in Scotland permeated through the entire United Kingdom.

Prior to the Reformation, we have already noticed the manner in which the faith of the Celts has evolved and grown. Now we will begin to look at the Celts more closely as they define their faith in creeds and take a giant step by putting their faith into action.

Mary died in 1558, and was succeeded by her half-sister Elizabeth (1558–1603), the daughter of Anne Boleyn. She was antipapal, although it was believed by some that she was bereft of any dogmatic religious convictions. She was bent on saving the church of anything that savored of popery. She was bound to bring the church back to what it was in 1553. Elizabeth was so cautious with her religious changes, and so clever in her dealings with Roman Catholic states, that the pope was not convinced until 1570 that she was an enemy of Rome.

There was a notion throughout the United Kingdom that Protestantism was an English Religion. Such a notion faded because of the belief about the origin of Welsh Christianity. According to the Welsh belief, the Celtic Church was a non-Roman Catholic Church whose purity had not been defiled by Romanish practices forced upon it during the time of Augustine. This belief was given prominence in *Epistol at y Cembru*, an introduction to the Welsh translation of the New Testament published in 1567.

> The Epistol was the work of Richard Davies, bishop of St. David's from 1561 until his death in 1581. The translation was prepared in obedience to a parliamentary statute. In 1563, the bishops of Wales and Hereford were commanded to ensured that a Welsh version of the Bible and Prayer Book would be available in every parish in Wales by St. David's Day, 1567.[1]

Parliament also noted that Welsh could also be the language of worship. Of course, this was ironic. It seemed that Parliament was authorizing Welsh for worship barely a generation after it banned the use of all Welsh in secular matters. To cover up this blunder,

Parliament enacted the Act of 1563 and insisted that the English Bible would also be available in Welsh churches in hopes that the Welsh would soon master the English language.

Since the Roman Catholic Church also contained Celtic people in their congregations, it is only proper to note that the Vulgate (the Roman Catholic Bible) by St. Jerome was in use in Celtic Catholic parishes in Britain. It was written in Latin and was completed in 405. Pope Sixtus V appointed scholars to revise the Vulgate in 1587, but after his death in 1590, many alleged errors were found in the work. Under Pope Clement VIII, there were further revisions in 1592 and 1598. The revision in 1598 became the official text in the Roman Catholic Church in Britain and throughout the world. The English translation of the Vulgate is called "The Douai" or the Douay Version, after the town of Douai, France, where it was first published.

No translation of the Welsh Bible in its entirety was available until 1588, when William Morgan, Vicar of Llanrhaeadrym-Mochant had his translation published. William Morgan did a worthy and commendable job on the Old Testament but, as he put it, he did little more than "cleanse" the New Testament. The Bible was as essential to the Welsh as Luther's Bible was to the Germans.

The educated clergy, other than those already named, preached in Welsh mostly in fear that the Roman Catholic Church would reassert itself again in Wales. There had been very little tradition of preaching, or the use of a homily in Catholic Wales, for Catholicism stressed the sacrament rather than the Word.

In Wales, as well as in other parts of the United Kingdom, there was a scarcity of clergy fit to be licensed as preachers; there were only about twenty in Wales, thirty or so in Scotland. The Anglican Church in England was ready to grab as many educated clergy as they could find from Cambridge and other universities to supply their vacant pulpits.

The followers of Calvin tried to transform the Church of England into a Presbyterian church. They demanded a bishopless church of intense moral consciousness. They embraced the doctrine of election and sought to place laymen under the strict discipline of the gospel, which was a system that Celt John Knox had partly begun in Scotland[2] and was completed by another Celt, Andrew Melville.

How did Calvin, his teaching, and lifestyle get into the United Kingdom? Lest we forget, many Celts remained in northern France up to about 1800. They had heard of Calvin and his *Institutes of the Christian Religion*. There is no mention of Calvin being on the soil of the United Kingdom, so it was thought that some of his followers were responsible for his message being heard and accepted there. After all, Calvin, having been born in France, was bound to be an influence there.

As far as the Celts were concerned, nothing had been written down concerning the Christian faith that was any better than what John Calvin wrote in his *Institutes of the Christian Religion*. Today some folks believe that *The Institutes* were only received and used by the Church of Scotland, the Celtic Reformed and Presbyterian branches of Christendom. Not so! As we will see, his beliefs were accepted by a majority of the Celtic denominations that were being born in the United Kingdom. There was even one Celtic church that bore his name. The name of this church as viewed today sounds like an oxymoron. The Welsh Calvinistic Methodist Church is a church of which we will hear of in more detail later in this chapter.

The style and competence of Calvin was appreciated by the Celts. Even greater appreciation was found in his common sense approach, plus his step-by-step presentation of the Scriptures and theological topics so they could be understood by common folks. Calvin claimed that the Bible had been withheld by the scholastics, monks, and priests of the Roman Church. The Celts understood Calvin's teachings, not as cold speculation to be used as psychological and sociological speculation, but rather as sincere, solid, and certain teaching that takes root in the inmost affection of the heart. Thus it lead to the transformation of life, but it must enter our heart and pass into our living. This is why the Celts accepted Calvin, for they saw what they termed a false piety, which to them did not belong in the church.

These are some of the basic tenets of Calvin on which many of the Celts hung their beliefs:

- He laid down a pathway to the reading of sacred Scripture for the simple and uneducated. He really "led his readers by the hand."
- His eloquence was bereft of intangibles, big words, and had passion tempered with intensity.
- He led us to a deeper knowledge and understanding of our Scriptures, and their uses within our personal lives, as well as in the church. He revealed to us the mind of the Author.
- Calvin revealed a sovereign God who demanded complete obedience and who would open up the belief in this kind of a God, through the life and merit of Jesus Christ and the power of the Holy Spirit, which could control and empower one's daily living, as well as assist one in formulating a personal theology.
- If we are led to Jesus Christ so that he might offer us access to God, then our relationship with God does not command cowering prostration before the power and might of a remote omnipotent God. Rather, it invites trust, joy, and thankfulness in the presence of the fountain of every good thing.
- We shall never be clearly persuaded, as we ought to be, that our salvation flows from God's free mercy, until we come to know and realize by our change and the newness of life that we experience.
- So this life of ours, dedicated to such a God, enhances our life in reforming the church, through the meaning of Scripture, so that our lives speak for themselves giving them a Christian credence.[3]

Calvin's effect on the life of the members of the early Celtic Church made a real difference in their belief, as well as in their ability to express their faith and grow.

When we discuss the Celtic churches and their problems with the English rulers and the Church of England, we must understand the situation that existed at this point in time.

The Celts did not consider the Church of England as a Celtic Church, though some Celts over the years have become a part of that church. The reason is that the Bretons, who were a part of the Celtic band, lived in the area of what is now called England. They betrayed their fellow-Celts in 1270, declaring that they did not wish to be a part of the Celts anymore, and changed their names to Britons. They gave their allegiance to King Edward and took part in the war against their own people in Wales, Ireland, and Scotland, thus making their fellow-Celts subservient to what is now called England.

The Church of England made it known to all people that not only were they bound to give allegiance to the kings of England, but since the kings of England were heads over the Church of England, all subjects without allegiance to the pope must give allegiance to the Church of England! This question has never been answered by Parliament: "Why was the Roman Catholic Church excepted and all other churches included?"

With this in mind, and noting the effect Calvin had in the life of the Celtic churches, one can readily understand the actions of the Celtic churches in certain situations where both the Church and the state seemed high-handed.

Now we can ask, "What were the results of the Reformation in the United Kingdom?" They have been variously estimated.[4] Some say, "The Reformation caused a split in the Church that has not yet been healed." But the Church had been split twice previously. The Roman Catholic, the Russian Orthodox, the Greek Orthodox, and now the Protestant Reformation made four parts to the Christian Church. Others declare, "The Reformation led to religious wars in the period 1546 to 1648."[5] But these religious wars were never fought on the soil of the United Kingdom!

The world has forgotten to look at the real reason for such a split that the Celts had from both England and the Roman Catholic Church.

Go back to the early foundation belief of the early Celts. "The Celts believed that power resided in the family and was a gift from the gods or the One God, and it was to the deities or the Deity they believed they were held responsible." Both England and the Roman Catholic Church believed and acted contrary to such a belief in power. They believed in a power to amass territory, and to amass people respectively, whatever the cost!

Let us take a good look on the huge positive side of the Reformation, which greatly transcends any negative outlook! The Bible was much more widely read by the masses of the people, and among the Protestants it was regarded as the only reliable authority in the realm of faith and morals. In addition, the teachings proved to be a guide to peoples' attitudes toward business and civil government, not only by the Celts and non-Celts but also by both Roman Catholics and non-Roman Catholics. The Reformation was, for the most part, a religious movement of a conservative nature and indirectly assisted in a movement for reform in the Roman Catholic Church. It has played the role of utmost importance in the lives of many individuals and nations. As years have passed, we continue to see the Reformation, both in Europe and in the United Kingdom, mature and evolve into a great moral and spiritual force in many nations.

Another basic part of both national history and church history needs to be noted here so we can more easily understand the Celts and their relationship to the crown, which includes both the government of England, and the Church of England. They both have been linked together for several years in a manner wherein the kings or monarchs of England had direct oversight and direction of the Church of England. In the earlier years, it was a direct oversight of the Church. Later "an archbishop was appointed by the crown to oversee the Church, but an archbishop was directly responsible to the crown."[6]

Ever since the Bretons, with the English army of Edward I, invaded and captured the Celtic countries of Wales, Scotland, and Ireland, and set themselves up as overlords, England's desire was to insist that these countries give total allegiance to the government, as well as the Church of England, over which it also held dominion.

Since this time, not only had these satellite countries of the Celts yearned and pleaded for their national independence from England, but they had repeatedly sought to be free from allegiance to, and subjection under, the Church of England. The subjugation and control of the government over the Celts has already been presented. We will now examine how the Celtic churches sought to thwart England's desire to control the Celtic churches as well.

Here again, we see emerging the old Celtic "power" concept. The Celts believed that they were already taken over by force, and now that force wanted to take over their most basic possession—namely their belief in their God and how they worshiped that God!

You will observe such actions by the English repeated over and over again. We will begin with the Puritans, with whom we are most familiar. You recall those people who, because of their desire for freedom to worship the way they pleased, came to America on the Mayflower, landed at Plymouth Rock, and began a new nation.

THE PURITANS

These people, who had their beginning in England, were so named because of their desire to lead lives closer to their Lord, whom they referred to as the Pure One. They were formally called Brownists after one of their earlier leaders, Robert Browne. They became inspired by their vision of the early Celtic church, particularly as that church was inspired by John Calvin. They were attracted by Calvin's reference to two Bible texts: The first was "These all died in faith, not having received the promises, but having seen them afar off, and were persuaded of them, and embraced them, and confessed that they were *strangers and pilgrims on the earth.*"[7] The other text was: "Dearly beloved, I beseech you *as strangers and pilgrims,* abstain from fleshly lusts, which war against the soul;"[8] Both these texts describe Christians as strangers and pilgrims. Feeling that this is what they were, in the sight of the Church of England and maybe others as well, they adopted the name Pilgrims and desired to worship in the manner of their beliefs.

These Celts, because their belief in power ran contrary to that of the English and because Celts were among this religious group, stood up for their right to worship as they chose.

However, at that time Queen Elizabeth, who considered herself the head of the Church of England, decreed that those who did not attend worship at the Church of England must pay a fine, and ministers who refused to conform to the creed and practice of the Church were to be punished.[9]

After the death of Queen Elizabeth, James I (1603–1625) continued to berate the Pilgrims for not conforming to the rule of Parliament, the king, and the head of the Church.

The Church of England called all of those nonconforming religious groups Separatists. A few of the Puritans set up their congregations in London and took the consequences. Others who lived near Scrooby moved to Holland. The remaining Puritans moved to Southampton, England and later sailed to America on the Mayflower in 1620. Much of this information is found in the autobiography of William Bradford who became the second governor of the Plymouth Colony. From this time on, no Pilgrim congregation could be found anywhere on British soil.

THE INDEPENDENTS—MOSTLY CONGREGATIONALISTS

These groups seemed to have their beginnings in England and Wales about the same time in the very late 1500s (circa 1595). They were given their names by Parliament and the Church of England. They believed that each congregation should be entirely independent. The Congregationalists, who accepted that name for their denomination, believed in the independence of each congregation. That group of early believers, however, composed what was called "church rules of governance," to which each congregation must conform. The Congregationalists in general refused to allow a great deal of authority to pastors and reserved much authority to reside in their board of deacons.

A majority of the Pilgrim fathers (about half) could be called Congregationalists. It was also partly through the influence of the Puritans that the Quakers and Congregationalists found their way to America and found religious freedom, for they had also been persecuted by James I.

Anabaptists and Baptist Churches

These two churches had their beginning in Germany and Switzerland in the early 1500s, and began their ministry in London in 1611. They enjoyed religious freedom until about 1627, when they were obliged to conform to the Parliament Act of Uniformity of Common Prayer of 1559 under Charles I.

The first of these two churches, which might also be called Independents, was the Anabaptists. They were so named because they had to be baptized all over again, and so they received the name Anabaptists, or Again-Baptists. The Anabaptists were given toleration by the Dutch Republic but were not treated so kindly in the United Kingdom.

Gradually the name *Ana* was dropped, and the new name of Baptist was put in its place. Baptism was only by immersion.[10]

The Baptist church movement gradually moved westward into Wales by 1692. During the time of William III and Mary II, Baptists were meeting in private homes, barns, or in the open air among the Celts. In 1695, chapels were built in Llanwenarth near Abergavenny, and later Baptists and other nonconformists became strong in Carmarthenshire, Glamorgan, and Monmouthshire.[11]

The Church of the Quakers

They were also called Independents and Quakers, out of ridicule, because they shook when they prayed. The real reason they were called Quakers was because an early leader, George Fox, told the congregation, "Tremble at the Word of the Lord." Earlier they called themselves Children of the Light, Friends, Friends in Truth, and later the Society of Friends, which is their present day title.

The Friends opposed the formal worship of most Christian groups. They believed that worship should be spontaneous, without a fixed ritual, an order of service, or a prepared sermon. Any person might preach or pray when they felt led. Both men and women were allowed to speak in worship.

These folks believed in simple living and strict honesty in business. They held that the truth should always be spoken. Because of this, they have always objected to taking an oath. They always used "thee," "thou," and "thy" when speaking to any individual.

The Friends disapprove of war and violence and have always been on the forefront of aid to people in need regardless of person, class, or position. The Quakers spoke out fearlessly for their belief that uniformity in religion was necessary. As a religious group, they were under persecution by Charles I and were the first to be granted religious tolerance by William III in 1689.[12]

THE ROMAN CATHOLIC CHURCH

Unlike all other churches in the United Kingdom, the Roman Catholic churches were not made to conform to the decree of Queen Elizabeth—to conform to the creed and practices of the Church of England or else. No one seems to know either the answer or the reason.

During that time, the leaders of the Roman Catholic Church were by no means idle. Not only had the great scholars and priests within the Church done much for reform even before the close of the fifteenth century but also in the first half of the sixteenth century. Another religious order was founded by the Spaniard Loyola, called the Society of Jesus or the Jesuits.

During this time another weapon was used by the Roman Catholic Church that consisted of a list of books condemned either entirely or in part by the leaders of the Church. Finally from 1545 to 1563, the Council of Trent convened, and a large number of reforms were made by the Dominicans and the Jesuits.

The official creed of the Church was put into writing so that hereafter everyone could tell exactly what the Church taught and stood for. Moreover, this Council issued a new translation of the Bible called The Vulgate.[13] (See p. 207)

The Presbyterian Church

This church in the United Kingdom was begun in Scotland under the leadership of such stalwarts as John Knox, Andrew Melville, George Wishart, and others. Each of them not only professed a very strong Celtic faith and background but also encouraged other Celts to hold fast to their heritage.

Those early Presbyterians declared their belief had a biblical foundation and that their form of government had its base in the Acts of the Apostles.[14] They claimed that the congregation in Jerusalem found it necessary to appoint certain persons as deacons. Their responsibility was to manage the finances of the congregation, take care of the poor, and to assist the local pastor in various duties. Appointed above the deacons were the presbyters called elders, chosen by the local congregation, and in their ordination like the pastors were responsible with the pastors as a session, for the total activities of the church.

The Presbyterian Church spread to Wales. Between 1660 through 1688 they were persecuted. The persecution varied from arbitrary insult to periods of imprisonment for those who belonged to the Presbyterian, Baptist, and Independent traditions. An additional complication was the situation in Scotland where the government was obliged in 1689 to recognize Presbyterianism as the official religion; it would therefore be perverse to continue to persecute the Presbyterians of England and Wales.[15]

One would think, after the death of Mary Queen of Scots and the persecution of the English government was ordered ceased, that persecution might abate and the Celtic Presbyterians in Scotland might have an easier time of it. Not so!

There was the continuous sniping and persecutions by the Roman Catholic Church, aided and abetted by the popes of Rome.

The English government found other ways to confound the Celts. The resurrection of the English government's disapproval of languages other than English again came to the fore. This became true, not only of litigation against Scotland for speaking Gaelic; they laid down the same law against the Welsh for speaking their language. They also bedeviled the Celts of Ireland for speaking Irish Gaelic. It was said that such a law was being reenforced because England could not speak or understand the languages, Gaelic or Cymraeg, and because through it these Celts might conspire against England.

English, by such insistence, became the primary language of both Ireland and Scotland even though Gaelic was kept alive in secret as a symbol of ethnic pride. Wales kept its language down through the years, not only in Celtic pride but in a strong attitude of "England be damned." In our present day, Celtic pride is bringing back the old Gaelic language, in both Ireland and Scotland, even though English remains the dominant language of the United Kingdom.

Ten years after the first general assembly of the Presbyterian Church in 1560, James I, King of England, an avowed advocate of the Church of England, demanded that all Scotland cease and desist giving allegiance to the Presbyterian Church and pledge their entire allegiance to the Church of England.

The Celts, who were followers of John Calvin, again made a counterproposal to transform the Church of England into a Presbyterian Church. They demanded a bishopless church of intense moral consciousness; they embraced the doctrine of election and sought to place laymen under the strict discipline of ministers of the gospel, a system which John Knox partially succeeded in creating in Scotland.[16]

In England the monarchs controlled the Church whereas in Europe the Roman Catholic Church controlled the monarchs.

An edict of James I in 1648 was carried out as super-implosion by the king so that the churches of Glasgow and St. Andrews were made bishoprics. All the Scottish bishops were required to be consecrated as bishops by the Church of England. It's strange that nothing was said about St. Giles in Edinburgh. Was it perhaps that John Knox served as pastor of the kirk?

Or was it that after the death of James I, Archbishop Laud pushed the Scots to the limit of their endurance? The famous stool throwing event at St. Giles brought the beginning of the end of the Anglicans and restored the Presbyterian Church to rule in Scotland.

OTHER PROTESTANT GROUPS FORMED IN THE UNITED KINGDOM

The Lutherans had no known Celts involved until they moved into the United Kingdom. Patrick Hamilton (1504?–1528) had visited Wittenburg, studied at Marburg, and began preaching the Lutheran doctrine. Nothing much has been said of the early beginnings of Lutheranism in the United Kingdom, except that some Celts stood by him declaring his right to his beliefs and to have freedom in worship.

He drew the wrath of the Roman Catholic Church, however. They burned him at the stake somewhere in Scotland in 1528.[17]

The Unitarians

There were no known Celts involved in this movement. In the period between 1534 and 1770, chemistry and physics were remarkably improved, and medicine was making progress. For the first time since the beginning of modern history, the scientists paid little attention to the authority of the church and its customs, the customs that *everybody* followed. They now began to blaze the way for a new system of thought.

This made the setting for the Unitarian Fellowship (never organized as a church). It began a widespread practice for scholars and their followers to preach their doctrine of toleration and skepticism. No longer bound by decrees of kings, no longer taught by the words of the Bible itself, philosophers and statesmen of the second half of the eighteenth century looked for other sources of inspiration. They had their beginning in London and exalted human reason to such an extent that they undermined the popular beliefs in religion and the truth of the Bible.

Some doubters had refused to accept the doctrine of the Trinity, which teaches that God is three persons in one God—God the Father, God the Son, and God the Holy Spirit. These scholars claimed that God the Father was the only member of the Trinity who was divine and that Jesus of Nazareth was no more than a human being. The Unitarians founded their Fellowship and received all those who insisted there was only One God.[18]

The Church of England

The Church of England is the official state church established by Parliament under Queen Elizabeth (1558–1603). The date is not clear. Some records show 1586, another shows 1583. In any case, the enactment took place during Elizabeth's reign. The Church of England is also known as the Mother Church of the Anglican Communion.

The doctrines of the Church of England were stated in *The Book of Common Prayer*, which claimed to teach and uphold the doctrine of the apostles and to be a branch of the universal Church of Christ. They believed, then and now, in both the Apostles' and Nicene Creeds. The church included both Protestant and Catholic teachings; however, in 1534, Parliament passed the Act of Supremacy, which made the king, rather than the pope, head of the Church.

After the death of Henry VIII in 1547, Protestantism spread rapidly throughout England; although for a few years, under Henry's daughter Mary, Protestantism was held in check. It was made a state church under Elizabeth. The official title of the new church was The Church of England, broken off from the Roman Catholic Church.

The Church of England retained the institution of bishop, and since the Latin word for bishop is *episcopus*, the word Episcopal is referred to as the Church of England. Later Episcopal became the title of what the Anglicans called the low church. The archbishop of the Roman Catholic Church is in Westminster Cathedral in London. The archbishop of Canterbury is over the Church of England, wherever it was situated.

In the centuries that the Church of England has existed, it has been controlled by the monarch of England. The king or queen not only acted as leader of the country but the director of the Church. This situation is just the opposite of the Roman Catholic Church in Europe, where kings were chosen and served at the behest of the Church. When they failed the Church, they were replaced by another sovereign.

After about 150 years, following the practice of the Roman Catholic Church in Europe, the rulers of England began to appoint a liaison between the monarch and the Church of England. Still the rulers of England were in total control of the Church in the name of the Archbishop of Canterbury.

In England at this time few people, if any, called themselves Celts; so really we can't call the spirituality that existed at this time in England, Celtic spirituality.

Another problem confronting the Church of England, through the years, seemed to be that no contemporary mission outreach, as we know it, has been reported. Church membership, affiliation, and growth appeared only to have come from edicts of the Church demanding people in all parts of the United Kingdom be a part of the Church of England and through family members who became of age. It wasn't until 1752 that people of the United Kingdom were allowed to worship as they chose. As a result, one can notice evidences of growth in every other church that was born on United Kingdom soil.

According to history, mission outreach as we know it (seeking to commit people's lives to God in Christ), was found in the Anglican Church when it became known as low church, and the Church of England became known as high church. A spiritual awakening took place when the Anglican Church was called the Episcopal Church. The Episcopal Church began to reach out to people and become involved in their community.

The Methodist Church

The Methodists became members of the Protestant church family through the preaching of John Wesley, a clergyman of the Church of England. He was not satisfied with conditions existing in his church. He claimed the church utilized too much empty formalism, had no spiritual outreach, and was minus a warm friendly feeling permeating the Church of England.[19]

In 1729, John Wesley and his brother Charles, George Whitfield, and some students formed what was called a Holy Club at Oxford University. Other students derided their methodical schedules of spiritual exercises and charitable duties and dubbed them "Methodists."

John Wesley did not simply resign from the Church of England. He tried for about ten years to reconcile and find religious satisfaction in the Church of England. In London in 1738, he does not say how, but his "heart was strangely warmed and he discovered an inner peace that came through God's mercy and grace." He dedicated his life to what he called "a personal holiness, with love and service to fellow human beings."[20]

John Wesley (1703–1791) and Charles Wesley (1707–1788) never planned to begin a new church, apart from the Church of England, but the evangelistic message of his preaching, his doctrinal emphasis, and his rigorous discipline caused the Church of England to make him unwelcome in Anglican pulpits. He and his brother traveled far and wide in order to reach the poor and the sick, who seemed to be neglected by his church, and allowed his followers to begin a new fellowship, which later became several churches throughout England. The name, which was derogatorily given, was graciously used as their church name "Methodist."

When they moved to Wales, joined some Celts, and organized churches in South Wales, "the Welsh Methodists appeared to be Calvinists and were closer to the nonconformists than were their English counterparts. Several nonconformists adopted some of the features of the Methodist way, with the emphasis on inner experiences, for example, the eloquent sermon, and the use of hymns of praise, rather than dirges and chants."[21] One must mention the number of hymns that were composed by the Wesleys, who enriched the hymnology of the church.[22] Among Charles Wesley's hymns are: "Come, Thou Long-Expected Jesus," "O For A Thousand Tongues," "Jesus, Lover of My Soul," and others.

The Methodist Episcopal Church

Strange as it seems, the same group of Oxford students who negatively dubbed the Wesleys as Methodists found reason to believe that some of the Methodist tenets of faith could be practiced within the structure of the Anglican Church, but not in the confines of the Church of England. They formed a church and called themselves the Methodist Episcopal Church.

The church's growth progressed slowly. Only a few churches sprang up in England. It was through a later migration from England to America, in the early 1800s, that this denomination was reported as flourishing.

"This new Protestant denomination, which separated from the Anglican Church, has ever since devoted itself to the needs of the masses of the people. These Methodists were not much interested in learned language or ceremonies but talked plainly of God's love for sinners."[23]

The Welsh Calvinistic Methodist Church

Although other churches in the United Kingdom were formed by Celts who were won over by Calvinistic doctrines and government for the church, the Welsh Calvinistic Methodist Church remained in Wales. Its Celtic spirituality has since expanded to the United States, Canada, Patagonia, and Australia, to name a few countries. This church is still predominantly active in these named countries.

Welsh Methodism is in origin independent of, and was organized prior to, English Methodism. Calvinistic Methodist groups were organized in Wales as early as 1736, three years before the organization of English fellowships by John Wesley.

In 1740, the great division between the Calvinists and the Arminians took place in the Methodist body in England, but the

Welsh Methodists were Calvinists from the beginning. The first general association or synod was held in 1742. Formal withdrawal from the Church of England did not take place until 1811, when the general synod met at Bala, where twenty-one persons were ordained to the office of ministry, and the church organization was established based avowedly on the New Testament.

Bear in mind that the ministers and members of this church were brought up under the influence of the Episcopacy, and yet, after due study of the Scriptures, rejected in toto that system of church government.

In 1823, a confession of faith was adopted, and in 1864, a general assembly was constituted. The word Methodist, in the name of this church, is to be understood in defining not its system of doctrine but methods of Christian life and work. In every church the elders are members of presbytery, which features a polity that gives the laity (men and women) an overwhelming influence.

Unlike the Presbyterian form of government, where all elders are members of presbytery and allowed to attend, only elders delegated by each session are allowed to vote. In the Welsh Calvinistic Methodist Church, all elders are members of presbytery, and *all* elders (active at the present time or not) are allowed to attend presbytery and vote.

These churches were transplanted to America by Welsh people who migrated to America around 1820. These churches sprang up in Ohio, Pennsylvania, Wisconsin, New York, and elsewhere in the midwest. In a published survey in 1986, there were, "based on first-hand information from 39 American states and 6 Canadian provinces, over 100 Welsh and Celtic congregations, and organizations, with more than 2,000 individual members."[24] The first church the author served after ordination (1946) was Bethania Welsh Calvinistic Methodist Church in Scranton, Pennsylvania, where he also served as the stated clerk of both the Welsh presbytery and synod.

As was the custom, prior to worship, the elders in turn led in prayer with and for the pastor, prior to taking their places together in the front pew of the church for worship. He happened to be the first pastor of that church who did not preach in Welsh.

In 1948, due to the lack of parishioners who spoke Welsh, and a number of clergy who could preach in Welsh, this presbytery was dissolved, and each of the parishes united with other denominations predominantly with Presbyterian or Methodist churches within their bounds; still keeping their heritage as Welsh Celts.

OTHER KINDS OF SPIRITUALITY AMONG THE CELTS

Spirituality among the Celts in the United Kingdom was more than just forming churches and proclaiming their faith and fighting for what they believed. We don't wish to make light of this accomplishment. However, we do not wish to hide other acts of Celtic spirituality either.

The Celts, in addition to establishing and promulgating the church with a "spirituality of the heart," also promoted the "spirituality of the hand and mind." Take a good look at the tremendous example of the Celts and the Salvation Army, although it was not their first act of service through their faith. We will note others.

You will not find this story of the Salvation Army in any English history text. Their history begins with only the London part of the story.

Salvation Army

It has been argued throughout the United Kingdom that the Salvation Army was not a church, so why include it here? Isn't it only a social service organization? The reason we are including it here is that it is an integral part of what we are calling Celtic spirituality!

William Booth (1829–1912) was thirty-five years old and wasn't sure he was really a Methodist though that was his background. He realized he was a Christian and wanted to serve people who were not only in need but also in despair. He felt they were pleading for a way out of their dilemma and believed that he had an answer.

The basis of the economy of the Welsh people was found in the coal pits of Wales, and these coal fields were almost stripped. Miners were laid off with no income! Only a few miners were left to close the pits.

The farms were not growing enough food to feed the people. London and neighboring areas were not much better off and could not help! Where would these people turn?

Into this mess came William Booth. During a revival in Cardiff, Wales, he talked to several people about their plight. He proclaimed, "We Celts have to take care of each other!" Someone in the audience replied, "It'll take more than a regiment to accomplish that!"

"We'll see to that!" Booth was said to have replied.

With the idea from this friend at this meeting in Cardiff, Booth fleshed out "an army of the Lord" in 1861, in a regimented and military style, with officers to train and minister.

He preached in Cardiff, not only concerning the need of a love and commitment to Christ and the Church, but he also taught sharing. He recruited people to eat a little something less so that others might eat a little something.

From Cardiff, Booth went to London in 1865, and in London he used the same program until he and his associates flooded the United Kingdom with headquarters in many cities, staffed with people who had abilities to help the less fortunate. Booth not only helped folks with physical needs but had an articulate ability to minister to their spiritual needs as well.[25]

The Celts to the Rescue

The center of the Celts' power resided in the family, and the Celts were known to have concern for families who were in jeopardy. Such was true of those during the potato famine in Ireland in 1840.

This famine caused the worst disaster in Irish history! About half the people lived on small tenant farms, sold their grain and cattle to pay their rents and other expenses, leaving only their potato crops for food. The Irish tenants were more callous and incompetent than their English counterparts. The country's problems were compounded by the vast population growth that took place during the early nineteenth century, rising from five million in 1801 to eight million in 1840, and consisting mostly of desperately poor families subsisting on potatoes. Disaster struck in 1845–1847 when the potato blight brought mass starvation and disease. The famine was both an economic and natural disaster. The blight affected not only potatoes. Another million people migrated, mostly to America and Canada.[26]

It was said that other Celts tried to aid the people in their plight, and shared what they had, which wasn't sufficient enough to do anything but prolong death. Both the government and the squire tenants were no help at all! The same was true of strikes because of poor working conditions in the pits of coal and ores. Quite often the only support or aid came from fellow-Celts, unless the squires or the government suffered.

Music in Worship

Music played a great part in the spirituality of the Celts, in both sacred and secular music, but especially in music related to the church.

According to our church history texts, and aside from the Celts, church music in worship goes back a long way. In the Old Testament we find ancient hymns, but no music is available for:

- "The Song of Miriam"
- "The Song of Deborah"
- "The Song of Barak"

No doubt there are others.

Previous to our present-day hymnals, we find what have been called "ancient chants and canticles," which go back as early as the fourth century, but with no music or tunes. The earliest examples of ancient chants and canticles found to be with music are:

- "Singing of Psalms"—Jerome—328.
- "Sabat Mater Dolorosa"—Thomas deClarno—1200s.

- "Dies Irae"—Thomas deClarno—1200s.
- "The Old Hundredth"—The Doxology—1551.
- "Singing the Psalms"—Scottish Psalter—1539.

Searching through church hymnals in our present time, we find:

- "The God of Abraham Praise"—Yigdal (Leoni).
- Hebrew Melody—Daniel Ben Judah—fourteenth century.
- "All Glory, Laud, and Honor"—St. Theodulph of Orleans. Written in the 800s; set to music 1615.

When we speak of ancient songs and hymns, it has been recorded earlier that the Celts sang songs of praise to their gods when they went into battles and when they returned. (See p. 65–66) The earliest records, by both Greek and Roman historians, report such happenings when the Celts fought the Hittites about 1650 and 1375 B.C. and the Galatians in 300 B.C. Like other bits of history, we have neither the words nor the music.

It is not generally known, but a fact nevertheless, that part singing had its origin and early development among the Cymry, or as the English called them, the Welsh. A famous Roman historian, Giraldus Cambrensis, writing in 1188, speaks of their skill in vocal music, which they sang in parts and not as elsewhere in unison. This skill and custom, developed through the ages, finds its expression today in the *Gymanfa Ganu,* the assembly or festival for sacred song.[27]

This institution in its present form is more than a century old and is expressive of the soul of the Cymry, or Welsh, since it gives an outlet to their fervent religious feeling through a medium they love best—the music of voices blended in harmony. It is, as it must be to the Welsh, a democratic institution, for persons of all positions in life take part in it. Four part singing (it has been known to be six- and eight-part harmony) of hymns and anthems has given the congregational singing of the Welsh people uncontested first place among the nations of the world.[28]

Rhif 301. Joanna. M. 20 (11au. 4ll.)

[Sol-fa musical notation table]

760 *Heddwch drwy'r Groes.*

f O GARIAD! O gariad
   Anfeidrol ei faint,
Fod llwch mor annheilwng
   Yn cael y fath fraint!—
Cael heddwch cydwybod
   A'i chlirio drwy'r gwaed;
A chorff y farwolaeth,
   Sef llygredd, dan draed.

Ni+ gallai'r holl foroedd
   Byth olchi fy mriw,
Na ;;wacl y creaduriaid,
   Er amled eu rhyw;
Ond gwaed y Messia
   A'm gwella'n ddi-boen,—
Rhyfeddol yw rhinwedd
   Marwolaeth yr Oen.

f Cydganed y nefoedd
   A'r ddaear ynghyd
Ogoniant tragwyddol
   I Brynwr y byd;
cres. Molianned pob enaid
   Yr Arglwydd ar gân,
Am achub anhydyn
   Bentewyn o'r tân! Amen.
      Ax., 1; MORGAN RHYS, 2, 3.

29

Note: Joanna (as it is known in Wales, St. Denio outside Wales) is the best known of Welsh tunes since its introduction in the English Hymnal in 1906 where it was first set to the words "Immortal Invisible, God only wise", and association that has gone everywhere that hymns are sung in English. It has considerable resemblance to the ballad entitled 'Can mlynedd i nawr' (a hundred years from now) which was popular in the early years of the 19th century. —Alan Luff

30

In 1811, the Welsh Calvinistic Methodist Church officially broke away from the Church of England. Why? Not only because of the church's inability to spiritually strengthen its members but because they could not find a priest or bishop who could sing the responses tunefully; and the congregational responses and participation in worship were nil.

Hymns already in print were hurriedly translated into Welsh, and challenges went out from the Welsh congregations to the national Eisteddfod in 1814, asking that competition be opened for the best hymn or anthem. Many hymns were placed in competition. The winner was announced, but each of the hymns were printed (Sol-Fa) and given to each congregation. It was shortly following this Eisteddfod, that a *Sol-Fa Hymnal* was printed. The Sol-Fa method was used in teaching congregations to sing in parts.

Following the secession from the Church of England, congregations used the word *capel* (chapel) to designate their place of worship from the word *eglwys* (church), which the Welsh used to refer to the Church of England.

It wasn't long after the secession from the Church of England that the chapels also began to write new hymns, as well as to translate into Welsh hymns that were already in use elsewhere. These hymns were written in the four-part harmony. When these hymns were ready, the congregations would remain following worship to rehearse these hymns for the following Sunday worship.

Following several of these after worship rehearsals, the chapels met together to sing these new Welsh hymns and anthems. At first they sang a cappella, using only a tuning fork. Later, when organs were available, people gathered at these meetings to sing hymns together. These gatherings became a regular practice and were called a Gymanfa Ganu. Such gatherings became a periodic affair and have continued in Welsh communities to this day. *"Byd gwyn fydd byd a gano, Gwaraidd fydd ei gerddi fo!"* ("Blessed is the world that sings, gentle are its songs!"

To the spirit of America, Canada, Australia, Patagonia, and the world, gallant Celtic Wales has contributed much. It is confidently believed that the Gymanfa Ganu is not the least among their Celtic gifts.

The Celtic Crosses

The cross, the sacred symbol of the Christian faith, signifies the symbol of redemption, Christ's death on the cross for the sins of the world. It comes in all types and shapes. Among the various crosses, we find the following:

The Greek Cross	The Maltese Cross
St. Andrew's Cross	St. Anthony's Cross
The Latin Cross	The Calvary Cross
The Patriarchal Cross	St. George's Cross[31]

The Cross for Christians arises from the cross that Jesus carried up the hill of Calvary. There are various shaped crosses, and there are many reasons for their formations.

The Celtic people gave us more than language, literature, and works of art. They gave the world more! They gave the world a special cross with a special meanings. They gave the world a Celtic cross, a special cross named after the early Celtic people, a cross with a circle superimposed, signifying eternity.

Most of the graves in the Celtic counties in Ireland, Scotland, and Wales are marked with a Celtic cross. What better cultural identity could any nation or people possess than a special cross of their own, marking their special faith?

The inspiration for the style is quite clearly the work of the bronzesmith and the goldsmith whose intricate designs were copied in stone. Presumably these great crosses of the ninth and tenth centuries were copies of wooden crosses whose arms were probably stabilized with cross-braces, making the circle of the crosses.

Many beautifully carved crosses are found in all parts of Wales and Ireland, but few remain at their original sites. Some have been irretrievably lost, and the rest are being carefully cherished, either by removal into churches to save them from the ravages of the weather or treasured in various museums.

There is still a fine old Celtic cross in the square of the city of St. David in southwestern Wales, which in early Welsh Christianity was a landing and meeting place for the early Celtic missionaries as they went to and from Ireland.[32] It has been called "the preacher's cross," honoring all servants of the church—past, present, and future.

There are several types of the Celtic crosses. (See p. 138–139).

1. *The plain Celtic cross*. There are no markings on these stone or metal crosses. They resemble a plain silhouette. They can be proportioned about two feet tall or, with a longer foot and base, can stand ten to twelve feet tall.

    They adorn certain places in a cemetery or a church yard. The smaller plain Celtic crosses, standing two to four feet tall, are mostly found on gravesites. Many of this type cross can be found today in Wales, Scotland, and Ireland.

2. *The Trinity cross* is a design distinctive from all the other Celtic crosses. This cross stands about twelve to sixteen feet tall. The author has only viewed this taller cross in Wales. It was thought to be from the ninth century A.D. It is a stone cross made from a slab about fourteen inches thick. Its base is about four inches wider on each side from its stem, which gradually narrows to the Celtic cross at its peak. In the three rectangular sections below are carved three separate Celtic engravings in continuous design, much like the designs found in *The Book of Kells*.

3. *Cross of the Scriptures*. This stone carving is normally over seven feet high, usually having a dominant circle to signify eternity, and interlaced with Celtic designs. Always carved in the circle is the Christ wearing a crown and holding a cross. In sections down the stem of the cross are depictions of events in the life of Christ. Atop of some Celtic Scripture crosses is a figure shaped like a house with people carved within. It is said this is to represent the "house of many mansions."

4. *Moone Celtic cross* may be found at Kildare, Ireland. This is one of the earlier Celtic crosses found in the United Kingdom. The Celts were tired of being warriors where lives were taken, and those who shared the gospel were called "soldiers of Christ." According to this Celtic cross, the twelve human imprints at the base represent the twelve disciples. The animals on the stem of the cross are to show the animals of sacrifice. The section above the disciples represents the Christ with a shepherd's staff. Other information regarding this Celtic cross seems not to be available.

5. *This Celtic cross of the twelfth century* is one of a very few Celtic crosses for two reasons: (1) The cross was carved into three pieces. Most others have been carved from one slab. (2) This cross is definitely Roman Catholic in symbolism. This cross presents the Christ to be dominant over His earthly vicar, the pope.

6. The Cwbelin Cross highlighted in the video of the 850th Anniversary Celebration of the Margham Abbey (1147–1197) in South Wales is presented in the inside cover of this book. The cross is the oldest Celtic cross, and is housed in the Stowe Museum in Port Talbot, which is adjacent to Margham Abbey.

There are many other Celtic crosses found not only across the United Kingdom but also around the world. They are found on altars or in chancels of many Christian churches. They mark the graves of deceased Christians and martyrs, or they stand in public squares announcing to all, "The Christ is both eternal and Lord over all." The Celtic cross cannot be mistaken because of its form. There is always a circle depicting eternity where pieces of the cross intersect.

Celtic Family Life and Lovespoons

Concerning family life among the early Celts, historians seem to have been divided. Some historians, who were only vaguely familiar with Celtic family life, were prone to cast a negative pall over this area of Celtic activity. Other historians, who didn't appear too positive, wrote in a more understanding manner, giving the Celts the benefit of the doubt.

It seems the early Celts, like the early Alaskan Indians, viewed the discipline of their children quite differently than those who were outside that particular culture. To the Celts and the Alaskan Indians, it was believed that discipline could be handled more objectively and without rancor or vendetta by someone outside the immediate family. The Alaskan Indians chose an uncle. The early Celts chose an aunt or uncle, or in some cases a trusted friend or neighbor. Usually those doing the disciplining were invited in by the parents of these children. Such discipline has been documented in Alaskan Native history. One can understand that those outside such a culture believing that their idea of disciplining was the proper way, were liable to report differently.

Be that as it may, from the early periods B.C., the Celts' family relationship—considering their family as a gift from the gods and being responsible to the gods for all gifts they have received—should be seen and understood as a key to their family disciplining and behavior. It is believed that failures in their family life, like ours, have been well-noted.

The Celts' early family life, like other earlier family groups, have believed that the keystone of the home was a proper marriage. It was believed that the best rationale for marriages was an arrangement by the families. Since it was proven over the years not to be the best arrangement in a majority of the cases, the children were allowed to decide who would be their wife, or who would be their husband, or whether some of the children might choose not to be married.

Within the family of the Celts, it was decided that there must be a better way to announce the betrothal or mark the engagement period rather than for these young people to just get married almost on the spur of the moment. This was where the novel custom of the Welsh lovespoon had its birth. The earliest lovespoon has been dated back to 1667.

Carving of kitchen utensils goes back a long way. People other than the Welsh, but including the Welsh, have been carving culinary pieces for centuries. Crude cooking utensils were formed from various metals during the Middle Ages. Close to the same time, kitchenware was carved from wood as were tureens, bowls, plates of different sizes, cups, and various sizes of spoons. Knives and forks were later forged from metals. It is not clear when the distinction between spoons designed for culinary use and those with romantic associations emerged.

It was thought to have come to the fore when parents decided to make their young men think seriously about marriage and had them carve a special spoon for the young lass in whom they showed an interest. At first they were not betrothal spoons given in place of an engagement ring but to show the lads interest in dating a young lass of his liking. Although there is historical evidence, there is much stronger evidence showing that some used these spoons as notices of betrothal, in a situation already in progress, but they were used basically denoting a desire for a relationship.

Imagine a young man who would work during the daylight hours, busily shaping a spoon in a small room lit only by candlelight or the glow of a fire. Of course, this could take some time, as he would want to make this spoon as beautiful and ornate as possible to impress the young lady. The carving time would keep both the lad and the lass from jumping into a quick marriage. It was also said that some parents recommended harder woods for the project, which would make the spoon much more presentable, knowing the project would take more time to complete. No doubt competition was involved for certain lasses, and the lads realized it.

Some lads were more adept at carving than others, and this not only led to having someone else do the carving, but it also led to professional carvers who would carve a spoon for a fee. The more intricate the design, the higher was the cost.

The author believes that the reader needs to view rather than just imagine what lovespoons look like. Here are just a few examples—some more ornate than others.

The design of the spoons meant to convey more than the gift of the spoon. Of course there was "P+N," within a heart, which were usually carved on trees. These spoons were made from a single piece of wood. The imagery on these spoons is hard to understand by the average observer. It can have so many meanings. There are a few samples below.

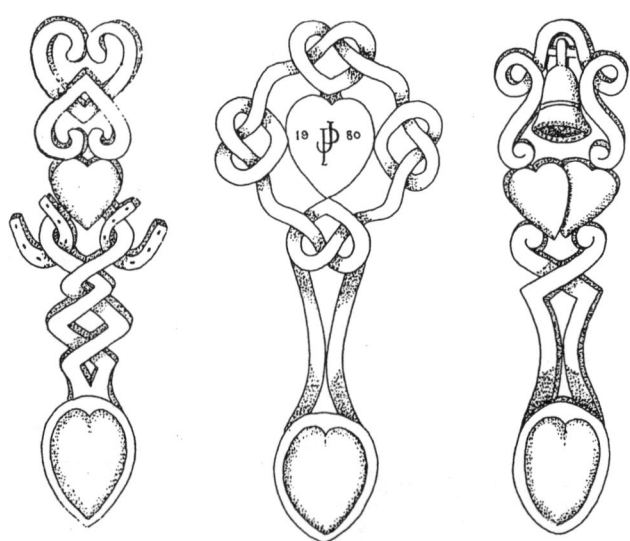

Here are some of the symbols and their meanings:

Hearts	Love
Crosses	Marriage and faith
Tools	I will work hard for you
Wheels	I will work hard for you
Bells	Marriage
Keys	Key to my heart and home
Locks	Safe and secure in your love
Balls in cage	Children or the desire for children
Chains	Union as the number of years together
Fruit	Fertility
Flowers	Fertility and beauty
Leaves	Fertility and beauty
Trees	A long and happy life
Anchors	Steadfastness, security
Rope	Joining together
Life symbol	This strange symbol is said to represent the nostril depicting the breath of life
Interlaced ribbon	Life everlasting taken from Celtic designs

Imagine you are a lad trying to impress a lass. What design would you carve in your lovespoon? Look at a catalog of lovespoons and imagine what each of them are trying to say.

Other cultures, patterning their lovespoons after the Welsh Celts, began to use their lovespoons to denote their time of engagement. In Egypt, instead of spoons, it was common for a bridegroom to present his bride with a pair of hand-carved knives in a sheath. Such were known as wedding knives.

The custom of lovespoons lasted only about a century, but they are now being used as family related gifts. For example, they are given for an anniversary, a wedding, a birth. They are also used as gifts on other occasions as well. They are gifts to bind people together, which still display the sentiment "I love you!"

First Half of This Century

World War II concluded the first half of this century in Great Britain. They had earlier endured invasions by the Saxons, the Vikings, and others, but this was an invasion encounter they had never ever faced before.

> One of the most important factors which fostered the peace movement of the 1930s was the belief that methods of warfare had become wholly barbaric. The fact that it was possible to bomb civilians from the air was the main reason for that belief. Official opinion held that 600,000 inhabitants of the cities of Britain would be killed by bombs during the first two months of a war against Germany. Thus there was craving to flee from the cities; the statistics of the railway companies show that 150,000 people migrated to Wales during the Munich crisis of 1938. Authorities believed that millions more would flee in panic if war were declared.[35]

The war had already moved at a rapid pace in a westerly direction across Europe. France's surrender left Great Britain with no allies in western Europe. Germany had crushed six countries in three months, and Hitler boasted that he would march into London in two more months. He ordered his command to plan an invasion of the British Isles, called Operation Sea Lion. But Hitler hoped that he could force Britain to surrender without invasion.[36]

Wales' appeal was based upon the assumption that it was too far to the west to suffer German bombing raids. The assumption proved to be unfounded. Cardiff suffered its first raid in June 1940. During the following fifteen months, 30,000 buildings were lost or damaged. Swansea suffered most severely between 1940 and 1943, with forty-four raids. A total of 369 people were killed. The entire town center was destroyed.[37]

In denying that political beliefs were acceptable grounds for exemption, the tribunals in Wales were probably mistaken for the Military Conscription Act of 1939 and 1945. These recognized wide categories of objection, especially toward conscientious objectors. In 1945, tribunals in Britain dealt with 59,192 objectors, three percent of whom received prison sentences. Once again there were more Welshmen and Scottish, in proportional terms, than were the Englishmen who refused to be conscripted, a fact which can be largely attributed to the strength of Christian pacifism.[38]

One can surmise that Christian pacifism, leading men to object to conscription, had its birth in the peace movement (1939) begun by the Celts. The Celts, because of their belief in power, joined with the Quakers and others who opposed any kind of military action or confrontation.

History at this juncture tells us that Celtic clergy on both sides of the Christian movement, Roman Catholics and Protestants of the United Kingdom, did their parts in the German invasion of Britain. They served in hospitals, drove ambulances, visited bomb shelters, acted as air-raid wardens, administering to the wounded and dying. They were also pastors and priests to congregations.

As an aside, we cannot overlook three matters that happened during this conflagration: (1) All references to the people involved in the United Kingdom's war with Germany were referred to as English or British. Reporters and historians never mention other citizens of what is also called the United Kingdom. Lest we forget, others fighting this battle were called Celts, Irish, Scots, Manx,

Cornish, and Welsh. These citizens dedicated themselves in this fight as well as the English! (2) In the record of this war, historians report events that bring merit or pity to the attention of the world as being the cause of the English or Great Britain. The United Kingdom is scarcely mentioned, except when eliciting help to do something, or noting you are part of us and your help is demanded; then this nation is referred to as the United Kingdom. (3) From the vantage point of the Celts, since the Bretons became Britains, England has used power to amass territories like the Greeks and the Romans, and others felt the fury of their fight. Now England experienced the fury and frustration that others felt when the Germans used that same type of power against them.

Now we see what transpires from this point to our time. Does Celtic Spirituality still continue? How? Where? Is it more active or less active? Did Celtic Spirituality evolve into anything meaningful? What about worship? Take a look at what has evolved!

CHAPTER 7

PRESENT DAY CELTS: OUR SPIRITUAL MENTORS? (1950–PRESENT)

The past is ours! It contains all that is worthy and imperishable in it; and therefore, the present and the future is ours too! Centuries have swept the past away a hundred signs of human devotion, and only one is left that we cherish, outside the cross for all to follow and honor and cherish. It is called "Celtic Spirituality."

—Paul F. Evans

As we approached the mid-century mark, the tourist centres in the United Kingdom took advantage of people who were becoming interested in their heritage. The Celts, especially those who emigrated from the United Kingdom to America, began to take a look at their heritage.

It was at this point that the church plays a strategic role. Although the governing bodies took a census, found the number of people in each shire, and marked the increases and decreases in population, there seems to be a lack of many shires failing to report births and deaths. The only other medium of reporting was found in church parish records, or by searching for the name in cemeteries in the communities where their loved ones were known to have lived. Here it was possible to find the year of birth and death and possibly the months and years of record.

Problems also arose in finding references through the church. Some vicars, pastors, and priests were poor record keepers. Records were lost by church fires. Old records proved to be unreadable because of fading inks. Records referred to cemeteries but did not mention what cemetery. Many people were not either members or attenders of a particular church. The Church of England's membership records seem to have been the best.

About the same time, heritage societies were formed and became a great factor in assisting in the search for many hard-to-find families. Through scientific methods they were helpful, especially in reading faded documents.

The Church of England, through the English Parliament (as noted earlier), ceased to report anything concerning Celtic history or the Celtic Church. This proves to be another stumbling block to seeking family names to add to one's heritage. Here one must turn to Celtic churches or the shire's recorder.

When people today talk about Celtic spirituality in our present time, they must return to the early beginnings of the Celts (circa 2250 B.C.) and trace their spiritual lineage to the present. Granted, there is not as much spiritual lineage as there is historical lineage. We must use the bits and pieces of spiritual lineage that we have been given and try to place them in perspective, as we have tried to do in this treatise.

People talking about Celtic spirituality agree, we must rely primarily on most of the words of other historians and consider their slanted interpretation of events. The Celts left no early historical documents, but passed information down from one generation to another, and in doing so left lasting faith impressions from one generation to the next.

Their definition of power was not only understood but exercised in such places as against the Roman invasion of the empire, and the Scots Confession, but also in the present feudal system under which they now exist without true freedom.

This power made a great impression on their children in reference to the importance of the family, their belief that the gods were personal and personable in their relationship to them, that the gods gave them all gifts, aided them with their problems, and held them accountable for all that they received.

> Their belief presented to the Celts through the Druids, that there were many gods simply because many gods were needed to handle all that was transpiring in the universe. Now they realized this one god could do it all alone. Add to that the fact that their belief led them to be the first practicing environmentalists. So when they were faced by the early saints, who confronted them with One God, who could do all these things that the totality of their gods accomplished, it became easier for them to believe in this one God. This One God could help them with their life's problems, provide them with a life after death. They realized that this One "God could do more than they could ask or even imagine."[1]

It proved to be a normal conversion to Christianity. The Celtic Church was born!

This conversion for the Celts, however, was not as cleancut as one would imagine. At first there was an admixture of mythology and monotheism. There was the further influence of the early saints and the influence of John Calvin (even though he never set foot on the soil of the United Kingdom). Add to this the working of God's grace and the power of God's Holy Spirit, and we have a Celtic spirituality that can only be expressed as "an evolutionary process," or as the New Testament declares, "they grew in grace and the knowledge of Jesus Christ our Lord."[2]

This Celtic Church, with its combination of mythology and monotheism, mushroomed and multiplied into groups of churches, worshiping God in a manner in which they were both comfortable and also able to hone their belief. Another turning point of their faith came at the Reformation in the United Kingdom and the Scots Confession. True, this turned into a confrontation and a division, but it sharpened their faith and led them into outreach and mission to their world, which to this point had been negligible.

Their outreach and mission included not only a desire to incorporate other individuals into the life of the organized church, and involve them in their work and ministry, but also in the building of schools, colleges, and universities. They took an active part in politics, including social ministries such as the Salvation Army. They took their faith with them wherever they went, making quite an imprint on their communities. Their faith and ministry evolved into this present-day structure. You can see how the evolution of this Celtic spirituality came about by referring to the "Church History—Celtic History Chronology."[3] (See the Addendum.)

Celtic spirituality did not come to a conclusion in the United Kingdom; it continues there. Celtic spirituality also has spread to and is active in Canada, Australia, Patagonia, the United States, and elsewhere. These countries have Welsh, Scottish, and Irish churches. There are also groups inside and outside these churches who are promoting their Celtic heritage and faith by singing choirs, Celtic societies, sports events, and international exhibits. So Celtic life and activities continue.

No one would say that Celtic spirituality concludes here. It continues! The life of the Celts has been born and is in the process of growing up. Some say the life of the Celts had died and was buried long ago. If so, the life of the Celts has been resurrected recently. The life of the Celts and Celtic spirituality will continue, either until the last Celt dies, or until the glory of God ceases to be revealed through their life and ministry!

The Reformation and counter-Reformation seem to be over. The people seem to be settled in their faith, and this is where I came in touch with both my Celtic background and my Welsh heritage. This span of life was opened by my grandfather, but the problem is: How much can a child remember between the ages of seven and eighteen? Further consider the author's association with the church and some of its parishioners over the years. Most of my association and reading has been with the Celtic Welsh.

At the beginning of this place in time, the bench marks of the church were basically Roman Catholic, Protestant, and none of the above. They each knew what they believed and why they believed it. For the most part, they were very sure of their faith, and both believed that the other was totally misled. The Catholics believed that they were the true and only Church, and that confession, purgatory, penance, and attendance at Mass were mandatory. The only responsibility of the lay people was to support the church with their money and attendance and lead the good life as prescribed by the Church.

On the other side of the coin, the Protestants were not protesters, as the Catholics claimed. Using the Latin of the Church (protest/protestare), they claimed instead that they stood up for something, and lay people had responsibilities in the church. Both churches were being instructed as to how to be Christian, and both were trying to evangelize each other. Neither side made much progress on evangelizing until each tried to convince those outside the church to come to be followers of Christ in their way.

In both camps the early saints, who were named by the people, were very influential. I believe it was at this time, when the Scottish folks wanted to make a point, they did so by changing their patron saint from Columba to St. Andrew. They became the first country to choose a disciple of our Lord as patron saint.

The author remembers from his seminary course in church history that both Ireland, which was predominantly Catholic, and Scotland, which was basically Protestant and reformed, opened their doors to each other. But their zeal for their individual faith remained strong! Wales, a few years later, found their faith crystallizing around John Calvin and John Knox. The Church of England also made themselves known. So to agree without becoming disagreeable was the cohesiveness of the true Celts.

The ethnic minorities in Ireland, Scotland, Wales, Britany, the Isle of Man, and Cornwall still recognized their own uniqueness. From the late eighteenth century they sought—and sometimes fought—to preserve their own individuality.

The individual characteristics of each Celtic region not only gave it an identity but also served as a reminder of the inheritance of the past. With the growth of nationalism in all areas, folk customs have been rescued from extinction and carefully nurtured to provide a new awareness of nationhood.

This is the heritage that the Celts kept on their shores, and this is the heritage that the Celts took with them on their migration to America, Canada, Patagonia, Australia, and wherever they made their new home. When the Celts migrated to their new homes, they took with them their culture, their literature, their music, and their spirituality!

Many Celts experienced hard times around 1840. The coal pits were cleaned out; fishing and farming places were overrun. The only folks who were able to stick it out were the rich landlords, those in politics, and those who had inherited much.

The setting sun in the west must have had an emotional appeal among primitive peoples, and it still has today. The feeling that beyond the Atlantic Ocean lay a miraculous land, like that which encouraged St. Brendan to make his voyage into the unknown, also inspired hundreds of thousands of Celts to leave their home an seek their fortunes in America, Canada, and Australia.

The majority of the immigrants to America were from the lower levels of the old world society. They offered themselves as farm workers and laborers. If they worked in the coal mine, like my grandfather, the coal mines were their destination. Most of them were fleeing from religious persecution or from famine. Migration was a hazardous business; as many as one-third died at sea from the overcrowding and squalor of the ships. Fortunately my paternal grandparents, and many others made it, or I wouldn't be here to continue the story of the Celts.

Extracts from a nineteenth century migration song are one of many such songs. Note the nostalgic words.

>Farewell to the groves of Shillelagh and shamrock,
>Farewell to the girls of old Ireland all around.
>May their hearts be as merry as ever I would wish them,
>When far away on the ocean I'm bound.
>O my father is old and my mother is feeble,
>to leave their own country it grieves their hearts sore.
>O their tears in great drops down their cheeks are a rollin'
>To think they must die upon a foreign shore.[4]

These migrant Celts brought with them their music, which inspired music; poetry that inspired poetry; sports that showed us how to win and how to lose and gave us the knowledge of competition. In fact they brought their whole heritage!

They also brought us great men and families who brought Celtic leaders to our shores, some of them carried in their parent's arms. Others were conceived there and born here, like my uncle Daniel, who died in infancy. There was Scottish-born inventor Alexander Graham Bell. Andrew Carnegie was of Scottish extraction. Others include Celtic Harry Lauder, contributor to American show business; labor leader John L. Lewis; and Thomas Jefferson, who was from Wales, gave us our Declaration of Independence. From Ireland came John Fitzgerald Kennedy, who became our first Roman Catholic president. This is just for starters! Wales also gave us Ian Woosnam, professional golfer, and Tommy Farr, a Welsh lightweight boxing champion. Scotland and Ireland gave us other prominent figures.

The Church came over too with all kinds of denominations to disseminate the gospel of love in Jesus Christ; Catholics and Protestants of different persuasions; Quakers, Methodists, Baptists, Presbyterians, Unitarians, and a denomination called the Welsh Calvinistic Methodist Church—a theological term, unheard of in many church circles.

Missionaries from Wales brought this denomination to America, and it had a large reception from Welsh-speaking folks in Ohio, Pennsylvania, New York, and Wisconsin. The Welsh synod of this denomination, which began in the mid-1800s, lasted until about 1948 when the need for a Welsh language church became unnecessary.

Of the Irish, Scottish, and Welsh who have many institutions and culture groups aligned with their Celtic background, I am more familiar with the Welsh.

I can share with you about several of the Welsh Celtic institutions:

- *Y Drych & Ninnau*—Two Welsh-American news publications.
- *St. David's Day*—patron saint of Wales—celebrated March 1.

- *The National Gymanfa Ganu Association*—Responsible for keeping Welsh hymn singing alive in America. It sponsors an annual national hymn-sing. In addition, each Welsh area sponsors its own Gymanfa.
- *Cambrian Societies*—Formed in 1918 in Wales celebrating the reinstituting the Society of the Bards, after King Edward I of England ordered all Welsh Bards slain in 1274. The society promotes all avenues of Welsh culture activities.
- *A National Eisteddfod*—Promotes Welsh culture through competition in vocal and instrumental music and elocution. It also keeps the Bardic tradition alive.
- *Cwrs Cymraeg* is a weeklong session held in several cities across the United States so people can learn their Celtic background, the Welsh Language, dances, traditions, educational institutions, etc.
- *Eisteddfodau* by mail is a new program. Contest parts are printed in *Y Drych* and *Ninnau*, time limits are set, and adjudicators are announced. Winners are notified by mail and in these two Welsh newspapers.
- *The National American-Welsh Foundation* makes available Welsh books and periodicals, historical trips in Wales, etc. The object of this foundation is to promote Wales and it people.
- *Women's Welsh Clubs of America* are federated to support the Welsh Home for the Aged.
- *Welsh Churches*—There are more than 2,000 Welsh churches across the United States and Canada, where worship is held regularly, and where the Welsh language may be heard and sung. One is Capel Cymraeg Bryn Seion, in the town of Beavercreek, Oregon, where the author serves as pastor. It was built in 1874, and has held continuous services of worship and annual Gymanfoedd since its inception.[5]

No doubt there are counterparts in other areas in the United Kingdom of the Celts to proclaim to the world what other Celts are doing that are not able to be listed here.

Present Day Celts:
Our Spiritual Mentors? (1950–present)

The Celtic churches in the United Kingdom of the Celts, I'm sorry to say, are not doing as well as the Celtic churches in America. Overseas, they are closing churches and uniting churches whose congregations are almost nil.

What's the problem? Do we need another revival to set in movement the churches there? That might not be the answer, but we need to understand the predicament of the church before we start any kind of movement, lest we lose the patient by our prescription.

From this vantage point, the reasons for the decline of the churches in the United Kingdom in numbers, acceptance, and power is the result of two generations' estrangement from the church. It is believed that is what is taking its toll in America. Thus estrangement has come, in part, from the humanistic approach to education, both inside and outside the Church.

For the most part, the thinking of those brought up in the Church has evolved into this kind of thinking:

> People no longer believe that Christianity is the only way to God; they don't even believe it is the best way to God. The way life teaches you is the best way, without even using God as a guideline or parameter. The Church doesn't mean anything to me anymore; in fact, it doesn't mean anything at all! It's OK for those that like that sort of thing, but count me out! These folks outside the Church live in a world of an intellectual relativism and cultural eclecticism. Somewhere along the way, the Church has failed these people. It has failed to provide them with the intellectual and spiritual resources needed in this post-modern world, including the most basic elementary beliefs of the Church. The only basis we have remaining is our Celtic heritage, in it is what little Celtic spirituality we may be able to find.[6]

Two generations ago, in the United Kingdom, churches that were weaned on the Reformers were still practicing the educational system of the Reformers. Such education focused on the study of classic texts that represented authentic models of good speech and writing. Students internalized these models through imitation and practice. Recitation, for example, was widely used, placing emphases on memorization and imitation, rather than personal creativity. Personal creativity came after the former, but not before!

The Reformers' theological convictions about the nature and purpose of the Church led them to stress the importance of baptismal catechesis in congregational life. Basic knowledge of the Bible, memorizing the Lord's Prayer, the Apostles' Creed, the meaning of the sacraments, etc. became as basic and necessary from the 1950s as they were earlier. The Reformers' vision of the nature and purpose of life remains as valid today as ever!

There's no reason that the internalization approaches of humanistic education cannot be replaced by forms of teaching consistent with the best contemporary research on human development and learning. To put it simply, one cannot think, speak, or act unless one has something to think, speak, and act with. Unless explicit attention is given to the acquisition of biblical and theological knowledge, the members of the Church will not be capable of using their faith to interpret their lives or their world. They will employ concepts from other areas of life in which they do not have competence!

Such is the case for catechetical learning. It is the core needed in the Church's teaching ministry, retrieving what is usable from the past while drawing on the best and most competent of contemporary research! Isn't such a plan worthy of being used to strengthen churches in all areas of the world, not just in the United Kingdom and America?

Isn't it strange? Three Celtic articles appeared in a July 6, 1996 newspaper:

> *Wiesbaden, Germany.* For those who had severe doubts that the Celts began their life and work here more than 2000 years B.C., German archaeologists displayed a newly discovered statue of a Celtic prince on Wednesday, calling it one of the most important archaeological finds in Europe in decades.
>
> The six-foot, 500-pound sandstone statue, in near-perfect condition, is believed to be at least 2,500 years old. It was discovered at a Celtic gravesite near Glauberg, northeast of Frankfurt . . .

Cardiff, Wales. "Storytellers Give Voice to Tradition." Bards, poets, singers, and musicians from across the globe gathered under the walls of a medieval castle in Wales to celebrate the Bardic tradition of storytelling. It might seem strange that people still want to listen in an age of watching television, but this is a unique art form whose time has come again.

London, England. "Imminent Return of Ancient Scots' Symbol Revives Debate." The Stone of Scone, a symbol of power at the coronation of British kings for 700 years, is to be returned to Scotland. Prime Minister John Major made the announcement this Wednesday to the House of Commons, stoking debate about whether Scotland should gain some form of independence. The Stone of Scone was returned in 1996 with pomp and circumstance.[7] (See the information on the Stone of Scone later in this chapter.)

- The author has a question: The Stone of Scone was a simple gesture in response to Scotland's request for her freedom. Some Scots claim it always had the Stone of Scone in its possession. Will England now crown her royalty in Scotland, or will she pay a price to lease the stone each time a royal coronation is held?

THE CELTS PROMOTE THEIR HERITAGE

Each section of the Gaelic culture is proud of both their corporate and their individual heritage. Each of the cultures began a national celebration of their culture as early as 1451.

The Scottish Gaelic Celebrations

From the borders of Shetland, from Lothian to the Western Isles, marks not only the beauty of the Scottish landscape—castles, abbeys, palaces, and Stone Age villages—but also exudes their Celtic history. Even villagers and townspeople today are exuberantly proud of their heritage, as are volunteers at tourist centres everywhere in Scotland. They are well-versed concerning their heritage.

Their art is not only displayed everywhere, but people are ready to share their knowledge, whether in a museum or a public arena. Their art, music, dance, and poetry are always on display in cities, towns, and villages, such as Glasgow, Perth, and Inverness. In most of these places, they are glad to help you honor their national Bard, Robert Burns. (They call him Bobbie.)

There is, of course, the national "Tattoo," held every year on the promenade in front of Edinburgh Castle. This is not only a brilliant drum and marching display but a review, almost in particular, of Scotland's military defense against both England and the Vikings.

The Tattoo would not be complete without the skirl of the bagpipe, Scotland's national musical instrument. It is believed that Celtic immigrants brought the bagpipe to Scotland nearly 2,000 years ago.[8] This most distinguished Tattoo exhibit would not be complete without a display of bagpipes and drums portraying precision marching.

Another big event in Scotland is the Scottish Games, which are also held wherever clans of Scots gather in the United States and Canada. In these games all eyes focus on the tossing of the *caber*. The cabers (poles) used in these games are fourteen, sixteen, and eighteen feet long and weigh approximately 180 pounds, which will test the strength and skill of any man. The score is marked by an end over end toss, beginning with the caber balanced in the contestant's hands perpendicular to the ground. The distance of the toss is not the prime factor in the score; taken into consideration is the straight direction of the toss. Each contestant is allowed three tries with each size pole, and the longest distance in these three tries is his score. The record for tossing the caber, with the eighteen-foot pole, is 47' 6".

At these games, the programs include the announcement, "The Scottish heritage is not complete without a large accent on the work of the Celtic Church." You will be shown John Knox's house on High Street in Edinburgh, where it is said, "He could look up the street to the castle and down the street to the needs of the people." They will show you where Mary Queen of Scots was imprisoned and where she lost her head; the Presbyterian Synod Office; the High

Kirk of St. Giles. They will encourage you to take in a showing of "The Covenanters Play," where the covenanter, the Rev. Alexander Pedan, wore both a wig and a mask to prevent persecution.

Folks proud of their church heritage will direct you to churches in their area that are partial structures, or still standing, which were part of the Reformation in Scotland or preceded it.

From June 10 to December 31 each year, the national museums of Scotland mount a major exhibition entitled, "The Wealth of the Nation." Among the relics and artifacts are those of Robert Burns, their national bard, and Robert the Bruce, their national freedom leader who was crowned Robert I, king of Scotland. People will hear of their spiritual leaders: John Knox, George Wallace, George Wishart, and a great spiritual leader from Iona, St. Columba, whose Monymusk Reliquary in which he carried the eucharist and holy oil to minister to the sick is found on display there.

The Stone of Scone

Before we talk about the Stone of Scone (pronounced SKOON), we must speak about coronation history, which precedes the Stone of Scone by decades. When earlier kings and queens across Europe and Asia were chosen, there were no coronation stones. These monarchs were crowned on soil brought from their own shire. Often they were crowned in another shire of their kingdom. When this happened, soil from their home shire would be transported to the shire where the coronation would be held. Such soil would be transported by horse and wagon over rough roads. By the time the wagon arrived, just enough soil remained to cover the place where the king or queen stood for the coronation.

Later on, in place of the soil, a large flat rock was used. The rock was easier to transport, and it presented a more powerful symbol for the coronation. What happened to these flat coronation stones, history does not tell us. Nor does history reveal how, where, or when this 400-pound Stone of Scone was secured. Nor does history reveal what kings or queens were crowned using this Stone of Scone (the Stone of Destiny). History just says kings and queens of Britain and Scotland were crowned using this Stone of Scone, a

400-pound red-gray sandstone rock that resided at Scone Castle north of Edinburgh.

There is a legend, which some folks call history. This stone was once used by the biblical Jacob as a pillow, on which he dreamed of angels climbing up and down from heaven on a ladder, known as Jacob's ladder.[9]

Legend says it was brought from the Holy Land and reverently carried through Egypt, Sicily, and Spain, reaching Ireland about 700 B.C. There it rested on the Hill of Tara, where ancient Irish kings were crowned. Celtic invaders were to have carried it off about A.D. 800 to a monastery in Scone, where it was lugged to Scone Castle, where Scottish and Pictish kings were crowned.

Later historians believed this as fact and insisted it was definitely a part of Scottish soil, even though geologists have proven that such a stone is not a part of the Holy Land geology. (See p. 130–131)

This much is true, and even substantiated by the British: Edward I, in his raid on Scotland in 1296, pilfered the Stone of Scone, bringing it back to England, where it was placed under the coronation chair in Westminster Abbey. It is now reported to weigh only 336 pounds. Was it dropped and broken on the way back from Scotland? Was it chipped so it could fit under the coronation chair?

Over the centuries, the English have stolen much, returned little, and very rarely said, "We're sorry." Indeed, the loot of the ages, from Egypt, South Asia, Greece, and other imperial outposts, continues to draw throngs to the British Museum in London.

The Scottish section in Parliament pleaded from the middle of June to Wednesday July 3, 1996 for their freedom and independence from England. After all, it was the seven hundredth anniversary of the time England took away their freedom and made them one of their feudal lords, so this was a perfect time to amend the wrong.

In the Scots' final statement, they brought up an act of Parliament known as the Treaty of Northampton (ratified in 1328) that, to put it mildly, was long overdue. This treaty promised to return the Stone of Scone immediately. Promises, promises, promises!

Completing their debate and plea, there arose raucous boos heard from Parliament, when Prime Minister John Major noted, "The cherished relic of Scottish history, the Stone of Scone, would be returned to Edinburgh on July 5, 1997!" There wasn't even a hint of giving them back their *freedom!*

Even then Prime Minister John Major, in making his presentation of the Stone of Scone, is quoted to have said, "The Stone will be returned to England whenever there is to be a coronation!"

Alex Salmond, leader of the independence-favoring Scottish Nationalist Party, in his acceptance speech is said to have made some retorts as follows: "What kind of a gift is this? What Scotland wanted was not just a symbol of power, but the substance of power, *our freedom!"*

I reiterate for the prime minister the Treaty of Northampton, which states, "When the Stone shall be returned to Scotland, Scotland shall be free!" Even a schoolchild can interpret English better than an educated prime minister! I would like to paraphrase Matthew 7:9, the words of our Lord, for the prime minister. "Or what man is there of you, whom if his 'protectorate' ask for 'freedom,' will give him a stone?" It is yet to be seen what will happen when the time comes for the next coronation.[10]

In September 1997, Scotland voted on what the English Parliament called the Devolution Referendum; meaning that certain stipulated rights, once held by the English government, were being transferred to the Scottish government, should they vote to accept them. Wales was also presented a Devolution Referendum noted in this chapter under the Welsh Celtic celebrations.

The Scots were given a full Parliament able to pass primary legislation on a host of subjects. It will also be able to raise or lower income taxes by three percent increments. It was passed.[11] It is thought that such a privilege was offered due to their continuous efforts for freedom.

The Irish Gaelic Celebration

Eire is the Celtic (Gaelic) name of Ireland, distinguished from Scoti, the Gaelic (Celtic) name for Scotland.

The Irish have carried their traditions and customs, relative to their heritage, far and wide.

The Gaelic Irish promote the wearing of the green, kissing the Blarney stone (in turn one will receive sweet flattering speech), and the wearing of the shamrock. You will hear repeatedly the fact that they stood up to and outlasted the British (for which they do not have a special but rather a continuous celebration). Only recently have they begun to celebrate their freedom from England. They had a prime celebration in 1921 and have celebrated continually since 1949.

Cities and towns throughout Ireland join in the A Tostal Festival that begins on Easter Sunday and lasts for three weeks. A Tostal, which means "Ireland at home," includes pageants, Celtic displays, and parades with colorful floats. The celebration marks many of the Celtic historical events of their country.

Left over from Ireland's early Celtic era are its round towers and elaborately carved Celtic crosses. (See Celtic crosses: 138–139, 229–232) Their round towers were used for both storage and viewing points in the wars with the British and the Vikings. But their Celtic crosses are their pride and joy, not only for their intricate carvings of biblical and historical moments, but also as focal points of worship in their churches and cathedrals. No other country honors, as do the Irish Celts, those early Celtic saints named by the people and those canonized by the Church.

One of their many religious festivals honors God's presence in their lives during the Great Potato Famine in 1840, despite the loss of lives and the vast number of folks who migrated to America and elsewhere to find a better future for themselves and their families.

Bringing back much of the Celtic lore were the Irish storytellers who dug deep into the past not only to entertain but also to promote and make alive an intricate part of their heritage. They told of fairies, little people, pagan gods (i.e., Banshees—women gods who warned people of death). They stressed their favorite *Cu Chulainn,* one of the most famous of the Irish legendary figures, a hero in the Cooley cattle raid.[12]

Northern Ireland, or the Irish Free State, has a great heritage also. Since 1905, when Arthur Griffith, a journalist, founded the Sinn Fein (meaning We Ourselves) political movement, this part of Ireland has been at odds with the English government about their desire for freedom.

They possess the same heritage that the Republic of Ireland possesses but were for some reason not included in the Republic. Like Scotland and Wales, they were considered part of the British Empire. The world newspapers recently have been focusing on the Irish Republic's desire for freedom, and their bombing and other disruptions in England, to gain attention to their plight.

The Welsh (Cymry) Celtic Celebration

In A.D. 1190, the Roman historian Giraldus Cambrensis had this to say about the Celtic Welsh: "They earnestly study the defense of their country and their liberty. For these they fight, for these they undergo hardship, and for these they willingly sacrifice their lives." Such was true because of the early Celts' belief about power. This belief in power formed the basis of their great heritage, which they received from the Druids and the Bards, and which is celebrated for us in the Eisteddfod.

The Eisteddfod is the final expression of all that is most vital and lovable in Welsh Celtic life. It reflects to perfection the Welsh Celtic character with its love of good company, gaiety, music, poetry, oratory, and intellectual rivalry. Where else would it be possible today to find audiences of 10,000 to 15,000 people, from all walks of life, listening with the keenest interest while choir after choir sings the same set piece, or competitors recite the same ode or sing the same song?

And where do vast audiences take real pleasure in listening to long and detailed adjudications of every piece? This is an annual national event of the Cymru for the purpose of reciting and reviewing their heritage. It is the earliest event in which any nation's heritage is presented in so many forms, and which has been continuously celebrated from early times to the present with only time off during the war years.

It is impossible to say when the first Eisteddfod was held. There are traditions that they were first held under the direction of the poet Taliesen at Ystum Llwydiarth in A.D. 517, with another under Maelgwn, prince of Gwynedd, on the banks of the Conway River in A.D. 540. The most important of the early Eisteddfodau for which records survive was the one held in 1451 at Carmarthen. The names of those who won prizes for best harpist (Cynfg' Bencerdd of Holywell), best singer (Rhys Bwting of Prestatyn), and Dafydd 'ap Edmwnd of Hanmer won the Bardic chair for poetry.

The Eisteddfod as we know it today dates back to 1568, when Queen Elizabeth issued a royal commission for the holding of an Eisteddfod.[13]

The national Eisteddfodau are held in August and alternately held in North Wales and South Wales. They were originally only open to citizens of Wales. But following the Eisteddfod in 1568, they have been open to other Celts (Scotland and Ireland), and at an early date, that has not been determined. The competition has been open to any Celtic organization worldwide.

The folks, other than those from Wales, are introduced in individual groups on stage and given a rousing Welsh welcome! In the most recent Eisteddfod, the participants came from Norway, Sweden, South Africa, Turkey, the United States, Australia, Patagonia, Canada, Korea, Argentina, Germany, and Italy. This gathering has been entitled *"Byd gywn fydd byd a gano, Gwaraidd fydd ei gerddi fo."* ("Blessed is a world that sings, gentle are its songs.") Nothing is quite like it! This is an international stage where combination of song, musical instrument, dance, and heritage is shared, transfusing music with emotion, understanding, and fellowship.

The Gorsedd of Bards (the Eisteddfod court) is responsible for both keeping and sharing, as well as safeguarding, the customs and rites of the Bards of all Celtic people. They also administer each Eisteddfod.

In addition to the Welsh national Eisteddfodau, other areas where Welsh people live are encouraged to hold Eisteddfodau in their region, honoring the heritage of the Cymry.[14]

The Devolution Referendum

This matter, on whether Wales should have its own Assembly, was held a fortnight after Scotland voted for such a referendum. While Scotland voted and won with a huge majority, the vote in Wales passed by only a 55 to 45 percent margin.

More people in Wales backed the Scottish-style Parliament than the talking shop Assembly (with very little power to do anything) actually offered to the Welsh. Opponents of any form of devolution were rather ingeniously able to argue against the Assembly on the grounds that it did not have sufficient powers to justify its existence, like the Scottish offer. Wales wasn't even offered any law-making or tax-varying powers, a model of government commonly described during the referendum. This is why the Welsh referendum was referred to as "nothing more than a toothless talking shop."[15]

Celtic Spiritual Awakening

According to Nora Chadwick, "The doctrine of Celtic spirituality has never been called into question."[16] Why? Because the Celtic Church became articulate from the beginning, not only to justify itself but to be dogmatic in a way that inspired growth, with continual implementation into the life of the community. Its spiritual life was one of evolvement in what one might call a continual spiritual awakening.

How did this happen? It happened through the manner in which the Celtic Church began and continued its missionary outreach. The Celtic Church did not so much seek to bring Christ to a community as to help that community to discover the Christ who was already there; not have to the community possess Him but to see Him as a stranger who wished to be their friend; they sought to liberate the Christ who was already there in all His richness!

The missionary endeavors of the Celtic Church in the sixth and seventh centuries saw the Celtic missionaries, going out of Iona in twos and threes, visiting the sacred groves, living alongside people with whom they wanted to share the good news of

Christ. They showed that the gods whom they worshiped pointed beyond themselves to the One God. These missionaries did not ignore nor did they disparage the beliefs of others. These missionaries had come from that same background, worshiped at similar rivers and oak groves, believed in the same multiplicity of gods, and simply shared the evolvement of their faith rather than demanding a direct response to their own. Could it be that Celtic missionary practices could be better used today?

If anyone is looking into the history of the United Kingdom, they will find very little about spiritual awakening. They will find only a series of community events that helped to revive spiritual lethargy and increase church membership for a short period of time. The Welsh revivals of 1859 and 1904–1905 are treated only as news. Any news about spirituality or a spiritual awakening must be found outside English history.

Up until 1850, the Celtic people in the United Kingdom, both Roman Catholics, the Church of England, and Protestant churches, needed a new outlook and direction for their calling and mission. This was provided by the Celtic Church of Scotland in "the Scots Confession."

Though it cost lives, confusion, and consternation, it was from this point in time that these churches found their place in Reformation Christendom and began to iron out the wrinkles in their faith. It was here that each began a more formidable presentation of who they were and where the priority of their mission centered.

What was accomplished from then to the present is amazing. We can only name the more prominent accomplishments in which the Celtic churches had a part: the two Welsh revivals in 1859 and 1904–1905. There was the formation of the Welsh, Irish, and Scots boards of education in 1919 and 1920. The Celts also entered into politics by electing David Lloyd George as both secretary of health and prime minister in 1916 and 1920 respectively, and promoted Neville Chamberlin for secretary of state in 1924. The Celts participated in the World Council of Churches in Jerusalem in 1928, and aided the Irish people in their potato famine in 1845–1847. Other Celts came to the aid in of the Welsh coal miners and their families in the depression in 1924, and helped to counsel and aid families in 1932, when the New York stock market crashed and affected all of the United Kingdom. A united group of Celts, both Protestant and Catholic, took part in the Ecumenical Movement when it began in 1937. They again participated in the World Council of Churches in 1938, and the Irish and Scottish Celts supported the Celts in Wales in the success of their Welsh Language Series on BBC, which began in 1938 and continues to the present time with various Welsh programming. The Scottish, Irish, and Welsh Celts played a great part in World War II both in the military and at home, beginning in 1940. British historians gave all the credit to the English military! United together, the Celts were able to pass the Folk Studies Act in 1946 and urge the National Council of Churches to be more inclusive of the Celts in the kingdom in 1950. In addition, Wales, Scotland, and the Irish Republic sounded off for their individual and corporate freedoms.

Someone seriously asked, in an account on Celtic history over the BBC, "Where would the United Kingdom be without the Celtic Church over the years to this present day?" In this call-in show, a person responded, "God only knows!"

Celtic people, eons before the Celtic Church came into existence and afterward, in spite of its faults and fusses, its differences and its deficiencies, its cohesion and its corruptions, by the grace of God the Celtic Church served well!

Let me conclude with this brilliant piece of prose entitled "Calvary," and attributed to St. Thegonnec of Brittany, circa 1980.

> They constitute a minority in the late twentieth century Western World . . . a series of minorities scattered in diverse nations. From antiquity to the present. They have been tossed this way and that in the storm-winds of international politics. And "the Celtic fringe"—the term used to describe them today—bespeaks factionalism and political insufficiency.
>
> Is there more to Celtic revival than nostalgia, more to their identity than wishful thinking? The Celts today can point as evidences to the Celtic languages they spoke: Irish and Scottish Gaelic, Mancs, Cornish, Breton, and Cymraeg, revived by

the poets and scholars, and now spoken daily by man living languages.

Another sign of Celtic life today, again in the cultural realm, is the survival of custom: dress, music, folklore, old Celtic names and places, and family traditions that are derived from old clans. But, the Celts do not base their identity on language and folklore alone. The Celts today may be a fringe group in France and Britain, and a scattered minority in the United States and Canada, as well as in other parts of the world—in Ireland they constitute a nation!

Whatever fate of the separatist movements in various nations today, the twentieth century has seen an example of a Celtic revival that is a political reality![17]

The long story of the Christian (Celtic) Church is a panorama of lights and shadows, of achievement and failure, of conquests and divisions. It has exhibited the divine life marvelously transforming the lives of people. It has also exhibited those passions and weaknesses of which human nature is capable. Its tasks have seemed, in every age, almost insuperable. They were never greater than at present when confronted by a materialistic interpretation of life, and when the furnace of almost universal war bids fair to transform the whole fabric of European, Great Britain, and American civilization. Yet no Christian can survey what the Church has done without confidence in its future.

Its changes may be many, its struggles great. But the good hand of God, which has led it hitherto, will guide it to larger usefulness in the advancement of the kingdom of its Lord, and toward the fulfillment of his prediction that if he be lifted up, he would draw all men unto him.[18]

Some Celt somewhere, be that person Breton, Gaelic, Mancs, Cornish, or Cymru, caught a glimpse of Celtic heritage in this:

A history is being relived!
A lost heritage
Is being wept after
With sad eyes and dry tears.

Present Day Celts:
Our Spiritual Mentors? (1950–present)

> A heritage
> That spoke beauty to the world
> Through dirty fingernails
> And endless alcoholic mists.
>
> A heritage
> That did cease communication
> Upon death, and nonetheless
> Tried to go on living
> *and did!*
>
> —Anonymous

God bless the author!

> We shall not cease from exploration
> And the end of all our exploring
> Will be to arrive where we started
> And know the place for the first time.
> —Anonymous

Afterword

Do you mind if I call all present-day Celts to read all they can of their early Celtic background to learn from and be proud of their heritage?

Do you mind if I invite all the non-Celtic crowd to not only learn from the Celts but to brush-up on their own heritage, for there is also a lot to learn there to make them proud too?

This is where I began; learning from stories my grandfather shared with me, adding to my heritage by reading Celtic background materials, building in myself a stronger and more durable Celtic spirituality. This made me proud!

Notes

Introduction

1. *Y Beibl Cymraeg*, Welsh Bible, NT, 57. Stonehill Green, Westlea, Swindon SN5 7DG. *The Bible*, Luke 2:1 ff.
2. *A Child's Nightly Prayer*, "Now I lay me down to sleep . . ." Written in Welsh.
3. Andrew Zenos, *Compendium of Church History*, 76.
4. Pastor, Welsh Chapel, Hill of Zion.

Chapter One

1. *World Book Encyclopedia* (Chicago, IL: Field Enterprises Educational Corporation), 5:158.
2. Simon James, *The World of the Celts*, 10.
3. *World Book Encyclopedia* and *World Dictionary*.
4. James, 11.
5. *World Book Encyclopedia* and *World Dictionary*.
6. *World Book Encyclopedia*, "Pre-Historic Man," 14:666–672.
7. Ibid., 668–669.
8. Ibid., 667.
9. John Davies, *A History of Wales* (Penguin Books, 1994), 7.
10. *World Book Encyclopedia*, "The Iron Age," 2:528–529.
11. James, 42–43.
12. *World Book Encyclopedia*, "Iron Age," 9:343.
13. Ibid., 360.
14. Barry Cunliffe, *The Celtic World* (New York: St. Martin's Press), 120–121.
15. Ibid., 120

16. Map—Migration of the Romans into and out of the United Kingdom.
17. *The Holy Bible,* "Hittites," Num. 13:29; Deut. 7:1; Josh. 24:11; Judg. 3:5; 1 Kings 10:29; 2 Kings 7:6; 2 Chron. 8:7; Ezra 7:6.
18. Gal. 3:1.
19. James, 12–13.
20. Nora Chadwick, *The Celts* (London: Penguin Press, 1971), 52.
21. James, 52.
22. *World Book Encyclopedia,* 16:724.
23. Strabo, *Geographica,* (17 volumes), 4, 1, 14.
24. Ibid., 4, 4, 2
25. Ibid., 4, 1, 2.
26. Ibid., 7, 3, 8.
27. Herodotus, *Histories,* 4, 49 and 2, 23.
28. *World Book Encyclopedia,* 14:146.
29. Diodorus Siculus, *Histories,* 5, 33, 34.
30. Strabo, 7, 3, 8.
31. Chadwick, 19.
32. See "Iron Age," this volume.
33. Cunliffe, 16.
34. Miles Dillon and Nora Chadwick, *The Celtic Realms,* 31f.
35. Cunliffe, 16–17.
36. Chadwick, 23.
37. Ibid., 23–25.
38. Cunliffe, 116–119.
39. James, 78–79.
40. Strabo, 4, 1, 2; James, 54–56.
41. Cunliffe, 114–115.
42. Julius Caesar, *The Gallic Wars,* 6, 13.
43. D. A. Brinchy, *Studies in Early Irish Law,* 18.
44. Dillon and Chadwick, 229.
45. Duncan Norton-Taylor, *The Celts: The Emergence of Man* (New York: Time-Life Books, 1974), 67.
46. John Davies, 92.
47. Ibid., 93.
48. *New World Encyclopedia,* 10:108.
49. Chadwick, 50.
50. Dillon and Chadwick, 43–45.
51. James, 64–65.
52. Ibid., 53.
53. Ibid., 130—Pix.
54. Chadwick, 20; 123–130.
55. Diodorus Siculus, *Library in History,* 5:29.
56. Gen. 22:1–14.
57. Caesar, 6, 16.

Chapter Two

1. Oliver Davies, *The Quest of the Spiritual*, 2.
2. Andrew C. Zenos, *Compendium of Church History*, chapter 7, 76.
3. "United Kingdom of the Celts," iii. The phrase I heard from my grandfather. I have no idea where he found it. It must have been written somewhere for him to quote it to me.
4. *World Book Encyclopedia*, 5:242.
5. Ibid.
6. Albert Hyma and J. F. Stach, *World History: A Christian Interpretation*, 136.
7. Ibid.
8. Duncan Norton-Taylor, *The Celts*, 101.
9. Strabo, *Geographica*, 4:4.
10. Cambrensis, Giraldus—twelfth century.
11. Nora Chadwick, *The Celts*, 131.
12. Strabo *Geographica*, 4:4, 3.
13. Simon James, *The World of the Celts*, 41.
14. 2 Tim. 6:7.
15. Giraldus Cambrensis, twelfth century.
16. Edward Jones, (Bardd y Brenin) *Men of Harlech* (Translation) *Musical Relicks of Welsh Bards*, 1784.
17. Julius Caesar, *The Gallic Wars* 6, 17.
18. James, 89.
19. See Chadwick, 174f.
20. Timothy R. Roberts, *The Celts of Myth and Legend*, 28.
21. In addition see Gerhard Herm, *The Celts*, 124–130.
22. Lucan, *Hercules*, 1f. See F. Benoit, *Ogam*, 17:268.
23. See "Celtic Gods": Chadwick, 141–185, 264–265. Dillon and Chadwick, *The Celtic Realms*, 28–30, 183; James, 88–89, 142–144, 161; Norton Taylor, *The Celts*, 91–95, 102. Specific animal totems.
24. Caesar, 6, 17.
25. Kuno Myer, *Introduction to the Ancient Poetry*.
26. Nora Chadwick, 47.
27. Ibid., 47–48.
28. Peter Berresford Ellis, *The Druids*, 232.
29. A Welsh Druidic Celebration.
30. Ward Rutherford, *Celtic Lore*, 117.
31. Barry Cunliffe, *The Celtic World*, 72.
32. Ibid., 72.
33. *World Book Encyclopedia*, 11:77.
34. Gen. 31:19.
35. *Matthew Henry's Commentaries*, 1:86.
36. Acts 17:22–23 KJV.
37. Lucan, Roman poet, A.D. 39–65.

38. See artist's drawing, 76.
39. Strabo, 4,4,6. Quoting Posidonius. See James, 93.
40. Nora Chadwick, 157–160, 227–228.
41. See Replica of the Temple, James, 142.
42. Diodorus Siculus, *Histories*, 6, 38.
43. Miranda Green, *The Celtic World*, 433.
44. Gen. 1:5.
45. Ibid., Genesis—1:5f.
46. Gerhard Herm, *The Celts*, 144.
47. *The Celtic Calendar*, (Annual). Address: 2973 Valentine Avenue, Bronx, New York 10458. FAX: 914-779-3710. Phone: 1-800-626 CELT.
48. Caitlin Matthews, *The Celtic Book of Days*, 41.
59. See gods and goddesses, 59.
50. Duncan, Norton-Taylor, 90–93. Matthews, "Mythological Harvest Days: July 31; August 1–2; September 28, 30."
51. Knud Rasmussen, *The Intellectual Culture of the Igulik Eskimo*
52. Ward Rutherford, *Celtic Lore*, 41.

Chapter Three

1. *World Book Encyclopedia*, "Stonehenge," 16:711.
2. Timothy Roberts, *The Celts in Myth and Legend*, 107.
3. *World Book Encyclopedia*, 16:711.
4. John Davies, *A History of Wales*, 10.
5. Ibid., 26.
6. Julius Caesar, *The Gallic Wars*, 5:20.
7. Ibid.
8. Tacitus, *Agricola,*, 24.
9. Caesar, *The Gallic Wars*, A Completion of Events.
10. Caesar, *The Gallic Wars*, Sacking the Druids at Mona.
11. Map—Invasion and Departure Routes of Julius Caesar.
12. Nora Chadwick, *The Celts*, Boudicca.
13. Caesar, 5:27.
14. John Davies, 29.
15. Nora Chadwick, *The Celts*, 83.
16. John Davies, 43.
17. Patrick Thomas, *A Candle in the Darkness*, 25.
18. John Davies, 64–66.
19. Dillon and Chadwick, *The Celtic Realms*, 113.
20. John Davies, Schematic, Royal Houses of Wales, 82–83.
21. See Chaucer's "Canterbury Tales."
22. See Williston Walker, *A History of the Christian Church*, "The Rise of the Papacy," 208f; Hyma-Statch, *World History*, 141, 155.
23. *The World Book Encyclopedia*, "The Magna Carta," 12:48.

24. Brian Davies, *Ninnau,* A North American Welsh Newspaper, October 1, 1997, 10. *New English Review,* Literary Quarterly in English. Chapter Arts Centre, Market Road.
25. John Davies, 148–149; 155–156.
26. Ibid., 156.
27. Ibid., 160.
28. Ibid., 161.
29. The Pledge of Allegiance to the American Flag.
30. Henry Wadsworth Longfellow, *Tales of a Wayside Inn,* "Paul Revere's Ride" presents the crux of the Revolutionary War.
31. Get a more in-depth picture with all the gore and intrigue. Read *The Brothers Gwynedd Quartet* and *The Blood of Shrewsbury,* both by Edith Pargeter. She also wrote under the name of Ellis Peters. These are listed as historical novels only because some characters cannot be verified.
32. *Worldbook Encyclopedia,* Bards, 2:78. John Davies, 347. Islyn Thomas, *Our Welsh Heritage,* 35–37.
33. Nigel Tranter, *The Story of Scotland,* 11.
34. Ibid., 74.
35. John Davies, 231.
36. Ibid., 233.
37. Ibid.
38. Ibid., 235.
39. Ibid.
40. *The American Dictionary,* "Mythology."
41. Ward Rutherford, *Celtic Mythology,* 21.
42. Ibid., 13.
43. Turn to pages 291–296 and view samples of these illuminated gospels with their explanations.
44. Anonymous, Irish Traditional, eleventh century.
45. An assortment of crosses including the Celtic crosses.
46. Ibid.
47. Ian Bradley, *The Celtic Way,* 1–2, 33f.
48. Bryan Davies, *Ninnau,* A North American Newspaper, October 1, 1997, 10. *New Welsh Review,* 17. A Literary Quarterly in English. Chapter Arts Centre, Market Road, Canton, Cardiff, Wales, CF5-1QE, United Kingdom.
49. Simon James, *The World of the Celts,* Drawing, 53.

Chapter Four

1. Isobel Wyatt, *Goddess into Saint.*
2. William Butler Yeats, *Collected Poems.*
3. Nora Chadwick, *The Celts,* 27.
4. Edward C. Sellner, *Wisdom of the Celtic Saints,* 21–27.
5. Timothy R. Roberts, *The Celts in Myth and Legend,* 27.

6. Barry Cunliffe, *The Celtic World*, 178.
7. Roberts, 26–27.
8. Chadwick, 179.
9. Ibid., 195.
10. See St. Patrick's Letter to Coroticus, Addendum.
11. An Early Gaelic Poem translated by Robin Flower.
12. Thought to have been from *The Famous Eulogy to St. Columba* by Bard Dallan.
13. Simon James, *The World of the Celts*, 172. Giraldus Cambrensis saw in Kildare, Ireland, twelfth century.
14. Additional Information: Nora Chadwick, *The Celts*, 249–252. Miles Dillon & Nora Chadwick, *The Celtic Realms*, 379–380, 387; James, *The World of the Celts*, 164, 173, 175. Janet Blackhouse, *The Lindsfarne Gopsels*, 7.
15. Dillon and Chadwick, *The Celtic Realms*, 205.
16. Andrew Zenos, *Compendium of Church History*, 73.
17. *The Law of 369*—Codex Theodosianus 16:2—Ayer, *Source Book*, 283.
18. Ibid.
19. Williston Walker, *History of the Christian Church*, 115f.
20. Zenos, 76.
21. Dillon and Chadwick, 228–229, 231. The Synod of Whitby—The Ester Controversy. Nora Chadwick, *The Celts*, 198, 207–272, 117–118. John Davies, *A History of Wales*, 77.
22. The author quotes from two lectures on "The Celts," who quoted these as being exact words from the mouth of Pope Gregory I.
23. Dillon and Chadwick, 230.
24. Ibid., parenthesis by the author for clarification.
25. Seminar notes from Pacific School of Religion, Berkeley, CA, 1995.
26. Bryan Davies, *Ninnau*, a North American Welsh Newspaper. October 1, 1997, 10. *New Welsh Review*, 17.
27. Ibid.
28. See Chapter 3, plus *The Brothers Gwynedd Quartet* and *The Blood of Shrewsbury*; both written by Edith Pargeter.
29. Brad Thompson, Editor, *Liturgies of the Western World*, 28, 40–41, 43.
30. The Council of Trent, 1542.
31. Davies, 239.
32. 2 Sam. 24:13.

Chapter Five

1. *World Book Encyclopedia*, 5:187.
2. Ibid., 15:223.
3. John Davies, *A History of Wales*, 239.
4. Hyma-Albert, *World History: A Christian Interpretation*, 70.
5. Nora Chadwick, *The Celts*, 47.

6. Davies, 257.
7. Ibid.
8. *World Book Encyclopedia*, 10:21.
9. Hyma-Albert, 248.
10. Davies, 263.
11. Ibid.
12. Ibid.
13. Ibid., 263–264.
14. *World Book Encyclopedia*, 3:293.
15. Ibid., 11:398.
16. Ibid., 3:293.
17. Hyma-Albert, 250.
18. Ibid., 250–251.
19. *World Book Encyclopedia*, 19:259; 259; 12:192.
20. Hyma-Albert, 251.
21. *World Book Encyclopedia*, 1:433.
22. Ibid., 7:115; 19:252.
23. Hyma-Albert, 252.
24. *World Book Encyclopedia*, 7:115.
25. Hyma-Albert, 254–256.
26. *World Book Encyclopedia*, 7:115–116.
27. Ibid., 19:259.
28. Ibid., 8:116.
29. Ibid., 18:284–285.
30. Hyma-Albert, 325. *World Book Encyclopedia*, 18:284–285.
31. *World Book Encyclopedia*, 5:75.
32. Ibid., 7:116.
33. Hyma-Albert, 390–392.
34. *New World Encyclopedia*, 5:75.
35. Ibid., 7:116.
36. Ibid.

Chapter Six

1. John Davies, *A History of Wales*, 242.
2. Ibid.
3. John Calvin, *The Institutes*.
4. Hyma-Stach—*World History—A Christian Interpretation*, 233.
5. Ibid.
6. *The Doctrine and Polity of the Church of England*, 39 Articles of 1563. John Davies, *A History of Wales*, 241.
7. Heb. 11:13, KJV.
8. 1 Pet. 2:11, KJV.

9. Hyma-Stach, 230. British Parliament, *Acts of Uniformity in Common Prayer,* 1559.
10. Ibid., 231.
11. Davies, 293.
12. *World Book Encyclopedia,* 6:459–461.
13. Hyma-Stach, 232.
14. Acts 6:1–4; 11:30; 14:23; 15:23.
15. Davies, 288, 293.
16. Ibid., 245.
17. Williston Walker, *A History of the Christian Church,* 416.
18. Hyma-Stach, 280–282. 17.
19. Ibid., 291–292.
20. Andrew Zenos, *Compendium of Church History,* 282–286.
21. Davies, 311.
22. Zenos, 280.
23. Hyma-Stach, 292.
24. Greenslade, *Welsh Fever—Welsh Activities in the U.S.A. and Canada,* Inside Cover.
25. Williston Walker, *A History of the Christian Church,* 551.
26. James, *The World of the Celts,* 180. *Worldbook Encyclopedia,* 9:338.
27. Islyn Thomas, *Our Welsh Heritage,* National Welsh-American Foundation, 26.
28. Ibid., 26.
29. *Caniedydd Cynulleidfaol,* Sol-Fa Hymnal, 284, Hymn 760.
30. Luff, *Welsh Hymns and Their Tunes,* 154–155.
31. *Worldbook Encyclopedia,* Cross Samples, 925.
32. Thomas, 19.
33. Perkins, *Lovespoons from Wales,* cover; 14.
34. Ibid., 14.
35. Davies, 600.
36. *Worldbook Encyclopedia,* 19:388.
37. Davies, 601.
38. Ibid., 599.

Chapter Seven

1. Eph. 3:30 RSV.
2. Ibid., 2 Pet. 3:18 RSV.
3. See the *Appendia.*
4. Extracts from a nineteenth-century Irish immigration song.
5. Each of these are advertised in North American Welsh Newspapers—*Y Drych* and *Ninnau.*
6. From an interview that the author had with an Irish lad at Holyhead before boarding his ship to Ireland in 1986.

7. *The Scranton Times*, Scranton, Pennsylvania—USA. 7/6/96.
8. *The Worldbook Encyclopedia*, 2:24.
9. Gen. 28 RSV.
10. Excerpts from news releases dated London. Found in *Washington Post* service and *Los Angeles Times*, 6/4/96.
11. *Ninnau* and *Y Drych*—Devolution Referendum (Scotland), August 1997 and November 1997 respectively.
12. Some of their legendary stories are found in *Celtic Lore* and *Celtic Mythology* by Ward Rutherford; *Fairy Faith in Celtic Countries* by W. Y. Evans Wentz. See listing in the bibliography.
13. Islyn Thomas, *Our Welsh Heritage*, 32–34.
14. Ibid.
15. *Ninnau & Y Drych*—Devolution Referendum (Wales), August 1997 and November 1997 respectively.
16. Nora Chadwick, *The Celts*, 210.
17. Though named St. Thegonnec of Brittany, this author found no way of substantiating his authenticity. This piece of prose was found in a copy of the English-Welsh newspaper *Y Drych*, minus the date it was published.
18. Williston Walker, *A History of the Christian Church*, 589–590.

Addendum

ADDENDUM

CELTIC HISTORY/CHURCH HISTORY CHRONOLOGY

CELTIC HISTORY	DATES	CHURCH/WORLD HISTORY
	Paleolithic (2,000,000–10,000 B.C.)	
	2,000,000	Earliest manmade tools
	100,000	Homo erectus defined
	40,000	Homo erectus-Neanderthal
	35,000	Homo sapiens become dominant
	Mesolithic (10,000–8,000 B.C.)	
	10,000	Ice Age begins to retreat

Celtic History	Dates	Church/World History
	Neolithic (8000–4300 B.C.)	
	8000	Ice Age ends
	8300	Wales and Britain free of glacier
	7000	Oldest human plaster statues
First immigration into UK	6000	First use of pottery
	Calcolithic (4300–3200 B.C.) *Traditional dating—Creation*	
First Cromlechs built	3500	
	Early Bronze (3,200–2,050 B.C.) Mesopotamians invent writing	
Early era of the Druids	3050	
	2950	Old Kingdom Pyramids (Egypt)
	2850	Palestine "urban age"
Beginning of Stonehenge	2800	
Traces of Humans found in UK	2550	
	2350	Traditional date of Great Flood
Early era of the Druids	2100	
Ritual shafts	2030	

Celtic History/Church History Chronology

Celtic History	Dates	Church/World History
	Middle Bronze (2050–1550 B.C.)	
Iberian Celts migrate into UK	2000	
Celtic belief in power	1800	
Storage Shafts	1800	
	1750	Hyksos invasion of Egypt
	1700–1400	Hittite Kingdom
Celts fought Hittites (moved)	1650	Abraham to Egypt
	1600	Eskimo culture—Bering Sea
Celtic Druid Laws	1600	
	Late Bronze (1550–1200 B.C.) Period of Exodus and Conquest	
	1550	Hyksos expelled from Egypt
	1500	Hittites (new kingdom)
Stonehenge Complete	1400	Amarna Period (Akhenaton)
Farming by Celts recognized	1400	Fall of Jericho
Celts fight Hittites again	1375	
Evidence of Urnfield Culture	1300	Ramses II (1290–1224)
	1290	Hebrew Exodus
	1250	Conquest of Canaan

THE CELTS

Celtic History	Dates	Church/World History
	Iron Age (1200–918 B.C.)	
	1200–1020	Period of the Judges
Celts coins, tools, jewelry found	1200	
Salt mining by Celts	1200	
Celtic materials—Hallstatt	1200–918	
	1125	Deborah
	1020–1000	Saul
Celts were wheelrights	1000	
	1000–960	David
Proto-Celts dominated Europe	1000–750	
	960–220	Solomon
	Iron Age II (918–587 B.C.)	
	918	Divided monarchy; prophetic
	850	Elijah
Hallstatt Era	750–450	
Celts bury swords with the dead	750	Hosea and Amos
	722	Samaria falls
Celtic church law	632	
More Celts migrate to UK	600	Marseilles founded
La Tene Culture, archaeologists	600–200	

Celtic History	Dates	Church/World History
	Exilic (587–539 B.C.)	
	587	Destruction of Jerusalem
	587–539	Babylonian Exile
	Persian (539–332 B.C.)	
Celtic language Gaelic and Cymraeg final	515	Zerubbabel builds Temple
	508	End Etruscan dominion of Rome
Celtic trade with Etruscans begins	500	
	460–400	Ezra and Nehemiah in Jerusalem
La Tene culture	450–50	
More Celts migrate into UK	400	
Celts invade Italy	400	
Celts ravage Rome	390	
	380	Rome rebuilt
	343–341	First Samnite War
	Hellenistic (332–63 B.C.)	
	323–198	Ptolemic rule of Palestine
	326–304	Second Samnite War
Celts meet Alexander the Great, Danube	325	

THE CELTS

Celtic History	Dates	Church/World History
	323	Death of Alexander the Great
Celts fight Galatians	300	Constantinople and Rome equal
Celtic Battle-axe People	300	
Celtic Temple dug-up at Heathrow (1940)	300	
	298–290	Third Samnite War
Celts sack Delphi	279	
	264–146	Three Punic Wars
Celts again advance on Rome, Telamon	225	
Celtic Beaker culture	200	
	198–167	Seleucid rule of Palestine
Celts beat Galatians at Olympus	189	
Celtiberians war against Rome	113	
Mining materials in the UK	100	
	Roman (63 B.C.–A.D. 324)	
	68	Agricola takes command in Britain
	63	Pompey takes Jerusalem/Rome
	55	Caesar's Expedition— the UK
	54	Caesar's Expedition— the UK
	46	Caesar invades the UK
	37–4 A.D.	Herod the Great

Celtic History	Dates	Church/World History
	4 B.C.	Birth of Christ (Traditional)
	29 A.D.	Death of Christ
The Iceni Celts—Boudicca's Revolt	60	Agricola Britain Legionary Legate
	61	Seutonius Paulus kills Druids at Anglesey
	66	Masada
	70	Fall of Jerusalem
Gnaeus Agricola conquered the Picts	80	
	93	Agricola dies
	122–125	Hadrian's Wall
	135	Second Jerish Revolt
	167	Maccabean Revolt
	244–284	Rome named British emperors
	306–337	Constantine the Great
	Byzantine (324–630 A.D.)	

First and Only Statement in Church History Texts about the Celts

	325–590	Nicene Age
	325	First Council of Nicaea
Revolt Magnus Maximus, Welsh Autonomy	383	
St. Patrick	390–461	
	390	Pelegian Controversy
	395	St. Augustine, bishop of Hippo
Celts arrive from France and Spain	400–600	

Celtic History	Dates	Church/World History
	400	Autustine (Theologian) "Doctrine of grace"
	405	St. Jerome Vulgate
	407	Emperor Horatius "Defend Yourselves"
	409	Last Roman detachment departs
	411	Council of Carthage
	430	Goths invade Britain
St. Celeste sends Paladius to Ireland	431	
St. Patrick's Mission to Ireland	432	
Caesar leaves UK	470	
Celts begin trade with Etruscans	500	
Celtic rites held	500	
Earliest Eisteddfod held	517	
St. David, Patron Saint of Wales	520[?]–589	
St. Colomba or Colum-Cille	521–597	
	540	Gildas—"Fall of Britain"
Taliesin composes early poetry	550	
	560	St. Martin founds Celtic monastery at Tours
Columba founds Celtic Monastery, Iona	563	
Death of Dwi Sant (St. David)—Wales	589	

Celtic History / Church History Chronology

Celtic History	Dates	Church/World History
Augustine Lands in England	597	
Welsh language wirtten down	600	
Augustine, Archbishop of Canterbury	601	
Augustine unacceptable Welsh Bishop	602	
	Arabic/Islamic (630–1516 A.D.)	
	610–632	Era of Mohamad Celtic Church
Celtic Church Law	632	
Synod of Whitby—Easter date	663	
Goidelic Celts to the UK	700	
	716–757	Hadrian's Wall erected
Iona celebrates Easter—Roman date	716	
	754	Second Council of Nicaea
Easter	768	
	778–784	Offa's Dyke
Celtic monastery at Lindesfarne	793	
	795	Vikings settle in Ireland
	805	Vikings invade Iona
First Celtic crosses	820	
Kenneth McAlpin—Pict king	844	
Rhrodri Mawr	870	

Celtic History	Dates	Church/World History
Hwyl Dda's law is folk law	880	
Soul friendship developed	900	
Hwyl Dda's law revised and enacted	910–950	
Book of Kells Manuscript	1007	
King Gruffudd ap LLewellyn, Wales	1039–1063	
King Gruffudd united Wales	1059	
	1066	Norman Conquest/Battle of Hastings
	1066–1071	Wm Conqueror sets Earldoms
	1087	Death of William I
	1087	Territory to his sons
	1087–1100	William II is king
	1090	England seized by Normans
Rhys ap Tewdwr, Welsh leader, dies	1093	
	1099–1291	The Crusades
	1100–1135	King Henry I to the throne
Welsh boundary set	1105	
	1135–1154	King Stephen crowned
	1154–1189	Henry II rules
	1170	Thomas aBecket killed
	1171	Henry II lord of Ireland
	1171	Prince Modoc discovers America

Celtic History / Church History Chronology

Celtic History	Dates	Church/World History
	1172	Thomas aBecket a Saint
First Eisteddfod in Cardigan	1176	
	1189–1199	Richard I is king
	1199–1216	King John rules
King Edward orders all Bards killed	1200	England begins feuday system
First Mass served in the UK	1200	
	1215	Magna Carta
	1216–1272	Henry III crowned king
Henry III names Great Britain	1267	
Llewellyn ap Gruffydd named prince of Wales by Henry III. All others came from Royalty!	1267	Treaty of Montgomery
Celtic Bretons become Britains	1270	
	1272–1307	Reign of King Edward I
	1272	Edward I invades Celtic countries
Robert the Bruce	1274–1329	
Llewellyn ap Gruffydd slain, ambush	1282	
End of Welsh rule	1282	
	1290	Robert deBaliol Scottish King
Stone of Scone stolen by Edward I	1296	

THE CELTS

Celtic History	Dates	Church/World History
	1301	Edward I makes son Edward II prince of Wales
	1307–1327	Edward II, King of England
Robert the Bruce defeats Edward I	1314	
Scotland decalres independence Eng	1320	
	1327–1377	EdwardIII, King of England
Robert I (Bruce), King of Scotland	1328	Treaty of Northampton
	1371	Stuart tartan formed
	1377–1399	Richard II reigns
	1399–1413	Henry IV, King of England
Owain Glyndwr declares himself Prince of Wales	1400	
	1413–1422	Henry V to the throne
Welsh literature increases	1439	
	1442–4761	Henry VI crowned
	1455	Gutenburg Bible
	1461–1470	Edward IV is king
	1470–1471	Henry VI, King of England
	1485–1509	Henry VII to throne
	Turkish Ottoman (A.D. 1516–1918)	
	1509–1547	Henry VIII crowned
	1517	Protestant Reformation begins in Germany

288

CELTIC HISTORY/CHURCH HISTORY CHRONOLOGY

Celtic History	Dates	Church/World History
	1520	Martin Luther excommunicated
	1524	English overlords overbearing
	1525	Zwingli—Liturgy "Word"
	1526	Diet of Speyer, Lutherans killed
	1528	Patrick Hamilton (Lutheran) burned
	1530	Augsburg Confession
	1533	Lady Jane Gray
England separates from RC Church	1534	Strasburg Liturgy, Bucer
English language mandatory in UK	1540	
England removes language barrier	1543	The Act of Union
	1545–1563	Council of Trent
	1545	Printing press invented
	1545	Calvin, form of church prayers
First books printed Welsh	1547	Clergy allowed to marry
First book of Common Prayer	1549	
Protestant English Prayer Book	1553	
	1553–1558	Lady Jane Gray lifespan
John Knox fled to Geneva	1554	
Scottish Reformation	1558	
	1558–1603	Elizabeth I crowned
	1559	Act of Uniformity of Common Prayer

Celtic History	Dates	Church/World History
First General Assembly Scot Pres	1560	The Scots Confession
	1563	The Heidelberg Catechism
Welsh Bible and Prayer Book Ch. Eng	1567	
National Eisteddfod	1568	Catholic Christian doctrine
	1572	St. Bartholomew's Massacre
First Welsh Bible (Independent)	1588	
William Herbert, first Welshman to address the House of Commons, Education	1590	
First Book of Discipline, Scotland	1592	
Independent Congretations	1595	
Book on Counter-Reformation, Welsh	1596	
	1598	Vulgate Bible official
	1600	Crown owns all ores underground
	1603	James I, King England/Scotland
The Bible—King James Version	1611	
	1618	Thirty Years War began
	1620	Pilgrims land in America
	1625–1649	Charles I rules England
William Morgan's Bible	1629	

Celtic History / Church History Chronology

Celtic History	Dates	Church/World History
First Welsh Church at Llanfaches (Independent)	1639	
Irish Massacres	1641	
Westminster Assembly, Dir. for Wor	1643	
Westminster Directory, Liturgy	1644	
Westminster Confession (Early Ed.	1647	
	1649	Cromwell takes 9/10 of Ireland
	1649–1653	Long Parliament
Act, Propagation of the gospel, Wales	1650	
	1653–1658	Oliver Cromwell rules
	1658–1659	Richard Cromwell rules
	1660–1685	Charles II reigns in England
Presbyterian Church to Wales	1660	
Welsh lovespoons started	1667	
	1685–1688	Reign of James II
	1688	Last of the Stuart kings
	1689–1702	William III and Mary II rule (William: 1689–1702; Mary: 1689–1694)
Baptists move to Wales	1692	
Promoting Christian Knowledge	1699	

Celtic History	Dates	Church/World History
Repudiation of transubstantiation	1701	
	1702–1714	Queen Anne ot the throne
	1707	England and Scotland united
	1725	Decline of spiritual life in UK
Celts deal with philosophy/theology	1725	
	1727–1760	George II is king
Welsh Calvinistic Methodist Church	1736	
People may worship as they choose	1752	
	1760–1820	George III reigns
Sunday schools began in Wales	1772	
	1775–1783	Revolutionary War
Sunday schools began in England	1780	
	1801	Ireland became part of UK
Welsh Calvinistic Methodists broke with the Church of England	1811	
Welsh Calvinistic Methodist Church ordination in Wales	1811	
Eisteddfod first for hymn and anthem competition	1814	
Baptist Missionary Society, Wales	1816	

Celtic History/Church History Chronology

Celtic History	Dates	Church/World History
	1820–1830	George IV is king
Welsh Calvinistic Methodists Confession of Faith	1823	Monroe Doctrine
Protestants allowed to hold office	1828	
Missionary organizations, Scotland	1830	English courts extend to Wales
	1830–1837	William IV rules England
	1837–1901	Queen Victoria on the throne
Sol-Fa method—singing in parts	1840	Archbishop Thomas a'Becket
Free Church of Scotland	1843	Parliament takes away Welsh language
	1845–1849	Potato Famine in Ireland
Evangelical Alliance, Wales	1846	
	1848	St. Fagans outdoor museum
Large migration to US and Canada	1850	Industrial Revolution, America
Y Drych Welsh/English Newspaper	1851	
Llangollen Eisteddfod International	1858	
Welsh Revival	1859	
Salvation army formed in Cardiff	1861	
Welsh Calvinistic Methodist Church—first general assembly	1864	
Salvation Army formed in London	1865	

Celtic History	Dates	Church/World History
Welsh church in Patagonia	1867	Oldest Protestant Church, Alaska
University of Wales, Aberystwyth	1872	
Welsh Sunday Closing Act	1881	
Bryn Seion Welsh Church, Beavercreek—oldest Welsh church in Oregon	1884	
Coligny calendar found	1887	La Tene artifacts appear
Welsh Immediate Education Act	1889	
Tenant farmers refuse to pay tithe to the church of England	1891	
	1901–1910	Edward VII reigns
Welsh Revival	1904–1905	
	1905	Sin Fein founded
	1907	Nat'l Library and Museum chartered
	1910–1936	George V is king
	1914–1920	World War I
Easter Rebellion v. Brits in Dublin	1916	
	Mandate (A.D. 1918–1948)	
Cambrian Society formed	1918	
Disendowment by Welsh Anglicans	1919	
Welsh/Irish education board	1919–1920	Irish free state fight Britain

Celtic History / Church History Chronology

Celtic History	Dates	Church/World History
	1920	League of Nations
	1920	Fascists come to power
Ireland freedom from Britian	1921	
Welsh Nationalist Party formed	1924	
	1925	Placid Cymru-Welsh nationalists
	1930	Labor Party dominates
	1931	Statute of Westminster (all denominations free)
	1934	Barmen Declaration
	1936–1952	George IV is king
Welsh language programs on BBC	1938	World Council of Churches
Peace movement in the UK	1939	Military Conscription Act
	1940–1944	World War II raids on UK
	1945	New industry encouraged in UK
Welsh and Irish folk studies	1946	Nationalized banks and railways
	1947	India and Pakistan free from England
	The Modern Era (A.D. 1948–Present)	
	1948	Social security in England
	1949	Advisory Council for Wales

THE CELTS

Celtic History	Dates	Church/World History
	1949	Ireland leaves Commonwealth
	1949	North American Treaty Organization
Britain National Council of Churches	1950	World Council of Churches
	1951	Minister of Welsh Affairs in UK Cabinet
	1952–Present	Queen Elizabeth II
	1954	South Asian Treaty Organization
	1955	Cardiff declared Welsh capitol
Westminster Confession of Faith	1958	
	1961	Lutheran Church in America
Presbyterian Brief Statement of Faith	1962	
Welsh Language Society	1962	Second Vatican Council/Pope John XXIII
	1962	School prayer unconstitutional
	1963	Elanor Roosevent died
	1963	Pope Paul VI
	1964	Racial civil disobedience
Established Secretary State for Wales	1965	Inter-Faith dialogue
Aberfan Colliery Disaster (Kills 116 children, 28 adults)	1966	Aberfan Colliery
Welsh Language Act Passed	1967	Presbyterian Confession of '67

CELTIC HISTORY/CHURCH HISTORY CHRONOLOGY

CELTIC HISTORY	DATES	CHURCH/WORLD HISTORY
	1969	Investiture Prince of Wales
Increased use of Welsh Language	1969	Welsh Tourist Board
	1970	Black Manifesto
	1970	Council on Church and Race
The Welsh Language Act	1973	
	1977	Sun Myung Moon Unification Church
World Mission Conference, Dublin	1977	Episcopal Church ordains women
Wales proposes "Freedom", defeated	1978	
Scotland's "Freedom", defeated	1978	
	1981	Marriage of "Prince of Wales"
	1982	New Welsh TV channel 4 BBC
	1982	Prime time viewing in Welsh
	1988	Beautifying mining areas
Eisteddfod competition by mail	1989	
	1993	"Tourism 2000" published by UK
Scotland's Freedom Proposal defeated	1995	
England returns Stone of Scone	1996	
	1997	British crowned colony of Hong Kong restored to Chinese Sovereignty

Celtic History	Dates	Church/World History
	1997	Wales referendum passed
	1997	Scotland Referendum passed
	1998	Prime Minister/Sinn Fein dialogue
	1998	Death of Princess Di, Princess of Wales

ADDENDUM B

KINGS IN THE UNITED KINGDOM

NAME	REIGN
Saxons	
Egbert	829–839
Ethelwulf	839–858
Ethelbald	858–860
Ethelburt	860–866
Ethelred I	866–871
Alfred the Great	871–899
Edward the Elder	899–924
Athelstan	924–940
Edmund I	940–946
Edred	946–955
Edwy	955–959
Edgar	959–975
Edward the Martyr	975–978
Ethelred II	978–1016
Edmund II	1016
Danes	
Canute	1016–1035
Harold I	1035–1040
Hardecanute	1040–1042

NAME	REIGN
Saxons	
Edward the Confessor	1042–1066
Harold II	1066
Normans	
Wm I, Conqueror	1066–1087
William II	1087–1100
Henry I	1100–1135
Stephen	1135–1154
Plantagenet Family	
Henry II	1154–1189
Richard I	1189–1199
John	1199–1216
Henry III	1216–1272
*Edward I	1272–1307
Edward II	1307–1327
Edward III	1327–1377
Richard II	1377–1399

* First King to be coronated at Westminster, London, with The Stone of Scone. Other Kings were coronated in Scotland!

Name	Reign
House of Lancaster	
Henry IV	1399–1413
Henry V	1413–1422
Henry VI	1442–1461
House of York	
Edward IV	1460–1470
House of Lancaster	
Henry IV	1470–1471
House of York	
Edward IV	1471–1483
Edward V	1483
Richard III	1483–1485
House of Tudor	
Henry VII	1485–1509
Henry VIII	1509–1547
Edward VI	1547–1553
Gray, Lady Jane	1553
Mary I	1553–1558
Elizabeth I	1558–1603
House of Stuart	
James I	1603–1625
Charles I	1625–1649
Commonwealth	
Long Parliament	1649–1653
Protectorate	
Oliver Cromwell	1653–1658
Richard Cromwell	1658–1659
House of Stuart	
Charles II	1660–1685
James II	1685–1688
William III	1689–1702
and Mary II	1689–1694
Anne	1702–1714

Name	Reign
Great Britain	
House of Hanover	
George I	1714–1727
George II	1727–1760
George III	1760–1820
George IV	1820–1830
William IV	1830–1837
Victoria	1837–1901
House of Saxburg-Gotha	
Edward VII	1901–1910
House of Windsor	
George V	1910–1936
Edward VIII	1936
George VI	1936–1952
Elizabeth II	1952–

Note: Robert the Bruce was named King "Robert I," who, by a simple act of Parliament was "dethroned."

Many other Kings were crowned in other parts of The United Kingdom but were never even recognized!

Worldbook Encyclopedia
Vol. V, p. 224

Addendum C

Celtic Poems

Poems from the Black Book of Carmarthen (8th Century)

The Advice of Addaon

> I asked all the priests of he world,
> The Bishops and Judges,
> What most profits the soul.
>
> The Lord's Prayer, The Beati and Holy Creed,
> All sung for the sake of the soul,
> Are best practiced until Judgment Day
>
> If only you shape your own path,
> And build up peace,
> You shall see no end to mercy.
>
> Feed the hungry and clothe the naked,
> Sing our in praise,
> For you have escaped the devil.

But the proud and idle, pain on their flesh
On account of excess,
Must be winnowed until they are pure.

Too much sleep, drunkenness and sipping the mead,
Too much pandering to the body,
That is their sweet bitterness before Judgment Day.

They who commit perjury for land and deceive their lord,
Who pour scorn on the humble,
Shall know regret on Judgment Day.

By rising for matins and by midnight vigils,
By praying to the saints,
Every Christian shall receive forgiveness.

Maytime is the Fairest Season

Maytime is the fairest season,
With its loud bird—song and green trees
When the plow is in the furrow
And the oxen under the yoke,
When the sea is green
And the land many colors.

But when cuckoos sing on the tops
Of the lovely trees my sadness deepens
The smoke stings and my grief is clear
Since my brothers have passed away.

On the hill and in the valley,
On the islands of the sea
Whichever path you take,
You shall not hide from the Blessed Christ.

It was our wish, our Brother, our way,
To go to the land of your exile.

Seven saints and seven score and seven hundred
And were without fear.

The gift I ask, may it not be denied me,
Its peace between myself and God.
May I find my way to the gate of glory,
May I not be sad, 0 Christ, in your court.

The Loaves of Taliesin

The beauty of virtue is doing penance for glory,
Beautiful too that God will save me.
The beauty of a companion who does not deny me his company,
Beautiful too the drinking horn's society.
The beauty of a master like Nudd, the wolf of God,
Beautiful too a man who is noble, kind and generous.
The beauty of berries at harvest time,
Beautiful too the grain on the stalk.
The beauty of the sun, clear in the sky,
Beautiful too they who pay Adam's debt.
The beauty of a herd's thick—maned stallion,
Beauty too the pattern of his plaits.
The beauty of desire and a silver ring,
Beautiful too a ring for a virgin.
The beauty of an eagle on the shore when tide is full,
Beautiful too the seagulls playing.
The beauty of a horse and gold—trimmed shield,
Beautiful too when bold in the breach.
The beauty of Einion, healer of many.
Beautiful too a generous and obliging minstrel.
The beauty of May with its cuckoo and nightingale,
Beauty too when good weather comes.
The beauty of a proper and perfect wedding feast,
Beautiful too a gift which is loved.
The beauty of desire for penance from a priest,
Beautiful too bearing the elements to the altar.

The beauty of a minstrel of mead at the head of the hall,
Beautiful too a lively crowd surrounding a hero.
The beauty of a Catholic priest in his church,
Beautiful too a chieftain in his hall.
The beauty of a strong parish led by God,
Beautiful too being in the season of Paradise.
The beauty of the moon shining on the earth,
The beauty of summer, its days long and slow,
Beautiful too visiting the ones we love.
The beauty of flowers on the tops of fruit trees,
Beautiful too covenant with the Creator.
The beauty in the wilderness of doe and fawn,
Beautiful too the foam—mouthed and slender steed.
The beauty of the garden when the leeks grow well,
Beautiful too he charlock in bloom.
The beauty of the horse in its leather halter,
Beautiful too the king's retinue.
The beauty of a hero who does not shun injury,
Beautiful too is elegant Welsh.
The beauty of the heather when it turns purple,
Beautiful too pasture land for cattle.
The beauty of the season when the calves suckle,
Beautiful too riding a foam—mouthed horse.
And for me there is no less beauty
In the father of the horn in a feast of mead
The beauty of the fish in his bright lake,
Beautiful too its surface shimmering.
The beauty of the word which the Trinity speaks,
Beautiful too doing penance for sin.
But the loveliest of all is honor and covenant
With God in the Day of Judgment.

The Feast of the Dead

Up from the Celtic twilight
Through the mists of no more time,
The undead walk among us

Addendum C
Celtic Poems

This kalend of wintertime.
When the monstered black sow of my homeland
Avoided the bonfires bright
For beyond the warmth of the coelcerth*
Hid the shivering terrifying night,
Where the forces of evil held audience
And for spirits the setting was right.

There's no Celt that feels not that there's something
That stirs 'neath the soul at this time.
It's edged all in black
With a sound that goes back
To the dark, between the fires of old!
Oh yes! We've a wonderful story
We Celts and our spirit beliefs;

So listen my friends, list now closely
To the tales of our Bards and our chiefs.
Tales of things that seem beyond reason,
Beyond understanding and life,
Of Ghouls and of Monsters and Spirits
And of music of draped harp and fife
We reach back to the mist shrouds of our mountains

Our valleys, our forests, our shores,
This eve we'll throw open our windows
This eve we'll throw open our doors
And thus will our New Year enter
And out old Celtic year go out.
But, forget not, my friends that tonight
The spirits of Annwn† are about.

* Bonfire †Netherworld

Tom Jones

Note:—October 31st, Halloween, is the Celtic New Year's Eve. November 1st, Celtic New Year's Day.

A Fourteenth Century Excerpt

>Who is your God? And where is he?
>Is it in the skies he is or in the earth,
>or under the earth, or upon the earth,
>or in the seas or in the streams?
>Is he young? Is he beautiful?
>Has he sons and daughters?
>Is he one of the everliving ones?

>>Lady Gregory
>>*Book of Saints and Wonders*

A Plaque At Ionia

>Deep peace of the running wave to you
>Deep peace of the flowing air to you
>Deep peace of the quiet earth to you
>Deep peace of the shining stars to you
>Deep peace of the Son of Peace to you.

>>The Iona Community

Some Celtic Epigrams

Weariness of legs after some active deed is better than apathy and weariness of spirit; weariness of spirit lasts forever, weariness of the legs lasts for only and hour.

>>Scottish Gaelic
>>15—16th Century

To be born Welsh is to be born privileged. Not with a silver spoon in your mouth, but music in your blood, and poetry in your soul.

>>Welsh
>>12th C.

Celtic Blessings

The Guardian Angel

Thou angel of God who hast charge of me
From the dear God of mercifulness,
The shepherding kind of the fold of the saints
To make round about me this night.

Drive from me every temptation and danger,
Surround me on the sea of unrighteousness,
And in the narrows, crooks, and straits,
Keep thou my coracle, keep it always

Be thou a bright flame before me,
Be thou a guiding star above me,
Be thou a smooth path below me,
And be a kindly shepherd behind me,
To—day, to—night, and forever.

I am tired and I a stranger,
Lead thou me to the land of angels;
For me it is time to go home
to the court of Christ, to the peace of heaven.

Blessing of Healing

I wish healing upon you
The haling of Mary with me,
Mary, Michael and Brighid
Be with me all three.

Your pain and sickness
Be in the earth's depths,
Be upon the grey stones,
For they are enduring.

Fly with the birds of the air,
Fly with the wasps of the hill
Swim with the sea—going whale,
For they are swiftest.

Be upon the clouds of the sky,
For they are the rainiest,
Be upon the river's current
Cascading to the sea.

Carmina Gadelica
Volumes 2 & 3
Translation — C. Matthews

Addendum D

Translation of St. Patrick's Works

The Letter to Coroticus

1. I Patrick, a sinner, very badly educated, in Ireland, declare myself to be a bishop. I am quite certain that I have received from God *that which I am*. Consequently I live among barbarian tribes as an exile and refugee for the love of God; God himself is the witness that this is true. It is not that I was anxious to utter from my mouth anything in so harsh and unpleasant a manner. But I am compelled by *zeal for God,* and the truth of Christ has aroused me out of affection for my neighbors and children for whom I *have given up* country and kinsfolk and *my own life even to death.* If I am worthy, I exist to teach tribes for my God, even though I am despised in some quarters.

17. Consequently I mourn for you, I mourn, my dearest. But again I rejoice within myseW I have not *labored* in vain nor has my pilgrimage been *useless.* And if this crime, so horrible, so unutterable, had to happen, thanks be to God you baptized believers have departed from this world to Paradise. I observe you; you are beginning the Journey to where *there will be no night nor mourning nor death* any *more, but you will rejoice like calves*

loosed from their tethers and you will tread down the wicked and they will be as ash under your feet.

18. You therefore will reign with the apostles and prophets and martyrs. You will receive eternal kingdoms, as he himself witnesses in the text *They will come from the east and from the west and will sit down with Abraham and Isaac and Jacob in the kingdom of Heaven. Outside are dogs and poisoners and murderers;* and *As for the liars and perjurers, their part is in the lake of everlasting fire.* It is not for nothing that the apostle says, *Where the good man will scarcely be saved, where will the sinner and wicked lawbreaker find himself?*

19. Now this is why Coroticus and his gang of criminals, rebels against Christ—how will they feel, since they distribute baptized women as prizes for the sake of a wretched temporal kingdom which of course may disappear in a moment? *Like cloud or smoke which is dispersed by the wind, so will* deceitful *sinners pensh from the face of the Lord.* The good however will feast in great confidence with Christ. *They shall judge nations and rule over* wicked kings for ever and ever. Amen.

The Confession

I / His Youth: His Capture by Irish Pirates; God's Goodness to Him

1. 1 am Patrick, a sinner, most uncultivated and least of all the faithful and most despised in the eyes of many. My father was Calpornius, a deacon, a son of Potitus, a presbyter, who was at the village of Bannavem Taberniae. He had an estate nearby and it was there that I was captured. At that time I was nearly sixteen years old. For I did not then know the true God and was carried away captive as had been so many thousands of people—it was according to what we deserved because *we had*

Addendum D
Translation of St. Patrick's Works

deserted God and we had not *observed his commandments* and we had not been obedient to our bishops who used to warn us about our salvation. So God *brought upon us the anger of his indignation and scattered us* among many *nations, even to the end of the earth,* where now I am to be found, in all my inadequacy, among foreigners.

3. So that is why I cannot keep silent, *and it is not expedient,* about the great acts of goodness and the great grace which the Lord generously gave me *in the land of my captivity;* because this is my repayment, after I have been chastened and have recognized him *to praise and confess his wonderful works* among every nation that is under the sky.

4. Because: there is no other God nor was there ever in the past nor will there he in the future except God the Father ingenerate, without beginning, from whom all beginning flows, who controls all things, as our formula runs: and his Son Jesus Christ whom we profess to have always existed with the Father, begotten spiritually before the origin of the world in an inexpressible way by the Father before all beginning, and through him were made things both visible and invisible; he was made man; when death had been overcome he was received into Heaven by the Father, and *he gave to him all power above every name of things heavenly and earthly and subterranean and that every tongue should confess to him that Jesus Christ is Lord and God;* and we believe in him and await his Advent which will happen soon, as *judge of the living and the dead,* and *he will deal with everybody according to their deeds* and *he poured out upon us richly the Holy Spirit* the gift and pledge of immortality, who makes those who believe and obey to be *sons of God* and *coheirs with Christ* and we confess and adore him, one God in the Trinity of sacred name.

16. But when 1 had come by ill luck to Ireland—well every day I used to look after sheep and I used to pray often during the

day, the love of Cod and fear of him increased more and more [in me] and my faith began to grow and my spirit to be stirred up, so that in one day [I would say] as many as a hundred prayers and nearly as many at night, even when I was staying out in the woods or on the mountain, and I used to rise before dawn for prayer, in snow and frost and rain, and I used to feel no ill effect and there was no slackness in me (as I now realize, it was because the Spirit was glowing in me).

17. And it was there that one night I heard a voice saying to me in a dream, "You have been right to fast because you will soon return to your country," and next after a little time I heard a Message saying to me, "Look, your ship is ready"—and it was nowhere near but lay perhaps two hundred miles away and I had never been there before nor did I have any acquaintance among the people there—and at last after a while I took to flight and deserted the man with whom I had been for six years and I came in the power of God who was guiding my way for a good purpose and I had no fear all the time until I reached the ship.

20. But that same night I was sleeping and Satan tempted me strongly, which I shall remember *as long as I shall be in this body,* and there fell on me something like a huge stone, and none of my limbs capable of moving. But how was it that it occurred to me, ignorant in spirit that I was, to call on Elijah? And while this was taking place I saw the sun rising in the sky and while I was crying out "Elijah! Elijah!" with all my strength, the next thing that happened was that the radiance of that sun fell upon me and at once dispersed from me all paralysis, and I believe that I was succored by Christ my Lord and his Spirit was at that moment crying out on my behalf, and I hope that so it shall be in the *day of my tribulation,* just as it says in the gospel, *"In that day"* the Lord testifies, *"it will not be you who will speak but the Spirit of your Father who speaks in you."*

23. And next a few years later I was an Britain among my parents who [had] received me for their son and earnestly requested me that I should now after all the troubles which I had experienced never leave them, and it was there that *I saw in a vision of the night* a man coming apparently from Ireland whose name was Victoricus, with an uncountable number of letters, and he gave me one of them and I read the heading of the letter which ran, "The Cry of the Irish," and while I was reading aloud the heading of the letter I was imagining that at that very moment I heard the voice of those who were by the Wood of Voclut which is near the Western Sea, and this is what they cried, *as with one voice,* "Holy boy, we are asking you to come and walk among us again," and *I was struck deeply to the heart* and I was not able to read any further and at that I woke up. God be "thanked that after several years the Lord granted to them according to their cry."

24. And on another night—I *do not know, God knows* whether it was in me or beside me—[someone was speaking] in the most elegant language which I listened to but could not understand, except that at the end of the speech he spoke these words, *"He who gave his life for you,* he it is who speaks in you," and at that I woke up full of joy.

25. And another time I saw him praying in me and I was as it were within my body and I heard above me, that is above my *inner man,* and there he was praying earnestly with groans, and while this was going on I was in amazement and I was wondering and I was considering who it could be who was praying in me but at the end of the prayer he spoke to the effect that it was the Spirit, and at that I woke and I recalled that the Apostle had said, *The Spirit assists the weaknesses of our prayer: for we do not know what it is right for us to ask for; but the Spirit himself intercedes for us with groans that cannot be uttered, which cannot be expressed in words;* and in another place, *The Lord our Advocate intercedes for us.*

34. And this is why therefore I give unwearving thanks to my God, who kept me faithful *in the day of my trial,* so that today I can offer to him confidently in sacrifice my life as a living victim to Christ my Lord, who *preserved me from all my difficulties* so that I can say as well, *Who am I, Lord,* or what is my calling, since you have worked in me with such divine power so that today I should regularly exalt and glorify your name wherever I happen to be not only when things go well but also in troubles, so that whatever may happen to me whether good or bad I am equally bound to accept it and always give thanks to God because he has shown that I should believe in him endlessly as trustworthy and he has taken notice of me so that in spite of my ignorance and [of our being] *in the last days* I should venture to undertake this task, good and wonderful as it is, in such a way that I should imitate those who the Lord had long ago foretold would declare his gospel *as a testimony to all nations* before *the end of the world,* and we see as a consequence that it has been fulfilled just so: you can see that we are witnesses that the gospel has been preached as far as the point where there is no one beyond.

37. I was even from time to time offered many gifts with weeping and tears, and I offended them, and also it was against the wish of some of my elders but by the providence of God I did not yield to them nor agree with them—no thanks to me, but it was God who prevailed in me and withstood them all, to enable me to come and preach the gospel to Irish tribes and endure insults from unbelievers, *to bear the reproach of my pilgrimage* and many persecutions. *even as far as being thrown into irons,* and to sacrifice my free status for the good of others, and, if I were worthy, I am ready [to give] my life unhesitatingly and willingly for his name and I want to sacrifice it there even if it involves death, if God were to kindly grant this to me.

41. And so it is that those in Ireland who had never had knowledge of God but up to now always only worshipped idols and

filthy things, how is it that recently a people of the Lord has been made perfect and are called sons of God [and] the sons of the Irish and the daughters of subkings become monks and virgins of Christ?

42. There even was one blessed Irishwoman, an aristocrat of noble race very beautiful and of full age, whom 1 baptized; and after a few days for a particular reason she came to us, she indicated to us that she had received a Message from an angel of God and he directed her that she should become a virgin of Christ and that she should draw closer to God: God be thanked, on the sixth day from that she happily and eagerly chose that [careen which all the virgins of Christ in the same way also choose— not with the consent of their fathers, but they even endure persecutions and false accusations from their relations and in spite of that their number continually increases (and I cannot reckon the number from those of our race who have been born there) apart from widows and people living a life of continence. But those among them who are held in slavery have the hardest time: they hold out steadfastly even against intimidation and threats; but the Lord has given grace to many of his maidservants for even though they are forbidden still they steadfastly maintain their imitation [of Christ].

59. And if I ever practiced this imitation with any success for the sake of my God, whom I love, I ask him that he may grant that I may spill my blood along with those [other] exiles and prisoners even though I may lack burial itself or my corpse may be most squalidly torn limb from limb by dogs or wild beasts or *the birds of the air may devour it.* I believe most confidently that if this were to happen to me I have gained my soul along with my body, because, without a shadow of doubt, on that Day *we shall rise* in the radiance of the sun, that is *in the glory* of Christ Jesus our Redeemer, as *children of the* living *God* and *coheirs with Christ and destined to be conformed to his image,* because we shall reign *from him and through him and in him.*

60. For the sun which we see rises every day for our benefit at his behest, but it will never reign nor will its radiance endure, but all who worship it will come to a bad end in wretched punishment as well. But we who believe in and adore the true sun, Christ, who will never die, nor will anyone die *who has done his will*, but *he will last for ever just as Christ lasts for ever,* Christ who reigns with God the Father almighty and with the Holy Spirit before ages and now and for all ages of ages. Amen.

CELTIC SPIRITUALITY: A SELECTED BIBLIOGRAPHY

Adam, David. *The Edge of Glory: Prayers in the Celtic Tradition.* Harrisburg, PA: Moorhouse Publishing, 1985. Traditional and modern prayers composed in the same style by this Anglican vicar, now of Holy Island.

Backhouse, Janet. *The Lindisfarne Gospels.* Phaldon Press Ltd, 1981. ISBN 0-7148-2461-5. An excellent history of Lindisfarne, the making of manuscripts and colored manuscript plates.

Bamford, Christopher and William Parker Marsh, Ed. *Celtic Christianity: Ecology and Holiness. An Anthology.* London: Lindisfarne Press, 1982. ISBN 0-940262-07-X. Lists many Celtic saints and examples of their writings. An excellent bibliography for additional studies on Celtic saints.

Best, Nicholas. *Celtic Britain.* London: Weidenfeld & Nicholson. Photographs of Celtic interest. ISBN 0-297-83488-6.

Bitel, Lisa M. *Isle of the Saints: Monastic Settlement and Christian Community in Early Ireland.* Ithaca, NY: Cornell University Press, 1990. Detailed analysis of scholarly research on early Irish monasticism and hagiography.

Bradley, Ian. *The Celtic Way.* London: Darton, Longman, and Todd. Reprinted. ISBN 0-232-52001-1. Bradley begins with the Celtic knot and uses it as the key to unlocking the Celtic way, 1993.

Cahill, Thomas. *How the Irish Saved Civilization.* NY: Doubleday, 1995. A popular and highly readable book tracing Ireland's role in transmitting the classical heritage of Rome into the Middle Ages; however, I believe the author misses giving credence to the Celts in Ireland, who were there long before the Roman influence became of any effect. i.e., St. Patrick, born in Wales, was a very effective Christian influence in Ireland, and like St. David, was recognized a saint by the people long before either of them were noticed by the Roman Catholic Church!

Caniedydd Cynulleidfol. An early "Sol-Fa" Welsh hymnal. The Bookroom of the Welsh Independents, Wales, U.K. 1920. This is a collection of "Sol-Fa Hymns," the type used in the early Welsh churches. The Sol-Fa method was used to teach congregations to sing in four- and six-part harmony and later used as a hymnal for "Gymanfoedd Ganu" gatherings.

Cantor, Norman F. *Civilizations of the Middle Ages.* London: Harper-Perennial, 1995. A fair secondary study in capsulized form.

Chadwick, Nora. *The Celts.* London: Penguin Press, 1971. A scholarly survey of Celtic archaeology, history, art, and literature.

Condren, Mary. *The Serpent and the Goddess: Women, Religion, and Power in Celtic Ireland.* San Francisco: Harper, 1989. A feminist reading of sexual politics in early Irish sagas and saints' lives.

Cunliffe, Barry. *The Celtic World.* New York: St. Martin's Press. 1993. ISBN 0-312-09700-X. Cunliffe is a noted archaeologist (professor of European archaeology, University of Oxford). Book is about a people whose roots were buried in the past, 1990.

The Ancient Celts. Oxford University Press, 1997. ISBN 0-19-815010-5. Most current word on Celtic tribes, presented in high academic style.

Davies, John. *A History of Wales.* Penguin Books, 1994. Originally published in Wales as *Hanes Cymru,* 1980; translated into English, 1990. Writes about the early Celts as early as 1600 B.C. Each chapter presents a segment of Celtic history up to 1974.

Davies, Mike. *The Welsh Lovespoon.* Cardiff, Wales: Mike Davies, 1996. The author is a professional woodcarver/sculptor who presents "the history of the lovespoon" with explanation of the symbols and examples of lovespoons in color.

de Waal, Esther. *Every Earthly Blessing: Celebrating a Spirituality of Creation.* Ann Arbor, MI: Servant Publications, 1991. A lively introduction to themes in Celtic spirituality by its best-known contemporary interpreter.

Ed. *The Celtic Vision: Prayers and Blessings from the Outer Hebrides.* Petersham, MA: St. Bede's Publication, 1988. Traditional prayers from the *Carmina Gadelica* as collected in the Scottish Highlands by Alexander Carmichael in the nineteenth century.

Dillon, Myles and Nora Chadwick. *The Celtic Realms.* London: Hazell Watson & Viney Ltd. 1967. ISBN 0-351-158-08-1. Presently out-of-print. Lists books and periodicals of earlier Celtic writings. This book is partly revised in Nora Chadwick's *The Celts,* found in this bibliography, 1967.

Ellis, Peter Berresford. *The Druids.* Grand Rapids, MI: William B. Eerdmans Publishing Co., 1994. ISBN 0-8028-3798-0. A fairly complete and informative work on the Druids.

Elwood, Louis B. *The Rebellious Welsh.* Los Angeles: Ward Richie Press, 1951.

Farmer, D. H., Ed. *The Age of Bede.* Harmondsworth: Penguin Books, 1983. Translations of four early medieval texts including Bede's *Life of Cuthbert* and *The Voyage of St. Brendan.*

Green, Miranda. *The Celtic World.* London; New York: Routeledge, 1995. ISBN 415057647 and 0415146275 (pbk). Includes a great bibliographical reference, maps, and index.

Greenslade, David. *Welsh Fever: Welsh Activities in the United States and Canada.* Cowbridge, Wales: D. Brown and Sons, 1996. ISBN 0-905928-56-3. The author toured the United States doing research on the Welsh and enclosed his findings in this book.

Herm, Gerhard. *The Celts: The People Who Came Out of Darkness.* New York: Barnes and Noble Books, 1993. ISBN 1-56619-218-8. This is a two-thousand-year epic story of the northern European civilization that rivaled Greece and Rome both for richness and for the best kind of power.

Hughes, Cledwyn. *Royal Wales—The Land and Its People.* New York: Roy Publishers. Published in Britain.

Hyma, Albert and J.F. Stach. *World History—A Christian Interpretation.* William B. Eerdmans Publishing Company, 1942. A compendium-type book. Well written but not as inclusive as it might be. A simple overview.

Jackson, Kenneth and Ed Hurlstone. *A Celtic Miscellany.* London: Penguin Books, 1971. Translated selections of Celtic poetry, prose, and saga written in a variety of languages from the sixth century to the present.

James, Simon. *The World of the Celts*. London: Thomas & Hudson, 1993. Well illustrated short entries on various topics with emphases on the art and archaeology of pre-Christian Celts in Europe, Britain, and Ireland.

Jones, William D. *Wales in America*. University of Wales Press, University of Scranton Press, 1993. ISBN 0-940866-20-X. Although this book is a singular feature of a Welsh settlement in the U.S. between the years 1860 and 1920, it offers many of the early Celtic traits passed down from one generation to another.

Lenny, Bob & Thomas, Patrick. *Teulu Teilo—A History of the Church in Brechfa*. Printed by Eglwys Sant Teilo, Brechfa, Wales, 1993. An excellent history of the church as well as a history of St. Teilo and the Celts in the area of Brechfa.

Luff, Alan. *Welsh Hymns and Their Tunes*. Carol Stream, IL: Hope Publishing Company, 1990. ISBN 0-916642-42-9, U.S. and Canada. A most excellent background on the Welsh, their faith, and their hymns. Most readable.

Mackey, James P., Ed. *An Introduction to Celtic Christianity*. Edinburgh: T & T Clark, 1989. Scholarly articles on topics ranging from St. Patrick to James Joyce, from medieval Welsh history to the "Carmina Gadelica."

Muller, Robert. *New Genesis—Shaping a Global Spirituality*. Garden City, NY: Image Books, A Division of Doubleday and Company, Inc., 1984. Robert Muller served in the United Nations and was fondly called "the philosopher of the U.N." and "its prophet of hope."

Norton-Taylor, Duncan. *The Celts: The Emergence of Man*. New York: Time-Life Books, 1974. Catalog #74-17779. Portrays the Celtic people and color portraits of their life and activities, as well as their life on the continent as well as in the United Kingdom.

Pargeter, Edith (Ellis Peters). *The Brothers Gwynedd Quartet*. Single volume, 1989. Headline Book Publishing Company PLC, London, ISBN 0-7472-32679. Originally printed in four volumes. Set in Wales in the Middle Ages, depicting the war against the Welsh by the English, who were seeking to acquire more land. It was entitled "a historical novel" because she couldn't substantiate some of the names included in this four-volume work.

A Bloody Field at Shrewsbury. Set in fourteenth century England during the reign of Henry IV. Headline Book Publishing, PLC London, W1P

Lindisfarne Gospels (600–695): Illuminated carpet-page or cover of The Gospel of Matthew with interlace in the Celtic tradition. Use a magnifying glass and catch the intricate drawings.

Lindisfarne Gospels (600–695): Illuminated initial page of John's Gospel. The opening words of the Latin text decorated with spectacular elaboration. "In principo era verbum et verbum erat opud D(eu)m. . . ." "In the beginning was the Word, and the Word was with God. . . ."

The Book of Kells (c. 800): This plate represents the incident of Christ's arrest. The assailants are pictured smaller than The Christ to show Christ's power over those arresting Him. This drawing depicts the Latin Scripture of Matthew 26:30, "And when they had sung a hymn, they went out to the Mount of Olives."

The Book of Durrow (680–720): The illuminated initial page of Mark's Gospel. Note the Celtic knots and characteristic Celtic style often seen on artifacts found at Hallstatt in Austria circa 1200 B.C. before The Book of Durrow. The Celtic knot was also from this period.

St. Teilo Gospels (Early 8th c.): These are considered to be Welsh Celtic Christianity's crowning achievements in Illustrated Gospels . . . known also as "The Lichfield" or "The Chad Gospels." Here we have what can be called a "darker carpet-page," in comparison to other carpet-pages presented in "Lindisfarne," "Kells" or "Durrow."

St. Teilo Gospels (Early 8th c.): In contrast to the other initial-pages we have see[n] we have not only a "lighter" initial-page, but one that is shown in book form, rather tha[n] just a single page.

7FN, 1989. ISBN 0-7472-3366-7. She also wrote *The Brothers Cadfael*, a series of novels, and imaginary reconstruction of monastic life in the twelfth century.

Patterson, Helena. *King Arthur's Return. Cistercian Studies Journal*, 1994. Blanford, 1995. A good account of the part King Arthur played in Celtic lore.

Perkins, D. C. *Lovespoons from Wales*. Domino Books (Wales) Ltd., 1989. A major source for teachers and parents. A pamphlet used in the national curriculum in Wales. Pictures, symbols, and history.

Powell, T. G. E. *The Celts*. London: Thames & Hudson Ltd., 1991. No ISBN given. An excellent presentation of the Celts from their early beginnings in social, spiritual, and political life.

Roberts, Timothy. *The Celts in Myth and Legend*. New York: Metro Books, 1985, ISBN 1-56799-092-4. Contains Celtic myths, Celtic heroes, and Christian saints.

Rutherford, Ward. *Celtic Lore*. London: Aquarian Press, 1993. ISBN British Library 1-85538134-6. A history of the Druids and their timeless traditions.

Celtic Mythology. London: Aquarian Press, 1987. ISBN British Library 0-85030-551-9. Depicts the influence of the Celtic myths.

Sellner, Edward C. *Wisdom of the Celtic Saints*. Notre Dame, IN: Ave Maria Press, 1993. Engaging excerpts from the lives of early Irish, Welsh, Scottish, and Northumbrian saints with an excellent introduction.

Thomas, Islyn. *Our Welsh Heritage*. Trucksville, PA: National Welsh-American Foundation, 1978. Celts from a Welsh vantage point.

Thomas, Patrick. *Candle in the Darkness: Celtic spirituality from Wales*. Llandysul, Dyfed, Wales: Gomer Press, 1993. ISBN 0-83683974-6. A picture of Celtic spirituality after the departure of Julius Caesar from the U.K. He has also published *The Opened Door*, a small booklet on Welsh Celtic spirituality.

Van de Weyer, Robert, Ed. *Celtic Fire: The Passionate Religious Vision of the Ancient Britain and Ireland*. New York: Doubleday, 1990. Delightful collection of tales, poems, and prayers with an appendix giving directions for a "Celtic pilgrimage" to ancient sites.

Walker, Williston. *A History of the Christian Church*. Charles Scribner's Sons, 1944. A Church History text.

Wentz, W. Y. Evans. *Fairy Faith in Celtic Countries*. Guernsey, Channel Islands: The Guernsey Press Ltd. 1911, ISBN 0-901072-51-8 (Colin

Smythe Ltd) and ISBN 0-319-00773-4 (Humanities Press Inc.) In the Dedication, the "AE" refers to an anonymous Irish Mystic (*Radiant Mysteries of the Old Gods of Ireland.*) The stories and history of the Celts who have retained the elements of their pre-Christian religion through oral traditions.

Zenos, Andrew C. *Compendium of Church History.* Philadelphia Board of Christian Education, 1938. He holds that the historical movement is both vital and organic. To my knowledge, this is the only church history text that mentions the Celts.

Index

A. a'Becket, Thomas, 121
Aberaeron, 156
Abraham, 24, 53
Act of February, 131
Act of 1563, 207
Act of 1673, 190
Act of Supremacy, 219
Act of Uniformity, 214
Act of Union, 132, 195, 197
Aerial Photography, 22
Afterward, 263
Agriculture, 23, 24, 26, 30, 38–39, 96, 102, 103, 113, 182, 194, 244
Aidan, (See St. Aidan)
Aldred, 158
Alexander the Great, 33
American Revolution, 196
Ana-Baptist & Baptist, 214, 216, 245
Anamchara, 165
Anatolian, 19–20
Anerin, 112
Anglesey (Mona), 105–106

Anglican Church, 169, 175, 181, 185, 188, 189, 195, 196, 199, 207, 219, 221
Anglo-Saxon Chronicle, 112
Anne Boleyn, 180, 206
Anne, Queen, 192, 193
Apologia, 182
Archaeologists, 22, 28, 30, 31, 35, 36, 51, 55, 57, 59, 70, 83, 84, 86, 100, 101, 104, 140, 153
Archbishop of Canterbury, (See Canterbury)
Ard, 25
Armaugh, 163
Aristotle, 183
Armenian, 19, 20
Augustine, (See St. Augustine)

B. Baltic, 19, 20
Bannockburn, 130
Bannavem Taburniae, 153
Barbarians, 34, 38, 39, 62, 108
Barbarica Conspirato, 108
Bards, v, 50, 53, 78, 110, 124, 128, 132, 134, 145, 255, 256

Battle Axe People, 36
Battle of Hastings, 118
Beaker culture, 36, 103
Belenos, 95-96
Beltine, 95-96
Bible, 28, 40, 53, 58, 81, 155, 156, 171, 174, 177, 184, 208, 211, 212, 216, 218, 231, 241, 248, 252
Bibliography, 317-322
Billfrith, 158
Blacksmiths, 25
Bodb, 80
Border Barons, 120, 122, 131
Boer War, 199
Book of Common Prayer, 219
Book of Discipline, 176
Book of Durrow, 137, 142, 157, 158
Book of Kells, 136, 137, 142, 157, 158, 231
Booth, William, (See Salvation Army)
Boston Tea Party, 196
Booty, 33, 62, 74
Boudicca, 48, 105, 107
Bradford, William, 213
Bretons, 19, 21, 39, 103, 108, 111, 112, 122, 124, 126, 127, 128, 169, 170, 208, 209, 211, 238, 259, 260
Brigantia, 70, 81, 95
Bronze Age, 22, 23, 74, 80, 83, 84
Brythonic, 21, 103
Burns, Robert, 250

C. Caesar, Julius, 20, 29, 31, 58, 61, 64, 67, 73, 76, 144, 146-150
  Invasion into the UK, 104-109
  Departure from the UK, 110-112

Calvin, John, 143, 173, 175, 208, 209, 212, 221, 222, 241, 243
Canterbury, 121, 152, 161, 220
Cambrensis, Giraldus, 63, 157, 227, 255
Cato, 40
Celtiberians, 24, 28, 35
Celts, xiv, 17, 19, 25, 28, 29, 30-32, 33, 34, 36, 39, 52, 54, 62, 92, 143
Celts (Afterlife), 53, 54, 60-61, 64, 66, 68, 74, 134, 206
Celtic Arts & Crafts, 23, 24, 36-37, 48, 102, 134, 206
  Articles (Newspaper), 248, 149
  Calendar (Coligney), 70, 91-92
  Coins, 39, 90
  Crosses, 88, 137, 138-139, 140, 141, 229-232
  Cult Practices, 90-91
  Education, 76, 183, 242, 246, 247, 248
  Family Life, (See Lovespoons)
  Fighting, 31, 51-52, 63-66, 82, 111, 132, 144, 169, 177
  Heritage, viii, ix, 78, 124, 144, 239, 240, 242, 244, 247, 249-251, 260
  Holy Ground, 83
  Horses (Training), 38
  Knot, 137, 140
  Law, (See Laws)
  Legends, 60, 68, 79, 102, 133, 136, 166, 254, 260
  Language and Lingusitics, 19, 20, 30, 31, 35, 38, 39-41, 55, 59, 91, 103, 109, 119, 112, 132, 206, 210, 245, 259

Literature, 75, 77, 79, 84, 112, 120, 124, 133, 182
Lovespoons, 232-236
Medicines, 78, 203
Mercenaries, 29
Names, 50–51
Poetry, 60–61, 75, 231, 250, 301-308
Power, 32, 33, 35, 49, 51, 54, 60, 61, 62–63, 68, 74, 76, 77, 83, 98, 99, 107, 109, 110, 116, 122, 125, 143, 144, 148, 164, 170, 177, 204, 211, 212, 217, 225, 238, 240, 241, 253, 255, 257
Primitive Celts, 19, 99, 103
Pronunciation, 18
Rites, 171–176
Revivals, 258, 259, 260
Saints, xiv, 70, 88, 121, 145, 149, 150–153, 154, 162, 166, 241
Seasons, 93–98
Spirituality, viii, xv, xvi, 55, 56, 78, 124, 140, 142, 143, 159, 164, 172, 224, 241, 242, 247
Tribes & Clans, 45, 49–50, 64, 66, 110, 144, 164
Wheelwrights, 30, 38
Women, 33, 42, 48, 60, 88
Worship, 68, 69, 73, 74–77, 82, 83, 102, 147, 159, 164, 177
Writing, 31
Cernunnos, 70, 82, 151–152
Chad Gospels, (See Lichfield Gospels)
Chadwick, Nora, 30, 35, 36, 48, 63, 75, 107, 114, 152, 157, 191
Chapter Notes, 265-273
Charles I, 187–188, 192, 215
Charles II, 189–190
Chronology (Celtic), 277-298
Chrysostom, 34
Churches
Celtic, iv, 97, 144, 148, 149, 150, 152, 154, 155, 159, 160, 161, 163, 165, 166, 168, 169, 180, 208, 210, 211, 240, 241, 257, 258, 259, 260
Roman Catholic, 40, 88, 148, 150, 151, 159, 160, 161, 163, 164, 165, 169, 171, 172, 174, 176, 177, 205, 207, 211
Church of England, 124, 165, 169, 173, 177, 188, 207, 208, 210, 211, 212, 213, 215, 216, 219–220, 228, 240, 243, 258
Cicero, 34
Classical Writers, 30*f*, 55, 84
Claudius, Caesar, 62
Coelfrith, 163
Columba, (See St. Columba)
Commonwealth, 180, 204
Confessio, 153, 310-316
Confession, 151, 168, 176, 177, 223
Congregational Church, (See Independents)
Corman, 152
Cornwall (Cornish), 19, 21, 40, 108, 111, 124, 125, 126, 127, 128, 131, 145, 169, 243, 259, 260
Constantine, 159
Council of Trent, 215
Cromlech Buildings, 102
Cromwell, Oliver, 187, 188
Cult of Mothers, 79
Cunedda, 115

Cunliffe, Barry, 31
Cynesii, 34

D. Dagda, 71, 79, 82
Danes, 114
Danube River, 34, 88, 90
Dark Ages, 124
David II, 131
Davies, Bryan, 123, 140
Davies, John, 119, 120, 124, 125, 147
Davies, Oliver, xvi
Davies, Richard, 206
Davies, Mike, (See Love-spoons)
deBaliol, John, 129, 130
Delphi, 28
Devolution Referendum, Welsh & Scottish, 253, 257
Diet of Speyer, 173
Dillon-Chadwick, xv, 84, 115, 124, 125
Dillon, Miles, 103
Diodorus Siculus, 30–35, 64, 90
Disraeli, Benjamin, 198, 199
Divine Right of Kings, 187, 188
Domesday Book, 118
Druids, 30, 34, 41, 42, 43, 45, 50, 53, 60, 61, 67, 69, 74, 77, 79, 89, 91–92, 96, 97, 100, 105, 106, 110, 126, 132, 134, 140, 145, 146, 159, 162, 255
Dykes & Walls, 113

E. Eadfrith, 158
Early European People, 19, 69, 75, 135, 141
Easter Sunday, 160, 161, 163, 254
Ecgberht or Ecgberct, 163
Ecology, 145, 148
Ecumerical Movement, 259
Edward I, 118, 120, 125, 126, 127, 128, 129–132, 134, 170, 172, 210, 252

Edward II, 129
Edward III, 129
Edward IV, 167
Edward VI, 173, 175
Edward VII, 200–201
Edward VIII, 202–203
Eisteddfod, 40, 228, 243, 247, 255, 256
Elizabeth I, 180–182, 206, 213, 215, 256
Elizabeth II, 203, 204
Ellis, Peter, 30, 53, 78, 100, 101, 152
England, 23, 25, 57, 59, 102, 110, 114, 122, 123, 124, 127
English Bible, (See King James Version)
English Prayer Book, 174, 182
Engravers, 26
Environment, 75
Episcopal Church, 219, 223
Epona, 72
Equinox, 78, 161
Esus, 72
Ethelwald, 158
Ethnic Minorities, 243
Excommuinication, 181

F. Farming, (See Agriculture)
Feudal System, 121, 127, 168
Fighting Naked, 31
Figures of gods, (See Household gods)
French Revolution, 196

G. Gaelic, 18, 21, 31, 39, 40, 50, 111, 114, 126, 169, 173, 217, 253, 259, 260
Galatae, 28, 32, 49
Galatians, 28, 53, 62, 64, 104, 177, 227
Galican Liturgy, 171
Gallic, 21

326

Gauls, 31, 58, 88, 91, 104, 124, 170
Geology, 22
George I, 193–194
George II, 194–195
George III, 195–196
George IV, 196–197
George V, 201–202
George VI, 203–204
Geology, 252
Germanic, 19, 20, 28, 39, 73
Gildas, 112, 115
Glaciers, 22, 99
Gladstone, Wm., 198
Glen Innes, 102
Gods and Goddesses, 42, 58, 64, 66f, 68, 73, 83, 99, 116, 127, 133, 145, 146, 148, 166, 168
Goidelic, 21
Gorsedd Prayer, v
Goths, 112
Great Charter, (See Magna Carta)
Greek Orthodox Church, 40, 210
Greeks, 18, 24, 32, 46, 49, 51, 52, 62, 66, 79, 80, 84, 125, 133, 177, 238
Green, Miranda, 97, 152
Gruffudd ap Cynan, 120
Gruffudd ap Llewellyn, King of Wales, 120
Gymanfa Ganu, 227–228, 229

H. Hadrian's Wall, 113
Hallstatt Culture, 24, 36, 64, 72, 82, 140, 141
Hamilton, Patrick, 175, 218
Harlech, Men of, 65–66
Harold, King, 118, 120
Head Hunting, 62
Healing, 81, 90, 147, 156
Heathenism, 133, 151, 159
Helenic Greek, 19, 20
Henfynyu, 156

Henry I, 120
Henry II, 121, 130
Henry III, 57, 122, 125, 134, 219
Henry IV, 184
Henry VIII, 174, 180
Herbert, William, 183
Herodotus, 34f
Hill Forts, 51
Hispano Celts, 21
History & Historians, xvi, 17, 19, 24, 28, 34, 40, 41, 46, 52, 55, 59, 74, 83, 99, 109, 112, 115, 119, 122, 123, 124, 126, 127, 140, 143, 149, 153, 159, 161, 163, 164, 169, 172, 180, 182, 204, 211, 220, 227, 240, 252, 257, 259
Historia Regum Britanniae, 122
Hittites, 20, 28, 29, 53, 62, 64, 104, 177, 227
Holy Grounds, 72, 83, 86f
Holzhausen, 85
Household gods, 74, 80, 86, 137
Huss, John, 143
Hwyl Dda, 115, 116

I. Ice Age, 22, 29
Iceni, 106, 107
Ibernians, 24, 35, 102
Illegitimate Children, 47
Illuminated Gospels, 157-158, 315-320
Illyrian, 19, 20
Imbolc, 94
Independent Churches, (Congregational), 188, 213–214, 216
Industrial Rebolution (British), 196
Indo-Europeans, 19–23
Indo-Iranian, 19
Iona, 152, 155, 163–165

Ireland (Irish), 21, 23, 24, 31, 40, 41, 59, 88, 99, 103, 107, 110, 111, 114–115, 118, 126, 128, 129, 133, 142, 153, 161, 170, 196, 225, 243
Iron Age, 22, 31, 36
Irish Celebrations, 253–255
Irish Home Rule, 255, 259
Italic, 19, 20
Isle of Man, (See Mancs)

J. Jacobite Rebellion, 193–194
James I, 184–186, 213, 214, 217, 218
James II, 190–191
James, Simon, 125, 149
Jenkins, Dafydd, 47
Jerome, (See St. Jerome)
Jewelry, (See Celtic Art)
John (King), 122
Justices of the Peace, 131
Justinian Code, 47–48
Jutes, 58

K. Keltic, xv, 19, 143, 159
Keltoi, 18, 28, 32
Kings in the United Kingdom, 299-300
King James Version (Bible), 184
Knox, John, 122, 123, 144, 168, 176, 208, 216, 217, 243, 250, 251

L. Labor Party, 201–203
Lake Maggiore, 21
Lares, 80
La Tene Culture, 24, 28, 36–37, 72, 82
Latin Mass, (See Roman Mass)
Laud, Archbishop, 189, 218
Laws, 41f, 75, 131, 148, 159, 164, 186, 196
Child Labor, 198

Druidic Laws, 46
Hwyl Dda's Law, 47, 116
Inside the Church, 44–45
Outside the Church, 43–44
Marriage, 45–47
Penitential Law of Cummain, 43
Legends, 60, 68, 79, 102, 133, 136, 166, 254, 260
Leptonic, 21
Letters to Coroticus, 309-310
Lindisfarne Gospels, 137, 142, 152, 157, 158
Lir, 72
Lichfield Gospels, (See St. Teilo & Chad Gospels)
Literature, 75, 77, 79, 84, 112, 120, 124, 133, 182
Liturgical Colors, 172
Llewellyn Ap Griffudd, 125, 126, 129
Lloyd George, 201
Long Parliament, 188–189
Luff, Alan, 228
Lugh, 69, 72, 82, 151
Lugnasa, 95–96
Luther, Martin, 207
Lutheran Church, 173, 218

M. McAlpin, Kenneth, 119, 130
McFergus, Angus, 130
Mabinogian, 134
Magna Carta, 122–123
Mancs, 19, 21, 39, 40, 59, 126, 127, 128, 243, 259, 260
Marcher Lords, 122
Mapinus, 70
Mary Queen of Scots, 176, 184, 206, 216, 250
Masons, 24
Matroma, 72
Megoliths, 102
Menevia, 155

Melville, Andrew, 176, 208, 216
Mercenaries, 29
Methodist church, 221–222, 224, 245
Methodist Episcopal Church, 222
Migration, 14, 26f, 47, 54, 103–104, 112, 124, 125, 129, 144, 244
Minerals & Mining, 102
Mona (Anglesey), see Anglesey
Monasteries, 149, 150, 155, 164, 173
Monks, 134, 136, 137, 151
Morgan, William, 152
Morrighan, 72, 80
Music in Worship, 222, 226–229, 255
Mystery Religions, 146
Mythology, 60, 76, 94, 96, 97, 132–136, 151, 165, 166, 241, 254

N. Naked Fighters, 62, 64
Name Recognition, 50–51
Neolithic, 22, 23, 83, 85, 100
New Stone Age, 22
News Items, 248–249
Nicene Age, 57, 158–163, 168
Nicene Creed, 159–160, 219
Nicene Council, 159–160
Noah, 20
Nodens, Nodons, Nudens, 71
Normans, 114, 115, 116–117, 120, 190
Norton-Taylor, Duncan, 60, 86
Nuclear Physicists, 22, 23

O. Offa's Dyke, 113
Offerings, (See Sacrifices)
Official Name, Britain, 58
Ogham, 102
Ogimos, 71, 82
Older Christianity, 152, 165

Oldest Language, 40
Old Stone Age, 22
Oral Tradition, 17, 31, 76, 134
Ordivices, 105
Oreign, 146, 148
Oswald, King, 152
Owain Hwyl Dda, 112
Oxen, 26
Oxford Dictionary, 18

P. P-Celtic, 14
Pagan Trinity, 72
Paleolithic, 22, 23, 80
Palladius, 153
Palmerson, Lord, 198
Pargeter, Edith (Ellis Peters), (See Bibliography)
Parliament, 58, 131, 132, 184, 187, 206, 219, 240, 252, 253, 257
Pater Noster, 147, 171
Paulinus Seutonius, 105, 106, 108,
Peden, Alexander, 251
Peel, Robert, 198
Pelham, Henry, 195
Penates, 80
Picts, 108, 111, 112, 119, 155, 252
Pillars of Hercules, 34
Pitt, William (Elder), 194, 195
Platius, Alus, 146
Pliny, 78, 84
Plow, 24, 26, 102
Pope, 118, 126, 148, 156, 162, 173, 177, 206, 210, 216, 219
Pope Calixtus II, 156
Pope Celestine, 153
Pope Celement III, 207
Pope Gregory I, 150, 162
Pope Gregory VII, 173
Pope Gregory VIII, 181
Pope Sixtus V, 207
Prayer Book (Protestant), 17

Pre-Celts (Brythonic), 24
Pre-Christian, 48
Pre-Reformation, (See Reformation)
Presbyterian Church, 175, 176, 207, 216–218, 223, 245, 250
Pride, Col. Thomas, 189
Prince of Wales, 125, 126
Protestantism, 173, 180, 189, 195, 205, 230, 258
Prys, John, 173
Puritans, 175, 184, 186, 188, 212–213

Q. Q-Celtic, 21
Quakers (Society of Friends), 214–215, 237, 245

R. Rasmussen, Knud, 98
Recorders, 239, 240
Rees, Alwyn, 102
Reformation, 57, 142, 143, 144, 154, 161, 168–171, 173, 177, 182, 205, 210, 211, 241, 242, 247, 258
Reformed Churches, 168
Reminder gods, 80–81
Renaissance, 182
Revolutionary War, 128
Rhodri Mawr, 115, 116, 119
Richard I, 122
Ring Forts, 136
Ritual Shafts, 84–85, 87
Robert I (King), 131
Robert the Bruce, 129, 130, 131
Robert II, 131
Roman Catholic Church, (See Churches)
Romans, 18, 20, 24, 32, 35, 46, 49, 51, 52, 58, 62, 66, 67, 79, 80, 84, 91, 125, 177, 238
Roman gods, 66–67

Roman Mass, 49, 151, 171, 172, 175, 177, 178
Rome, 108, 133, 152
Rutherford, Ward, 86, 133

S. Sacrifices, 84, 90, 177
St. Aidan, 130, 152
St. Andrew, 154, 242
St. Augustine, 150, 152, 161, 163
St. Columba, 136, 154–155, 163, 242, 251
St. David, 155–156, 174
St. Elmo, 150
St. Frances of Assisi, 150
St. Giles Cathedral, 218, 250
St. Gregory, 20
St. Jerome, 207
St. Jude, 150
St. Non, 155
St. Patrick, 95, 153–154, 306–311
St. Paul's Cathedral, 199
St. Teilo Gospels, 137, 142, 158, (Also see Lichfield Gospels and Chad Gospels)
Sacrifices, 225
Salmond, Alex, 253
Salisbury Plain, 100
Salt Mining, 39
Salvation Army, 224–225, 242
Samhain, 70, 79, 94
Samniae, 88
Saul, King, 102
Saxons, 18, 20, 58, 111, 112, 113, 118, 124, 125, 170
Scientists, 20
Scotland (Scottish), 21, 23, 39, 40, 59, 108, 110, 113, 114, 118–119, 128, 129, 130, 131, 142, 154, 175, 176, 208, 243
Scots Confession, 176–178, 240, 241
Scottish Celebrations, 249, 251, 258

Sectic, 18
Sellner, Edward, 167
Shamans, 75, 97–98
Shela-na-gig, 79
Silures, 105
Sin, 68, 84, 168, 177
Sinn Fein, 255
Singing in Battle, 62, 65–66
Slavonic, 19, 20
Sol-Fa Hymnal, 228
Solstice, 101–102
Soul Frinedship, 149, 165–168
Stamp Act, 196
Statuary, 88
Statute of Westminster, 202
Storage Shafts, 84, 86f
Stone Age, 24, 103
Stone of Scone (Stone of Destiny), 119, 122, 130, 131, 249, 251–253
Stonehenge, 69, 77, 78, 85, 100–102, 135
Stowe Missal, 171
Strabo, 32, 33, 39, 64, 77
Switzerland (Helvetia), 21
Synod of Whitby, 151–153, 161

T. Tacitus, 77, 104, 105, 107
Taliesin, 112, 145, 256
Taranus, 71
Temples, 84, 86, 88, 89, 147
Tertullian, 146, 147
Teutates, 72
Thomas, Patrick, 110
Timulus, 38
Tocharian, 19, 21
Tolstoy, Count L.N., 17
Tonsure, 161
Totems, 73, 75
Trantner, Nigel, 130
Treaty of Northampton, 252
Treaty of Montgomery, 125
Treaty of 1673, (See Act of 1673)

Trinity (Pagan), 80
Tumulus, 38
Tyrhenians, 34, 35

U. Unetice, 38
Unitarian Fellowship, 218–219, 245
United Kingdom Official, 57
United Kingdom of the Celts, 39, 41, 47, 57, 58, 59, 98, 100, 109, 111, 125, 144, 169, 173, 204
United Kingdom of Ireland, 140
Unknown God, 81
Urnfield People, 36

V. Victoria, Queen, 198–200
Vikings, 114–115, 125, 157, 170, 250
Vulgate, 157, 207, 216

W. Wales, 23, 24, 59, 71, 99, 101, 102, 103, 109, 110, 111, 112, 115, 118, 119–121, 122, 123, 128, 129, 131, 132, 134, 147, 153, 155, 169, 170, 243
Wallace, William, 129, 251
Walpole, Robert, 193, 195
War, (See Fighting)
Wats, Dyke, 113
Welsh, 21, 31, 40, 79, 110, 115, 119, 125, 131, 132, 142, 163
Welsh Bible, 207
Welsh Calvinistic Methodist Church, 179, 208, 222–224, 228, 245
Welsh Celebrations, 255–257
Welsh Chapels & Churches, 207, 229, 246
Welsh Christianity, 206
Welsh N. T., 182, 206
Wentz, W. Y. Evans, 166
Wesley, Charles, 221

Wesley, John, 221, 222
Wessex Culture, 37
William I (Conqueror), 110, 116, 120
William II, 120
William III and Mary II, 190, 191–192, 214, 215
William IV, 197–198
Wishart, George, 176, 216, 251
World War I, 201
World War II, 236, 259
World Council of Churches, 258, 259
Worship, 42, 51, 74, 83, 84, 135, 223, 241

Y. Yeats, William Butler, 145, 146, 166

Z. Zenos, Andrew, xv, 57, 159
Zwingli, Ulrich, 143

To order additional copies of

The Celts

Their Spirituality and Their Place in History

Send $29.95 plus $4.95 shipping and handling to

Books Etc.
PO Box 4888
Seattle, WA 98104

or have your credit card ready and call

(800) 917-BOOK